Learning Organizations in Practice

D0550204

For further information on these titles and other forthcoming books please contact

The Product Manager, Professional Books, McGraw-Hill Book Company Europe, Shoppenhangers Road, Maidenhead, Berkshire SL6 2QL, United Kingdom
Telephone 01628 23432 Fax 01628 770224

Learning Organizations in Practice

MICHAEL PEARN
CERI RODERICK
CHRIS MULROONEY

McGraw-Hill Book Company

London · New York · St Louis · San Francisco · Auckland
Bogotá · Caracas · Lisbon · Madrid · Mexico · Milan
Montreal · New Delhi · Panama · Paris · San Juan
São Paulo · Singapore · Sydney · Tokyo · Toronto

Published by McGraw-Hill Book Company Europe
Shoppenhangers Road, Maidenhead, Berkshire, SL6 2QL, England
Telephone 01628 23432
Fax 01628 770224

British Library Cataloguing in Publication Data

Pearn, Michael
  Learning Organizations in Practice. –
  (McGraw-Hill Developing Organizations Series)
  I. Title II. Series
  658.3124

  ISBN 0–07–707744–X

Library of Congress Cataloging-in-Publication Data

Pearn, Michael
  Learning organizations in practice / Michael Pearn, Ceri Roderick,
Chris Mulrooney.
       p.   cm.
  Includes bibliographical references and index.
  ISBN 0–07–707744–X
  1. Employees – Training of. 2. Continuing education.
  I. Roderick, Ceri. II. Mulrooney, Chris. III. Title.
  HF5549.5.T7P355   1995
  658.3'124–dc20   95–5588
                                                                      CIP

12345   CUP   998765

Typeset by Computape (Pickering) Ltd., North Yorkshire
and printed and bound in Great Britain at the University Press, Cambridge

Printed on permanent paper in compliance with ISO Standard 9706

Contents

Series preface

The McGraw-Hill *Developing Organizations* series is for people in the business of changing, developing and transforming their organizations. The books in the series bring together ideas and practice in the emerging field of organizational learning and development. Bridging theory and action, they contain new ideas, methods and models of how to get things done.

Organizational learning and development is the child of the organization development (OD) movement of the 1960s and 1970s. Then people like Schein, Beckhard, Bennis, Walton, Blake and Mouton *et al.* defined a *change technology* which was exciting and revolutionary. Now the world has moved on.

The word 'technology' goes with the organization-as-machine metaphor. OD emphasized the *outside-in* application of 'behavioural science' which seems naive in the context of the power-broking, influence and leverage of today's language. Our dominant metaphor of organizations as organisms or collective living beings requires a balancing *inside-out* focus of development and transformation of what is already there.

Learning is the key to our current dilemmas. We are not just talking about change. Learning starts with me and you, with the person—and spreads to others—if we can organize in ways which encourage it.

Learning is at a premium because we are not so much masters of change as beset by it. There is no single formula or image for the excellent company. Even the idea of 'progress' is problematic as companies stick to the knitting and go to the wall. Multiple possible futures, the need for discontinuity almost for the sake of it, means that we must be able to think imaginatively, to be able to develop ourselves and, in generative relationships with others, to continuously organize and reorganize ourselves.

Organizations are unique, with distinctive biographies, strengths, opportunities. Each creates its own future and finds its own development paths. The purpose of these books is not to offer ready-made tools, but to help you create your own tools from the best new ideas and practices around.

The authors in the series have been picked because they have something to say. You will find in all of the books the personal voice of the writer, and this reflects the voice which each of us needs in our own organizations to do the best we can.

As the title of their book suggests, Michael Pearn, Ceri Roderick and Chris Mulrooney are concerned to make a contribution at the applied end of the broad church of the organizational learning/ learning organization 'movement'. This book will delight those who yearn for straightforward ways of getting started on the task of enhancing the learning capabilities and capacity of their organizations. It is very accessible, well laid out and easy to read.

Rather than telling people what a learning organization is, Pearn, Roderick and Mulrooney encourage the reader to participate with their colleagues in creating a view of what this means for themselves. The authors then offer a sequence of building blocks illustrated with case examples and practical processes and techniques—which they prefer to call tools—which they have used for helping organizations towards this goal. Many of these tools were developed as part of a two-year project with a consortium of eight major UK organizations.

In welcoming Michael Pearn and his co-authors to this series, I hope that their contribution will encourage all those who are trying to bring about the realization of the learning organization vision.

Mike Pedler.

About this book

Not so long ago, the notion that an organization could learn would have been greeted with something approaching derision. Learning is something done at school; adults grow out of it; learning is for children, whereas training is for grown-ups. Perceptions, however, are changing thanks to a major insight. The capacity to learn, individually and organizationally, is an asset which may turn out to be priceless. Much of the debate and published literature in recent years has focused on what is frequently referred to as 'the learning organization'.

This book does not contain a recipe for the learning organization or, indeed, all the steps that might be considered necessary for becoming a learning organization, for it is our view that learning organizations set out to achieve the unattainable, and that it is the quest that is important and not the arrival. To have arrived is the equivalent of saying: 'We've done it! There is nothing left to learn.'

This book offers tried and tested tools that facilitate different kinds of learning at different levels of the organization. It offers walking boots and a compass but not a map. The creation of the map is the prime responsibility of the organization's visionary and strategic leaders and there are already many books on the nature of the vision and how it can be achieved.

The learning organization or a learning organization?

This book is not about *the learning organization*. We are not sure if there is such a thing as *the* learning organization in the sense that the possession of a number of characteristics means that an organization is entitled to be called *the* learning organization. We are sure, however, that some organizations are better at learning than others. Some learn better at the macro level, making long-term strategic decisions which exploit and even anticipate changes in their external environment; some learn better at the micro level by harnessing and making use of the intelligence of *all*, or at least most of, their employees. Some learn better at both levels. Some learn more quickly than others, and some are good at learning from hard experience and transferring that learning to where it is needed. Some organizations have learned how to renew themselves and have managed their own renaissance, e.g. Rover Group. Others have learned to transform themselves continuously rather than wait for external pressures or a crisis to trigger the need for critical action, e.g. 3M. This book is designed to help the reader make intentional and conscious use of concepts and practical processes that will help the organization learn more effectively.

In a world that changes at an ever-accelerating rate, some organizations survive and thrive and others stagnate and die. With ever-faster change as a permanent fact of life for all kinds of organizations, there is a growing need to make intentional use of learning processes to help ensure that they continue not only to survive but also to thrive, by reacting effectively to whatever the future may bring, but also helping to shape that future. In this sense all organizations need to be learning organizations. Organizations which are not learning as fast as they could or should, and have not ensured that they continue to learn, risk becoming less effective, becoming unhealthy, and eventually ceasing to exist.

This book is not about *learning organization theory*, by which we mean the rapidly growing body of published books and articles on the subject of why it is considered necessary to become a learning organization. For readers who want to know what is being said on the subject we have included an Annotated Bibliography of the key works up to September 1994. This book offers descriptions of practical processes and techniques (we prefer to call them tools) which we have used to help organizations move towards becoming learning organizations. The book is not intended to inspire through the creation of a vision of how organizations in the future should be. We leave that to others, for example, Handy (1992) and Lessem (1991). Instead we have set out to describe a framework of practical steps, and a range of tools which will increase an organization's commitment to maximizing the pay-off from improved learning at all levels. The organization may or may not consciously have signed up to the idea of the learning organization. In our view that does not matter.

Overview of the book

Chapter 1 describes the changing national and global context which has necessitated the quest for organizations of all kinds to become quicker and better at learning. We also describe the distinctive features of our approach which is evolutionary and participative rather than radical and prescriptive.

Chapter 2 examines the significance of learning for an organization and relates it to the organization's vision and its core values. It also examines six different levels of learning within the organization. The chapter also encourages a healthy scepticism about the idea of learning organizations.

Chapter 3 does not define a learning organization. Instead it takes the reader through a series of exercises which gradually expand a number of underlying factors and considerations that need to be taken into account when conceptualizing a learning organization. It argues that conceptualizing a learning organization is better than trying to define it.

Chapter 4 contains a description of a project to create a set of tried and tested tools which would enable organizations to optimize the pay-off from increased or improved learning at individual, group, or organizational level. The chapter also contains a 'working approach' for a learning organization. We stress that the approach is not a definition with the implications of prescription and correctness, but rather a working model or framework to guide action. The chapter contains an overview of actions for a learning organization which include workshops for top management, carrying out a learning audit, reviewing the role of the human resources (HR) function, and upgrading individual learning skills.

Chapter 5 contains descriptions of a process for raising awareness of the critical significance of learning by carrying out audits and surveys of the state of learning in the organization. Chapter 6 describes workshop processes for creating an implementation plan and Chapter 7 focuses on practical measures to help managers manage learning more effectively, in terms of both their own learning and that of their teams.

Chapter 8 details ways to support and sustain learning, including shadowing, mentoring, learning contracts, and self-development, as well as a selection of instruments that have been designed to facilitate learning. Chapter 9 discusses the implications of moving from a training orientated culture to a learning culture.

In Chapter 10 we reflect on some of the lessons we have learned from our practical involvement with organizations seeking to enhance their competence to learn, and finally in

Chapter 11 we allow ourselves the luxury of speculating about some of the themes that underlie the learning organization concept.

Throughout the book we have provided examples to illustrate the practical application of the techniques we describe. We have also provided an annotated bibliography of key references on learning organizations for those who wish to explore particular topics in more detail.

References

HANDY (1992) *Managing the Dream: The Learning Organization*, London: Gemini Consulting.

LESSEM (1991) *Total Quality Learning: Building a Learning Organization*, Oxford: Basil Blackwell.

Acknowledgements

Many people have contributed to this book. In particular we would like to mention Robert Wood and Johanna Fullerton who were part of the Pearn Kandola team which created the first edition of the Toolkit for a Learning Organization (1993) which has now been replaced with Tools for a Learning Organization (Pearn and Mulrooney, 1995). Much of our early work on Developing Skilled Learners was carried out in collaboration with Sylvia Downs and Patricia Perry who pioneered techniques such as the Keys to Understanding, and who created several of the instruments described later in this book.

We would also like to thank our clients, and in particular the sponsors of our work in developing the Toolkit. We would like to mention Ed Williams and Keith Robson (Marks & Spencer), Colin Ions and Alan Taylor (Courage), Laurence Moss (Colgate-Palmolive), Jim McCready and Barry Kimber (Shell UK Ltd), Jenny Rogers (BBC), Keith Moultrie (NHS Training Division), Graham Vitty and Carole Singleton (Glaxo Manufacturing Services), and Paul Phillips (National Westminster Bank). We have also learned from the NHS Trusts who took on the task of piloting the Learning Organization Toolkit.

Other people from whom we seemed to be learning as fast as they seemed to be learning from us include Alan Herringer, Paul Christie and Dave Reed at Southern Life in Cape Town, David Goodman and David Heath at 3M, Paul Hughes at BNFL, and Marcia Carey-Ray and her team at Motorola, and Barry Kitson at ICL.

We are grateful to all these people and their teams for contributing to our learning, just as we hope we have contributed to theirs. We would also like to thank the companies who gave us permission to name them in the case studies presented in this book.

The list on page 13 and Figs 2.1, 3.1, 4.1, 4.3 and 4.4 are

xiv   *Acknowledgements*

extracted from *L'Autoformation dans l'Enterprise* by Philippe Carré and Michael Pearn, Editions Entente, Paris 1992, and are reproduced with permission.

The Learning Climate Questionnaire Profile Charts used in Figs 5.1 and 5.2 are reproduced with permission of The Employment Service and Newland Park Associates Limited. Figure 11.1 is extracted from *Managing the Mosaic* by Rajvinder Kandola and Johanna Fullerton, 1994, IPD Publications, London. We are grateful to the publishers for permission to reproduce these figures.

Finally, a special thank you to Sandra Macleod, who not only typed the manuscript but also kept us in check during hectic schedules, for her patience, forbearance and hard work, and also for her suggestions and improvements to our work.

1   Our approach to learning organizations

In this chapter we

- look at the changing global context in which organizations operate
- identify some of the reasons why learning has become an important issue for organizations seeking to survive and thrive in an unpredictable world
- describe our particular approach to becoming a learning organization.

Global change and global learning Many books have described the rapidly changing world in which organizations of all kinds have to learn not only to survive but also to thrive on uncertainty and ever more ferocious global competition (cf. Kanter, 1989; Drucker, 1993). Some of the key points made by these writers underline the need for an organization to learn not only to live with these 'conditions of the modern world' but also to learn to take advantage of them.

Typically we are reminded that the predictability horizon is getting closer and closer. New products used to survive long enough to repay their research and development costs. Increasingly, the technology that was exclusively available to large organizations can quickly be copied and replicated by small companies all over the world, so that the competitive edge that may have taken years to develop could be lost within a matter of months, as IBM discovered to its cost. Peter Senge (1990) notes that, as the world effectively shrinks and even the smallest companies can obtain whatever skills and technologies they require at a reasonable cost, the only source of competitive advantage is an organization's ability to learn rapidly and react more quickly than its competitors to a fluid market. Familiar technology that has evolved over decades, if not centuries, can now be superseded in a matter of a few years, for example hundreds of years of technology enshrined in the printing press and the mechanical watch mechanism yielding with dramatic speed to the computer and the quartz movement respectively.

Typical of the more startling developments are the facts that:

- There are more scientists and technologists alive today than have existed in the whole history of humanity.
- Global competition is becoming more and more fierce.
- The educational level and the aspirations of the workforce are changing dramatically.
- Some 'developing' countries are aiming to reach levels of national educational achievement superior to those of the industrialized nations of Western Europe.
- The average lifetime of the largest industrial enterprises is probably less than *half* the average lifetime of a person in an industrialized society.
- Development projects are now so complex that new ways of learning and managing are essential to their success.

Numbers of scientists and technologists

There are more scientists and technologists alive today than have existed in the whole history of humanity (Bengtson, 1992). In the last couple of decades there has been an explosion in knowledge and innovation. The RSA report *Tomorrow's Company* (1994) states that 'every year around the world as much new knowledge is gained from research and development as the sum total of all human knowledge up to the 1960s'.

Global competition

Global competition is becoming more and more fierce. This is dramatically manifested by the extreme variation in manufacturing labour costs between countries which increasingly have access to the same manufacturing, information and materials technology. Former West Germany heads the league at $25 per hour, with France, Japan, and the United States at about $17, and the UK at $13. These countries must compete with Taiwan ($6) and countries like Poland ($3) and Indonesia, where the labour rates are even lower (RSA, 1994). It is claimed that Japanese car manufacturers can produce cars of comparable quality to German cars in a quarter of the manufacturing time and with lower hourly labour costs. In order to continue to compete, organizations need to learn how to reorganize, reduce costs, innovate and create new opportunities for gaining competitive edge (Kanter, 1989).

Changing aspirations The educational level and the aspirations of the workforce are changing dramatically. With each generation there is a growing demand for increased autonomy and self-expression and improved quality of life. This is associated with an expectation of greater involvement in decision-making and increased responsibility at work. When Adam Smith, in *The Wealth of Nations* (1776), spelled out the division of labour into simple replicable steps, he cannot have imagined that the model of the hierarchical, multi-level, authoritarian organization which evolved would have lasted until the end of the 20th century or that it may well persist into the 21st. This despite the phenomenal growth in literacy and quantum leaps in technologies of manufacturing, materials, communication and information. What may have been necessary for a labour force of barely literate and ill-informed workers in the 18th and 19th centuries has become increasingly inappropriate today, where organizations need to tap into what is most valuable about human beings—their commitment, understanding, innovation and creativity—using their brains instead of just their hands. Organizations need to learn to take off the blinkers of over 200 years of experience and challenge conventional wisdom to develop new organizational models. Above all, the leaders of organizations (of all kinds) need to create organizations that people want to work in, where they can feel pride, and where they can achieve a sense of well-being and fulfilment within the context of work. If this kind of alignment between individual and organizational aspirations can be achieved then the qualities of a great team (cf. Senge, 1994) can be acquired, viz. a clear sense of purpose, pulling together, feeling valued and doing something worth while. Such teams can achieve great things and sometimes are unbeatable.

Educational aims of developing countries Some 'developing' countries are aiming to reach levels of national educational achievement superior to those of the industrialized nations of Western Europe. For example, Taiwan (like France) has set itself the goal of 80 per cent of all school-leavers having university entrance-level qualifications by the end of the century. In developed countries, so-called knowledge workers and skilled service workers already form the majority of the labour force (Drucker, 1993). With the high transferability of information and other technologies, and the fact that manufacturing technology can be developed and used anywhere in the world, countries like Taiwan will pose an ever-stronger competitive threat to high-labour-cost, traditionally organized companies.

As Rosabeth Moss Kanter (1989) put it in her influential book *When Giants Learn to Dance*, the challenge of the 1990s is to 'produce more with less'. In other words, greater output of higher quality must be achieved while using fewer resources. To fail to do so will necessarily mean the decline and death of an enterprise, which will succumb to relentless growth in competition in local, national and global markets.

Lifetime of industrial enterprises

The average lifetime of the largest industrial enterprises is probably less than *half* the average lifetime of a person in an industrialized society. Advances in communications and manufacturing technologies are such that competitive advantage in specialized markets which can take years to achieve can be overtaken in a matter of months. As a result the competitive pressure on companies will become ever more extreme. The failure rate of major companies was revealed in a study carried out by Royal Dutch Shell (de Geus, 1988). One-third of the Fortune 500 industrial organizations listed in 1970 had ceased to exist by 1983. By contrast, a small number of companies had survived 75 years or longer. Perhaps they knew something the others did not. More recent analysis of the original 500 companies has revealed that a further third had also ceased to exist by 1993 (Hooker, 1994). Size, current financial performance, and strength in the market-place is clearly no guarantee of future success.

Shortening cycle times

Development projects are now so complex that new ways of learning and managing are essential to their success. Boeing's development of the new 777 aircraft was achieved in record time in large part by abandoning traditional hierarchical, compartmentalized, demarcated approaches to the control of projects of this scale. Open collaboration, sharing, an attitude of 'no secrets' and, perhaps most importantly, putting *learning* explicitly on the agenda, were the means by which this vastly complicated enterprise achieved success.

Learning at the national level

There has also recently been a significant public enquiry by the Royal Society of Arts into the nature of Britain as a 'Learning Society'. The report, *Profitable Learning* (Ball, 1992), follows from an earlier report, *Learning Pays* (Ball, 1991), with a ten-point action plan to help create a learning society in the UK, in which the vicious circles of the 20th century—low productivity and profits, low investment, low standards, low skills—will be replaced by the virtuous circles of the 21st century. These are seen as high aspirations, high standards, high skills, high salaries, high satisfaction (see Figures 1.1 and 1.2). The *Learning Pays* report asserted that the creation of a learning society should be the UK's highest national priority. The argument was clearly expressed: 'Those nations that invest in learning gain economic, social and personal benefits for their citizens: those that fail to do so suffer decline.'

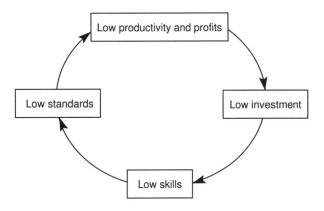

Figure 1.1   The vicious circles of the 20th century

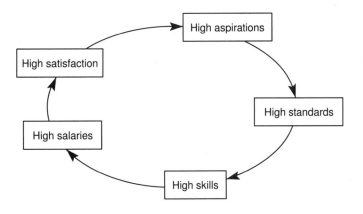

Figure 1.2   The virtuous circles of the 21st century

The report argues that at its best learning is continuous and often informal, whereas existing models of education and training overemphasize the initial and formal aspects of learning. The report's three major findings are that:

1. learning pays;
2. in a learning society the principle of lifelong learning should be the informing idea of education;
3. that it is the supply side of education and training that must change first if a true learning society is to be created.

In our view, a useful way of looking at the concept of a learning organization is as a microcosm of a learning society.

If industrially developed economies fail to develop, or only gradually evolve, as learning societies, it becomes even more important that employing organizations and institutions become learning organizations, if only to compensate for the inadequacies and inflexibility of the formal education and training systems and to develop people with the confidence and ability to adapt and to learn on a lifelong basis. To the extent that organizations can develop people to meet their own needs, they can become self-contained islands of learning and adaptation, but the process would be easier and more productive if it was located within a society that also placed a high value on lifelong learning, adaptation and change, thus equipping its citizens to cope with an unpredictable world.

Distinctive features of our approach

The most distinctive features of the approach which we describe in this book are that it

- is values-driven;
- employs participatory methods;
- is evolutionary;
- is based on principles of learning.

Values-driven

The approach described in this book has not stemmed from formal theories of learning or human behaviour, or from a systematic review of research on cognitive processes, or of organizational behaviour. Instead it has evolved piecemeal and has grown organically. It has its roots in research on individual learning, and the development and evaluation of methods and processes designed to enhance learning. Perhaps more importantly it has evolved from years of experience of working with groups of human beings, working with them to enhance their learning both as individuals and as teams trying to learn more effectively. Underlying the evolutionary approach that we have adopted is our basic training as occupational psychologists, which has probably caused us to pay more attention to behavioural rather than structural and organizational aspects of learning.

The set of values which has guided the development of our work is evolving all the time and may one day turn into a theory of human learning in organizations. For the moment they are simply a set of things we believe in. Even at their best, theories are only of value to the extent that they help us understand the world better and lead to actions and interventions that are more helpful than the alternatives. It is perhaps not insignificant that it was in France that one of the authors first came across the now familiar challenge:

It's all very well in practice but will it work in theory?

It does, of course, raise the question of whether an effective approach can be developed which guides action in the absence of formal underpinning theory. Our view is that implicit theory is sufficient to initiate a process and that the insights gained from experience may enrich the theory which itself suggests lines of action that can be taken. At the end of the day evaluation is necessary to determine whether desired outcomes have been achieved.

The values that have guided our work

- Most people prefer to have control over their destinies and their immediate environment.

The experience of working in organizations often detaches people from themselves and their personal (non-work) lives. We have heard people say of their managers: 'they just don't know what it's really like'; 'they don't really understand because they never listen to us'. Another symptom of this detachment is the often held view that something management is committed to just cannot work, and that everyone knows it except, apparently, the management team. Work can become detached from the rest of people's lives because they are often required to do things that they do not fully support or understand. It appears not to matter too much because 'it has always been like this' and as a result a norm of uninvolvement, disempowerment, even cynicism develops in organizations.

- The failure to mobilize people's intelligence and wisdom is wasteful in the extreme.

Certain groups of people stand out as extreme examples of the waste and neglect of human talents because they are typically under-represented in well-paid secure jobs or they are under-represented in key decision- and policy-making roles. In different contexts the neglected and under-utilized groups will, frequently, be women, sometimes men, often ethnic minorities, and depending on context certain religious groups, age groups, people with disabilities and so on. These groups reflect the diversity of human beings as employees, as customers and as partners.

In addition there is another kind of waste that arises from the organization of work and of jobs which makes people passive when they prefer to be active, subordinated when they work best among equals, acquiescent when they would prefer to challenge, and fearful when they would prefer to be confident. Too many organizations are stuck in a mould of operating that is derived from 18th- and 19th-century models of work organization and the strictures imposed by economies of scale, or merely decades of habit. The creative energy and commitment that would arise from further involvement would be intrinsically rewarding to the individuals and also to their organizations.

- Given a choice people would prefer to organize work closer to the way they organize and run their own lives.

For many people, there is a huge gap between their experience of work, where they spend a large part of their lives in a passive role, and their private lives, where they exercise choice, have responsibilities, prioritize, allocate and use resources, plan for the future, and are guided by or seek a sense of purpose in their lives. For many people at work the biggest decisions they are allowed to make are trivial compared to those they routinely make in their private lives. People learn to survive by acquiring the habits and the behavioural norms of the organization they find themselves in. If this means exercising one's intelligence only so far as it is tolerated, or not rocking the boat, then that is what many people will learn to do in the interests of security. To do this suppresses a natural desire to question, query, challenge and create, which at one level or another comes naturally to most human beings. There is a risk that we have built, and have become accustomed to running and being employed by, organizations that are incapable of making the best use of human talents and which fail to give dignity to those involved.

• Treating people with dignity is not only intrinsically motivating, it also brings rewards for the organization.

One of the best ways in which to treat someone with dignity is to encourage them to learn and to make use of that learning to the benefit of themselves and the organization. There is a risk here of caricaturing the differences between work and private life but we have spent years in the presence of people in all sorts of organizations who were utterly frustrated by their employing organization and who felt bitter and unable to change things. We have also seen highly able people trapped low down on the promotion ladder because they made the mistake of criticizing or challenging in a way that made others feel uncomfortable. We also have seen whole groups of workers written off and wholly underestimated by their managers. Top managers cannot know all the answers, nor can any one group within the organization. A partnership between functions and across different roles must be preferable to the now increasingly anachronistic division of labour between managers who think, plan and organize and workers who merely do the work.

Our thinking is motivated not by a desire to impose our values, but by our belief that it should be a prime objective of any organization to tap into and harness the intelligence and collective wisdom of everyone involved and to stimulate the continuous learning of everyone who contributes to that organization. If an organization succeeds in doing this it not only helps secure its own future but also provides a working environment that gives dignity to work. We believe that an organization which succeeds in unleashing its human potential will also succeed as an organization.

Participatory methods A distinctive feature of our approach is the use of group processes and exercises to enable groups to work out their own conclusions. More often than not groups can be equipped for a task, e.g. analysing the significance of learning for the organization, without the need for formal presentations on the subject. In our experience it is rare for a presentation on a proposed solution or way forward to capture the imagination and commitment of a whole group. This is because:

• a message the group works out for itself gains more commitment than one that is offered to it;
• a formal presentation is often not in the language that would come naturally to the group itself;

- a presentation, of necessity, makes assumptions about the audience's perspectives, experience and expectations;
- presentations often offer more information and ideas than the group is ready for or capable of learning, and so key messages can be lost;
- frequently a more didactic approach can set up a resistance in a group which is not equipped to handle open debate.

This is not an argument against more prescriptive methods *per se*, but only about their timing. In our view there is no single definition of, or prescription for, a learning organization that will meet all requirements. Instead it is preferable to allow groups to build up their own understanding as a means to increasing their commitment. Similarly, equipping a team to carry out their own analysis of need and to devise a plan of action for themselves will gain more commitment and support for the plan than trying to impose one.

Our approach is essentially one of empowering through participative methods. It is not however entirely participative because there are elements of knowledge built in, sometimes implicitly, to the various exercises and tools that we use and encourage others to use. The underlying philosophy is to create commitment through shared understanding and then to equip individuals and teams to use a range of practical tools. Where they go from that point cannot be specified or predicted, but the commitment to take action that grows from an understanding that has matured within the group will achieve longer-lasting results than systems, however elaborate and sophisticated, that are imposed from above or by a key group of people.

Evolutionary

Because our processes make use of participative methods, our approach is vulnerable to the criticism that it does not do enough, that it stops short, and that it cannot deliver everything that the organization might need. This is both a strength and a weakness. It is a strength in the sense that there is a commonly held mind-set that an approach should be complete and prescriptive if it is to be helpful. Unfortunately this can pander to those who want experts (internal or external) and consultants to tell them what should be done and how it should be done. It is often difficult for them to accept that they themselves or their teams are the best people to make such judgements once they have been equipped with conceptual frameworks and practical tools that can help bring about levels of involvement and commitment that develop their own momentum.

The approach described in this book is not a system, nor is it complete. The set of participative processes will continue to grow, as will the diagnostic tools and aids to learning, but there is no expectation that at some point in the future the processes and tools will be complete and offer one-stop shopping for busy managers seeking quick solutions to entrenched and systemic problems. There will always be a need for inputs and support from other sources, according to the mature judgement of the organization involved. This book does not describe systems thinking, scenario-planning, and other methods for surfacing mental models, or techniques for exposing paradigms, or for encouraging greater creativity and innovation in teams. It is unlikely that one book could offer all that an organization managing the complex processes of becoming a learning organization would need. (We have, however, included a detailed annotated bibliography to help you address issues outside the scope of this book.)

Comparing the recent contributions of Edgar Schein (1993) and Peter Senge's *Fifth Discipline Fieldbook* (1994) nicely illustrates this point. In his earlier book Senge (1990) powerfully argued that the five disciplines of a learning organization are:

- personal mastery
- team learning
- mental models
- shared vision *and most powerful of all*
- systems thinking.

The new fieldbook is immensely rich in ideas, theory-building, and practical processes and exercises to help organizations practise the five learning disciplines, representing as it does the contributions of 57 people. By contrast, Edgar Schein in a relatively short article offers his thoughts on the role of leaders in a perpetually learning organization. He makes several useful points, many of which coincide with our own thinking, arguing that:

- leaders must learn something new;
- leaders must create a change management group;
- the change group must go through its own learning process;
- the change group must design the organizational learning approach and create task groups;
- task groups must learn how to learn;
- task groups create specific change programmes;

- there must be extensive and intensive communication throughout;
- mechanisms for continual learning must be created.

The most distinctive contribution here is the emphasis it places on the importance of leaders and change management groups self-consciously experiencing new learning as part of the overall process. It is not sufficient that some people are told of the consequences of other people's thinking and/or learning and are then expected to have the same level of commitment.

Schein offers a programme for change which places emphasis on the importance of learning for the organization. In the work we have done with organizations we offer, among other things, processes that allow managers and others to examine and *explore concepts for themselves* and in this way to develop an *internalized understanding* of the significance of learning at all levels of the organization.

It is often said that the most dangerous time for a teacher is when he or she becomes respected and his or her ideas are accepted without challenge. It would be wiser to accept that there are not and should not be gurus in the field of learning organizations. The concept itself is dynamic, organic and unfolding, and it would be foolish for an organization to believe that one person has all the answers, or that anyone should seek to have all the answers. The closest thing to having all the answers lies in the creation of capacity in an organization to think for itself, persistently to question and challenge its own beliefs and assumptions, and to work out its own solutions. Ideally, this should be based on shared understanding of complex issues and the creativity and commitment that comes from collaborative working of people with a common vested interest in the survival and continuing success of the organization of which they form part.

Intentional use of learning processes as a unifying theme

Nowhere in this book or in our work with organizations have we attempted to define learning as a process. Sometimes it has been necessary to create a group process that attempts to distinguish learning from other processes such as training or development of people, but in almost all cases groups already have enough tacit knowledge to identify how learning, for example, can be blocked, or for that matter to itemize its critical role in contributing to organizational effectiveness now and in the future. It is not necessary to become embroiled in precise academic discussions over the definition of learning. It is sufficient to point out to those whose mind-set expects or even requires a formal definition before they can take something seriously that for most of this century researchers, and philosophers for even longer, have been disagreeing over the precise definition of learning. In reality there is no one definition that meets all requirements. Instead there can be many different levels of definition and many different definitions (we prefer conceptualizations) co-existing on the same level. Rather than risk becoming stuck on the quest for a precise definition, it is better to enrich a group's conceptual framework for thinking and talking about learning in a way that is sufficient for the purpose.

Underlying themes in our approach to learning include (Carré and Pearn, 1992):

- people learn in a variety of different ways
- making the learning process conscious or explicit helps learners exercise greater control over their learning
- individuals and groups can learn to become more effective learners
- both individuals and organizations can be blocked in their learning without even realizing it
- a systematic audit or analysis of learning blockages or of the learning climate is usually helpful in gaining commitment, understanding the problems, and in planning action
- managers need help in changing their behaviour to support and encourage learning
- a coherent strategy combining the introduction of organizational and individual enhancers to learning needs to be combined with a systematic analysis and removal of both individual and organizational blocks to learning
- the role of training and of trainers needs to be reviewed within the framework of a learning organization.

In the next chapter we

- describe the use of our techniques and processes to develop an understanding of the significance of learning for organizational effectiveness and renewal

References

BALL, C. (1991) *Learning Pays*, London: Royal Society of Arts.
BALL, C. (1992) *Profitable Learning*, London: Royal Society of Arts.
BENGSTON, J. (1992) Paper presented at Eurotecnet Conference, Montpellier.
CARRÉ, P. and PEARN, M. (1992) *L'Autoformation dans l'Enterprise*, Paris: Editions Entente.

DE GEUS, A. P. (1988) 'Planning as learning', *Harvard Business Review*, March–April, 70–74.

DRUCKER, P. F. (1993) *Post-Capitalist Society*, Oxford: Butterworth Heinemann Ltd.

HOOKER, S. (1994) Paper presented at a Motorola conference. *Making the Learning Organisation Work*, Paris, 19–20 April.

KANTER, R. (1989) *When Giants Learn to Dance: Mastering the Challenges of Strategy, Management and Careers in the 1990s*, New York: Simon and Schuster.

RSA (1994) *Tomorrow's Company: The Role of Businesses in a Changing World*, London: Royal Society for the Encouragement of Arts, Manufacturers and Commerce.

SCHEIN, E. H. (1993) 'How can organizations learn faster? The challenge of entering the green room', *Sloan Management Review*, Winter.

SENGE, P. M. (1990) *The Fifth Discipline: The Art and Practice of the Learning Organization*, New York: Doubleday.

SENGE, P. M. *et al.* (1994) *The Fifth Discipline Fieldbook*, London: Nicholas Brealey.

SMITH, A. (1776, reprinted 1994) *Wealth of Nations*, New York: Random House.

2 Understanding learning in organizations

In this chapter we

- examine some of the thinking behind the concept of learning organizations
- argue against thinking in terms of *the* learning organization
- pose 20 sceptical questions
- briefly describe the origins of the concept
- highlight the links between organizational vision, values and behaviour
- describe six levels of organizational learning
- examine four ways of thinking about learning organizations which use the six levels in different ways.

The core idea behind the 'learning organization' is that organizations of all kinds will not survive, let alone thrive, if they do not acquire an ability to adapt continuously to an increasingly unpredictable future. Reg Revans long ago argued that

> An organization's rate of learning must be equal to or greater than the rate of change in its external environment.
>
> (Revans, 1982)

This has always been true. The difference today lies in the rapidity of change and the increasingly unpredictable nature of the environment. The capacity of an organization to learn may, as Ray Stata has concisely expressed it:

> become the only sustainable source of competitive edge,
>
> (Stata, 1989)

Learning organizations are now much talked, and written,

[handwritten margin notes: "Statement from Assignment", "Pearn agrees"]

about. But is it meaningful to talk about *the* learning organization?

Why it is wrong to talk about *the* learning organization

If the focus of attention is on *the* learning organization one is tempted to ask the wrong sort of questions:

- What is *it*?
- How can you tell if you are *one* ?
- Who knows what *the* learning organization is?
- How do you become *one*?
- What do you do after you have become *one*?

These questions tend to arise when something can clearly be specified and described as a steady state. Consequently, the questions generated tend to focus on how you get there. By contrast, when the focus is on learning as a dominant feature or attribute of an organization the questions that arise are different, more sceptical and perhaps even healthier. It is paradoxical to be dogmatic about learning organizations. The sorts of questions that should be posed include:

- Is there such a thing as a learning organization?
- What is different about so-called 'learning organizations'?
- Is it a meaningful, and therefore, helpful concept?
- Is a learning organization different from a self-renewing organization?
- Is it just organizational development wrapped up in new clothes?

These questions allow a more challenging and constructive examination of the general idea of learning organizations. Below we offer 20 questions you might try asking.

Twenty questions to ask about learning organizations

- What do learning organizations do that others do not?
- What do organizations which do not learn effectively look like?
- What do organizations that learn effectively do differently?
- Are there different ways of being a learning organization?
- Are there different kinds of learning organization?
- Do you have to want to be a learning organization in order to become one?
- Do you have to call yourself a learning organization in order to be effective at learning?

- How can an organization tell if it is learning effectively?
- Can an organization succeed without being a learning organization?
- Can you be a learning organization without realizing it?
- What else might we be besides being a learning organization?
- Is there a difference between being a learning organization and maximizing organizational learning?
- What are the drawbacks to becoming a learning organization?
- What are the benefits of becoming one?
- If it is a question of self-transformation and renewal, isn't it true that a lot of companies managed that in the past without calling themselves learning organizations?
- Why the emphasis on learning instead of change and adaptation?
- Does its chief value lie in aspiration rather than achievement, as in total quality?
- Must a prescribed path or set of steps be followed?
- How does the process of becoming a learning organization differ from TQM or business process re-engineering?
- Is the decision to become a learning organization self-justifying or must a business case be made?

There are no universal answers to many of the questions posed above, but they do represent issues which an organization must consider as part of the process of examining the concept. Different answers will be developed by different organizations. Later in this book we describe processes which will help organizations examine these issues and form their own answers. Underlying these processes is the firm belief that answers and solutions which are developed by the people most involved have more power and lasting impact than those that are offered or imposed by outsiders. The best conceptualization of what it means to be a learning organization will be the one that the organization arrives at itself.

Origins of ideas about learning organizations

The concept of a learning organization, or 'the learning organization' as it is often called, first acquired prominence in the UK with the work of Pedler and his co-workers in the late 1980s culminating in the publication of their book, *The Learning Company* (Pedler *et al.*, 1992). Pedler and his team produced the oft-quoted definition of a learning organization:

det

> an organization which facilitates the learning of all its members
> and continuously transforms itself   (Pedler, *et al.*, 1992)

What is important about this definition is the emphasis on self-transformation. An organization can be very committed to training and development (as in the well-documented cases of Kodak and IBM) and yet be vulnerable to complete failure because the organization as a whole has not acquired a capability of transforming itself in the face of ever-faster changes in its external environment. Some organizations actually see the change coming but cannot adapt fast enough; others are taken completely by surprise and are suddenly overcome by competitors or by other dramatic changes in their markets, in various technologies, and even in socio-political contexts.

De Geus (1988) highlighted that companies do not learn and adapt very quickly with the startling statistic that one-third of the 1970 Fortune 500 no longer existed by 1983. Additional strength to this argument at this time came from the struggle for survival faced by several of Peters and Waterman's (1982) so-called 'excellent' companies.

At about the same time, Peter Senge's seminal article in the *Harvard Business Review* (1990a) and his book, *The Fifth Discipline* (1990b), began to raise awareness that:

- there is an important sense in which organizations as a whole learn;
- some organizations are a lot better at learning than others;
- organizational learning is critical to the survival and success of organizations in the future.

Senge's Definition

Senge sees a learning organization as one which is 'continually expanding its capacity to create its future'. There is a slight difference in emphasis from Pedler's definition in that Senge emphasizes *expanding capacity* whereas Pedler lays stress on continuous self-transformation. Either way, the commitment to becoming a learning organization requires radical shifts of thinking and behaviour.

Possibly one of the most useful conceptualizations has recently been produced by Dixon (1994). According to Dixon, learning organizations make:

> intentional use of learning processes at individual, group and system level to transform the organization in ways that are increasingly satisfying to [all] its stakeholders.   (Dixon, 1994)

We find this succinct formulation appealing for four reasons:

- It emphasizes the intentional use of learning processes which are often not well understood by organizations or by those in them who are responsible for bringing about change.
- It covers individual, group and system level learning thus embracing all spheres of learning in the organization.
- It refers to the critical outcome of self-transformation rather than externally enforced change arising from impending crisis.
- It refers to the satisfaction of all involved: employees, shareholders, suppliers, other partners, the community, and so on.

The insight that complete organizational learning is crucial to survival and success in the future has been expressed in a variety of ways. Peter Senge notes that the only source of competitive advantage is an organization's ability to learn and react more quickly to a fluid market than its competitors. In his view, in the future there will only be two kinds of company: failures which die suddenly or slowly, and learning organizations.

What seems to distinguish surviving and adapting organizations from the rest is the ability to capture relevant learning to their own advantage. Some organizations may have done this intuitively or even unconsciously in the past, but the rate of change in technology, markets and so on is so fast that organizations increasingly need to learn more systematically and to regard the learning of the total organization as a key part of its corporate mission. Stahl *et al.* (1992) have expressed this point well in their notion that in order to be successful in the future organizations need to 'form the strategy, structure and the culture of the enterprise itself into a learning system'. Garratt (1990), in a similar vein, has identified three characteristics of learning organizations:

- They encourage people at all levels of the organization to learn regularly and rigorously from their work.
- They have systems for capturing the learning and moving it where it is needed.
- They value learning and are able continuously to transform themselves.

So far, we have examined the origins of the concepts underlying learning organizations and different views of what learning organizations should set out to do.

Organizational vision and supporting behaviour

Key features of a learning organization are its vision of how it wants to be and a clear articulation and understanding of its purpose or mission, and the ways in which these manifest themselves in values and behaviour:

It may help to examine the components of the complex set of relationships linking an organization's mission and vision with espoused values and desired patterns of behaviour:

Mission	What the organization is there to achieve, why it exists, its purpose.
Vision	The idea it has of itself at specified points in the future: 5 years, 10 years, 20 years, or more. What it is aspiring to achieve.
Values	The guiding principles which should help determine choices, decisions, policies and behaviour and which flow from the mission and vision for the organization.
Objectives	The specific goals it has set itself and the strategy by which they will be achieved.
Behaviour	The forms of conducive and supportive behaviour which all members of the organization in different contexts should display.
Relationships	The nature of relationships, e.g. between stakeholders of different kinds, between functions, between managers and their teams, between colleagues, etc.
Actions and outcomes	The specific outcomes which taken together add up to the overall effectiveness of the organization over a period of time and help it move towards its vision and the fulfilment of its mission.

There is a complicated and subtle relationship between the components (Figure 2.1). A clearly understood, articulated and shared mission, vision and values should be the source of the objectives and strategy created by the organization. Stemming from both the vision and the mission should be a set of values and desired behaviours which support the achievement of objectives. The behaviour and relationships lead to actions and outcomes which help achieve the mission in line with the values.

In a learning organization one might expect learning to feature prominently, for example:

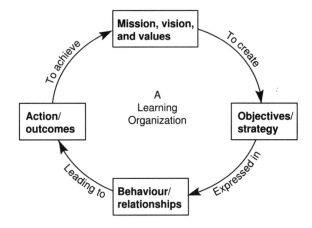

Figure 2.1   Links between mission, strategy, behaviour and outcomes (from Carré and Pearn (1992), reproduced with permission)

Mission	To learn faster than our competitors, and to form all our processes into comprehensive learning systems. To establish learning as an inspiration and source of fulfilment for all.
Vision	To have created the capability to transform continuously within 5 years, and be the kind of organization that people want to work for because they believe in it.
Values	To value challenge and contention. To appreciate and harness diversity. To be open and honest. To treat everyone with dignity.
Behaviour	To act with autonomy and to support self-development. To learn openly from mistakes. To continuously improve. To learn routinely from actual as well as simulated experience. To challenge and question continuously.

The point here is not that learning should dominate one or more of the areas, but that learning (its importance and achievement) ought to be a prominent feature. The key thing to note about a learning organization is that it exists only as a set of complex relationships which link the organization's vision, mission, values and behaviour to desired outcomes and results.

An understanding that sustained continuous learning and adaptation within the enterprise are critical, not only for meeting organizational objectives but also for identifying the objectives, should be at the heart of the enterprise's mission and vision. It should be a key determinant of the organization's culture, which manifests itself in the values and in the types of behaviour which are encouraged and reinforced as a means of achieving desired outcomes.

Levels of organizational learning

Some organizations may be better at achieving effective learning at some levels, but not at others. In our view, learning manifests itself critically at six different levels (see Figure 2.2). These levels are described here in a way which accentuates the differences between them. However, in reality there is considerable overlap between levels.

Figure 2.2   Levels of learning in a learning organization

Individual learning

It has always been recognized that individual employees have individual learning needs. Invariably these have been satisfied by the provision of formal vocational education and job-related training, but increasingly self-directed learning and self-development in which traditional formal training may only play a small part have become more common. The individual may have a need to acquire new skills, or to understand new processes. Many organizations are well equipped to meet individual training and development needs, whether through traditional classroom-based instruction, using multi-media methods (involving CBT, CAL or interactive video) and/or through open and distance learning provision.

An organization which, through its history and culture, has not placed a high value on individual learning may have acquired a workforce which is passive, fearful and reluctant to change. By contrast a workforce of motivated, energetic and confident learners is likely to be a workforce which uses 'its head', reacts to problems positively, and learns from mistakes, instead of concealing them or fearing punishment if mistakes are discovered. Enhancing the readiness and competence to learn of all employees and not just key individuals (top managers, researchers) or people with specific needs, is an important step towards becoming a learning organization.

Group or team learning

Whereas employees may have learning needs as individuals, there is another sense in which, as a member of a work group, or of a production or service unit, there will be a need for team-based learning to occur, which transcends the learning needs of the individual. As we will see later, there are also positive benefits to learning collaboratively; some actually learn better this way.

With the increasing recognition of the benefits of cross-functional, customer-focused teams and also of flexible self-directed or self-managed teams, attention needs to be given to the process and outcomes of learning as a team and not just individuals who make up a team.

Cross-functional learning

The third level of learning is the complex set of learning needs at the functional or departmental level. An example would be the need to develop a stronger customer orientation in a manufacturing department, or the need to understand and learn to co-operate effectively with departments with which there has been little or no co-operation in the past. Advances in information technology have brought previously separate and dispersed groups or functions into closer contact with each other, because of the massive increase in the capacity for storage, processing and retrieval of shared information. (The Boeing 777 project we mentioned earlier provides a good example of this.) Learning to work together, understanding each other, and working within a common and shared vision across diverse departments, or operating companies within the same group, is a critical level of learning for many organizations.

Organizational learning (internal)

The fourth level of learning covers the organization but focuses on learning *within* the organization. Here the emphasis is placed on ensuring that learning and adaptation are highly valued and reinforced within the organization and that all opportunities are taken to ensure that sustained learning and adaptation occur in the interests of the organization's quest for efficiency, innovation, quality gains, competitive edge, etc. For example, the Rover Group established the Rover Learning Business to achieve just such aims.

Organizational learning (current external realities)

Level five is outer-directed in the sense that the organization as a whole needs to learn continuously about the environment in which it is operating and in which it hopes to continue to operate in the future. It is very important for an organization to ensure that it is capable of assessing and understanding current trends in external markets, and of responding to new technologies and socio-political factors that change the environment in which it operates. The organization needs to ensure that changes are detected, understood and absorbed in such a way that it can respond constructively and resourcefully rather than being swept along by unanticipated events.

Organizational learning (future possibilities)

At level six, the organization needs to take a longer-term view of itself and the environment in which it operates. It must develop a broader picture of global markets, socio-political issues and other trends in technology and population patterns. The predictability horizon for many organizations is closing in, and they may be unable to predict with accuracy the state of their external reality only a few years ahead. Learning to cope with an unpredictable future is a key learning task.

Argyris (1991) has argued that top managers are often not well equipped to learn in this fashion because they are used to building on success and are therefore inclined to continue with modes of thinking and behaviour that have worked well for them in the past. There is also an important sense in which only so much can be learned from experience. Some things cannot be experienced (e.g. future possibilities) and can only be imagined or simulated by means of special techniques such as scenario planning (de Geus, 1988). In addition, special techniques may be necessary to bring to the surface and challenge underlying assumptions or mental models which determine (often unconsciously) the way an organization thinks about itself, its role and its future.

Level six is mainly carried out by the top management and leaders/directors of organizations. In a sense they learn *on behalf* of their organization and the results of their learning and adaptation are turned into transformational strategies and long-term objectives for the organization. Levels one to five focus on adaptive learning and transformation *within* the organization, though there is a sense in which these levels are also important for an understanding and appreciation of the 'bigger picture' (level five), both globally, nationally and internationally, to be developed within all employees in the organization.

Four kinds of learning organization

Building on these six overlapping levels of learning in organizations, we believe there are at least four ways of thinking about learning organizations; each one combines the levels of learning in different ways:

- A critical mass of effective learners
- A specially created environment which fosters learning
- A micro-learning organization
- A macro-learning organization.

A critical mass of effective learners

To the extent that policy-makers lack the confidence and motivation to learn and to test and challenge their own assumptions and mind-sets, an organization has acquired a learning handicap. To the extent that very few, if any, employees are confident and motivated to learn and to challenge assumptions, the organization has learned to live with a double handicap. If only key individuals (such as board-level directors, members of a think-tank or special project teams) are open to new learning, from whatever source, they will be keen to encourage others to accept or adopt their vision. If some people have been cast in, or have assumed, the role of learners on behalf of the organization, they will often want to tell others what is right or good for them, because they have done the learning for them. With the benefit of this learning they feel wiser and better informed and they see the challenge as transferring their wisdom into the heads of the less gifted. Several *'hazards to learning'* result from this approach:

- It encourages the vast majority of employees to be passive and not think for themselves.
- With passivity comes tolerance of the status quo, which may be acceptable in the short term, but can become a handicap in the long term.
- It perpetuates the view that some people do the thinking for the organization and lowers expectations of what the rest have to offer.
- A habit of not reflecting and challenging at work can develop, either because it is not encouraged or because it is reacted to negatively as threatening, disruptive, inconvenient or even disrespectful of those in authority.
- People who have grown accustomed to passivity and not using their brains at work will tend to react negatively to change out of fear and frequently a lack of understanding of the bigger picture.
- There is also frustration that the things that most people do

routinely in their private lives like planning, organizing, thinking ahead, taking on complete responsibility for their actions, are not encouraged at work or only tolerated to a limited degree.

The advantages of encouraging all members of an organization to become active, confident and motivated learners are, according to a group of line managers in the UK brewery Courage Limited, that they will:

- think more for themselves
- accept change more readily
- challenge more
- improve things for themselves
- seek out learning opportunities
- seek to improve themselves through learning
- learn new techniques and processes more quickly
- shorten training times
- achieve optimum levels of performance more quickly
- make fewer unproductive mistakes
- learn better from experience.

The group of line managers strongly felt that encouraging and sustaining learning of the whole workforce would bring lasting benefits.

This type of learning organization is likely to focus its learning efforts at levels one and two. Although there are clear benefits to be achieved from developing a mass of effective learners, these benefits can be undermined or even eliminated if the surrounding environment for the learners is not also specifically created to be supportive.

A specially created learning environment

A training school or learning centre, or even a short course, could be described as a specially created learning environment. The physical facilities and their layout, the availability of individuals who are there to bring about learning in others, the structuring of the day into 'lessons' or tutorials, and the expectations of those who are there to learn (students, trainees, course members) are all geared to the achievement of learning. Whether or not the learning objectives are achieved in the most effective manner is a separate issue.

When new technology is being introduced, or a green-field site is created, there is often a reorganization of work practices. Typically there is a higher level of autonomy, with traditional authoritarian supervision being replaced by empowering, facilitating team leaders or team managers. This is often associated with increased output and/or improved quality and by a higher level of employee involvement, openness, trust and continuous improvement. In many ways a conducive learning environment is created, even though there may have been little explicit focus on learning processes.

The key objective is the achievement of a highly motivated sub-group of people who are expected to spend more time than previously organizing and planning their own work, and finding new ways to improve things in a supportive and receptive local environment. The problems arise when that is as far as it goes. In one organization we worked with, a supportive learning environment had been achieved in one part of a factory and with considerable success, but the rest of the factory did not understand or appreciate what was going on and were resentful of the appearance of special privileges. As a result they did not co-operate, and accepted without challenge a wide range of critical and unflattering allegations about the unpopularity and ineffectiveness of the new department and its new working practices. In effect the rest of the factory spread rumours about the failure of the new way of working and, unconsciously or otherwise, made it harder for the new department to succeed within the wider factory system. The negativity expressed by the rest of the factory was even displayed by members of the management team responsible for other parts of the factory. Although the new department and its new way of working was declared a success, it seemed more like an oasis in the desert with sand dunes constantly encroaching. The factory had unwittingly created a negative reaction and an unnecessary new hurdle that had to be overcome. Too much focus had been directed at levels one, two, and to a lesser extent four, but the vital step of creating structures and processes to facilitate cross-functional learning was omitted.

A micro-learning organization

We see a micro-learning organization as one that believes that it should actively encourage learning and the acquisition of learning skills in all the people that make up the organization. It can achieve this by concentrating primarily on formal mechanisms for delivering training and development, and through extensive commitment to open learning. There is full commitment to training and development of all employees, which is efficiently delivered, monitored and evaluated.

In a relatively stable external environment where changes can be seen or predicted within a time-frame which would enable the organization to change direction, the micro-learning organization will benefit from a culture and structure, and policies and practices, which encourage and sustain the learning of all employees. The organization learns to be efficient within the framework it has created or indeed accepted for itself. The micro-learning organization seeks to make use of the talents of all its members, but does not seek to examine and challenge its own fundamental assumptions or paradigms as Barker (1994) put it. The micro-learning organization can operate well at levels one to four, but may not be good at assessing the true nature of its current external reality. It may, for example, believe that its market domination is unassailable and that there will be indefinite demand for its products or services. A micro-learning organization does not seriously examine the kind of organization it might or should be in an increasingly unpredictable future. This is the work of a macro-learning organization at levels five and six.

A macro-learning organization

The macro-learning organization differs from the micro-learning organization in that it constantly examines its external environment, both present and future, to determine whether it should change direction. The macro-learning organization builds in processes for thinking about its future and evaluating options, and seeks not only to react to future developments, both predicted and unpredictable, but to influence them. It can only do this by thinking long term, but what is long term to some will seem short term to others.

Even organizations which are successful in anticipating changes in markets and technology which overwhelm their competitors must also be good micro-learning organizations. Otherwise the strategic advantage gained at the macro-level can be gradually undermined and competitive edge can be systematically eroded by higher costs and failure to tap into the wisdom and intelligence of everyone in the organization. Many organizations are effective macro-learners but are weak at the micro-level. Similarly many organizations are good at the micro-level but their life-span is threatened by weakness at the macro-level. The combination of organizational learning competence at the macro- and the micro-levels is the winning combination. Such organizations are learning effectively at all six levels.

In the next chapter we

• describe a number of processes that you can use to help you and your colleagues work out a concept of a learning organization which will help you develop your own idea of a learning organization instead of one being imported from elsewhere. This conceptualization will help your organization to achieve the benefits of learning.

References

ARGYRIS, C. (1991) 'Teaching smart people how to learn', *Harvard Business Review*, May–June, 99–109.

BARKER, J. L. (1994) *Paradigms*, New York: Harper Business.

DE GEUS, A. P. (1988) 'Planning as learning', *Harvard Business Review*, March–April, 70–74.

DIXON, N. (1994) *The Organizational Learning Cycle: How We Can Learn Collectively*, Maidenhead: McGraw-Hill.

GARRATT, B. (1990) *Creating a Learning Organization: A Guide to Leadership, Learning and Development*, Cambridge: Director Books.

PEDLER, M., BURGOYNE, J. and BOYDELL, T. (1992) *The Learning Company*, Maidenhead: McGraw-Hill.

PETERS, T. and WATERMAN, R. (1982) *In Search of Excellence*, New York: Harper and Row.

REVANS, R. W. (1982) *Origins and Growth of Action Learning*, Bromley: Chartwell-Bratt.

SENGE, P. M. (1990a) 'The leader's new work: Building learning organizations', *Sloan Management Review*, Fall, 7–22.

SENGE, P. M. (1990b) *The Fifth Discipline—The Art and Practice of the Learning Organization*, New York: Doubleday.

STAHL, T., NYHAN, B. and D'ALOJA, P. (1992) *The Learning Organization—A Vision for Human Resource Development*, Brussels: Commission of the European Communities.

STATA, R. (1989) 'Organizational Learning—The key to management innovation', *Sloan Management Review*, Spring, 63–74.

3 Conceptualizing learning organizations

In this chapter we

- describe how to brainstorm the benefits of encouraging and sustaining learning in all employees
- offer two dimensions which can be used to categorize the organization into one of four learning types
- describe the INVEST model which can be used as a way of diagnosing the organization's performance as a learning organization
- describe a group exercise which develops understanding of learning organizations in such a way that a group can create its own conceptualization
- examine four important dimensions on which learning organizations vary.

? learn from mistakes

Understanding organizational learning

Lessons gained from personal experience are more likely to be remembered and internalized than principles or theories learned by other means. Winston Churchill in his autobiography *My Early Life* expressed it concisely when he said: 'I love to learn but I hate to be taught'. Many successful entrepreneurs claim that their most valuable lessons resulted from their biggest mistakes. One difference between them and others is that they learned from their mistakes, whereas the others did not.

In our view, many top managers (and maybe even writers on the subject) are happy to talk about the value of learning to the organization without fully understanding what they are saying, because they have not developed a deep and internalized understanding of learning in intellectual, emotional and behavioural terms. For this to happen managers need to learn consciously about learning and its importance to their organizations.

In our experience when a formal definition of the learning organization is offered to a group of managers they are unlikely to accept it. They are more likely to: ask why this definition and not another; be reluctant to accept it because it is couched in unfamiliar language; waste a lot of time arguing over the detail and as a result miss the key concept; and may end up paying lip-service to it in order to move on to what they see as more pressing issues.

A powerful process is to ask them to work out a concept for their own organization, but first they need to be equipped for the task. The first step is to establish the link between learning and organizational effectiveness. This can be achieved by using a participative, structured brainstorming technique called *Understanding Organizational Learning*. It involves using the Keys to Understanding method which we describe in more detail in Chapter 7.

This is how it works. Ask the group to form pairs and one trio if necessary. Give them a worksheet with the following questions on it, each question with a response box about half a page in size:

- What purposes can be served by encouraging and sustaining the learning of *all* employees in the organization?
- What would be the consequences for your organization of not succeeding in encouraging and sustaining the learning of *all* employees in the organization?
- How could you tell if you were succeeding in encouraging and sustaining the learning of *all* employees in the organization?

Normally we ask the pairs to address questions 1 and 2 first, allowing them about 10 minutes to jot down all the thoughts that occur to them. When they have finished, all their thoughts are listed on a flipchart using a strict procedure which is designed to ensure that thoughts are collected in without comment, judgement, or evaluation, however irrelevant, frivolous, or provocative some of them may at first seem.

Once the list has been produced the group reacts and discusses the ideas in it. In almost every case the group is impressed at the significance of learning for the organization. This is a connection they had not previously made, as learning was something they typically associated with school and university rather than the world of work.

We ran this exercise for a group of 50 line and HR managers in the European Division of Motorola, the international electronics and wireless communications company. They produced a total of 72 separate ideas which were classified into nine headings. The main argument was that learning was critical to organizational success as it helped achieve and sustain competitive edge without which the organization could not survive and thrive. It would also help develop a flexible and adaptive workforce which would continuously improve its performance and challenge the *status quo*, thus becoming more motivated and fulfilled. A sharper vision of possible futures, improved communication and transfer of learning within the organization were also seen as key benefits of encouraging learning in all employees.

The nine headings (with illustrative examples) were:

1. *Learning is critical to competitive advantage*
    'learning is what will make the difference in the future: it will help us achieve and retain competitive edge'
2. *A quicker responding organization*
    'better anticipation: a constant state of readiness for change'
3. *An adaptive workforce*
    'adaptive to new requirements (thinking not just doing)'
4. *Improved performance (innovation, challenges to* status quo*)*
    'increased productivity and efficiency; continuous improvement'
5. *Increased pride and dignity*
    'commitment, growth and fulfilment'
6. *Sharper focus on the long term*
    'pushes us into longer-term views; we will expand our own horizons'
7. *Improved communication and knowledge transfer*
    'better networking; help create a questioning culture'
8. *Better teamwork*
    'more synergy, empowerment; a collaborative work environment'
9. *Superior workforce*
    'attract and retain better people'

In response to the question about the consequences of failing to encourage and sustain the learning of all employees, the group of managers produced about 60 distinct responses. Their ideas were grouped into six distinct categories:

1. *Loss of competitive advantage*
   'missed opportunities, lost markets, and reduced profits'
2. *Loss of good people*
   'difficult to attract and retain'
3. *Stagnation*
   'rigidity and control, repetition of mistakes, and passivity, low energy'
4. *Demotivation*
   'loss of morale, no pleasure, training a chore'
5. *Loss of know-how*
   'poor use of experience, lower skill level'
6. *Follower not leader*
   'isolation, poor image, loss of innovation and creativity'

The question 'How can you tell?' produced a wide range of responses, ranging from measures of organizational effectiveness (e.g. profitability) to aspects of culture (autonomy, encouragement) and specific behaviour (e.g. ask more questions, challenge the *status quo*).

The process of asking open-ended questions about Purposes (question 1), Consequences (question 2), and Checks (question 3) (page 31) is part of the Keys to Understanding technique. The process generates a large number of ideas because:

- The group gives all its ideas on a topic before further information is given or evaluations are made. Giving information in advance can stifle creativity and inhibit receptivity.
- Working in pairs encourages discussion and sparks off new ideas.
- Worksheets are used to enable people to formulate their ideas, as reflection before speaking tends to improve the quality of ideas produced.
- All the ideas (one from each pair in turn) are written on flipcharts, without evaluation or discussion, to avoid pre-judgement and demotivating some members.
- Ideas that appear on the surface to be the same are explored by the group facilitator to ensure that additional or new concepts are not missed.

Generally, the totality of ideas produced is greater than any one member of the group or external expert could generate. The group is often impressed by its own output. The process 'opens people's minds', or enriches their conceptual framework, before approaching and dealing with a complex issue. The method (i.e., the form of the questions, the worksheets and the procedure for collecting in responses) can be taught to, and used by, managers to encourage creative problem-solving in groups and as a means of developing understanding of complex concepts or issues.

Another type of question used in the Keys to Understanding technique is the *comparison* or contrast question. For example, what do you think are the differences between a learning organization and an organization that does not learn well? This question would not work well unless preceded by the other questions about possible purposes and consequences of not succeeding.

When posed this question, a group of managers in Marks & Spencer, the well-known retail organization, produced the following list of positive and negative signs:

Positive signs	*Negative signs*
• fewer layers of management	• heavily hierarchical management structure
• everyone has a brain, and is encouraged to use it	• 'managers think and workers do' mentality
• people learning *all* the time	• we've always done it this way
• it is recognized that workers know things bosses don't know	• learning means training, of the formal kind
• genuine teamworking	• 'not invented here' mentality
• people are encouraged to manage themselves	• specialization defines work organization
• continuous improvement as an imperative	• training is something which is done to you
• work is more enjoyable *and* productive	• people matter less than technology
• questioning and experimentation encouraged	• past experience is what counts, not learning
• employees share progressively in decision-making	• your supervisor always knows best
• employees respect one another	• learning is a luxury
• training is learner-orientated	• learning is for school, work is about getting things done

- top management keen to change.

- 'if it ain't broke, don't fix it'

- decisions based on assumptions, not evidence.

From this starting point it is possible to move forward on the basis of a shared understanding of the significance of learning for *this* organization, rather than using time to argue over competing definitions. In practical terms, this exercise is used to set the agenda: the identified benefits, consequences and signs of success providing the focus for future activities.

Rating the organization

Are we already a learning organization? Two diagnostic processes will help to determine the answer.

A two-dimensional model

Having established the actual or potential benefits of encouraging and sustaining learning in all parts of the organization as well as the consequences of not succeeding, it is helpful to try to position the organization in terms of learning. This can be done initially by providing ratings on two separate dimensions. Ask each individual in the group to rate the organization (and/or their part of it) on two dimensions:

- The extent to which the *general environment* (including structure and culture) of the organization enhances, supports and sustains the learning of all employees (however they wish to define this).
- The extent to which *the workforce as a whole* is confident, motivated and competent to learn.

On both dimensions, the highest possible score is nine and the lowest, one. If the rating is in-between, a number between nine and one should be given, but not a five, to discourage sitting on the fence. The combination of ratings on the two dimensions positions the organization in one of four quadrants (see Figure 3.1).

- A stagnated organization
- A frustrated organization
- A frustrating organization
- A learning organization.

These dimensions are admittedly crude, but for the purposes of an awareness-raising workshop they combine to give an

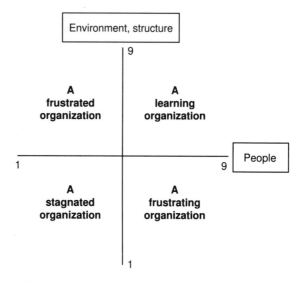

Figure 3.1   Four types of organization resulting from the interaction of two dimensions (from Carré and Pearn (1992), reproduced with permission)

overall view to the group which is sufficient to gain their commitment to further examination of the idea of learning organizations.

A stagnated organization relies solely on past experience for present solutions and all decisions come from management ('who know best'). The workforce is passive and uninvolved; it does not want to change and adapt (i.e., learn). There is no encouragement or incentive in the system and there are few, if any, opportunities for self-development. The employees are not motivated to learn and adapt; the structure and general environment of the organization inhibit learning.

A frustrated organization thinks it is doing the right things but the employees are fearful and lack confidence in their ability to cope with change and new working practices. This is despite the fact that management exhorts and encourages, provides access to open learning and has removed practical barriers to adaptation and change. In other words, all the right things are being done by management, but there is or has been little involvement of the people most affected in the design of the process. Their fears, needs and ability to contribute constructively to the design of solutions have been ignored.

A frustrating organization fails to recognize that its employees are skilled, energetic and keen to take on new learning. The system or structure provides little opportunity for self-development, access to training, or open learning. Formal training has low status and low priority for management. There is a wide gulf between the managers and the managed.

A learning organization has a strong vision of its future. All individual and group potential for learning and adapting at all levels is being fully utilized in the interests of setting, meeting and reviewing organizational objectives. Environmental and structural blocks to learning have been identified and removed. Strong enhancement and structural support for sustained continuous learning have been put in place at all levels.

Analysis of an organization's perceived position on the two dimensions can produce some interesting insights. Consider the coordinates for Company A (Figure 3.2).

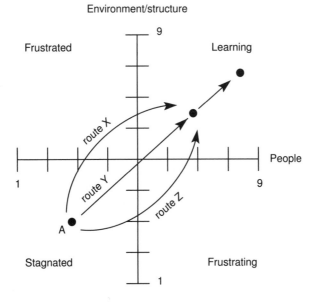

Figure 3.2   The coordinates for company A

By this analysis the organization has been diagnosed as somewhat stagnated, neither the general environment nor the workforce receiving high ratings. The group is recognizing that the situation could be a lot worse, but also recognizes that there is considerable room for improvement. The current position of Company A raises the question of the best route to be taken. Route Y aims to move directly to an improved position on both dimensions thus positioning the organization in the lower left-hand sector of the learning organization quadrant as a first step to moving diagonally to the upper right-hand side. This could be difficult to achieve, as it requires coordination of diverse initiatives over a protracted period. Route X requires putting in place support mechanisms, for example the development of a culture that supports and rewards learning, and other structural and organizational changes to enhance learning. The danger is that many organizations become stuck in the 'frustrated' quadrant thinking that enough has been done and it is therefore the fault of an apathetic and intellectually defective workforce if more changes and improvements are not achieved. If the organization recognizes that improvement on both dimensions is needed and that being positioned in this quadrant is a transitional state, then it is less likely to remain a frustrated organization. Route Z entails recognizing the talents and energy that already exist in the workforce and building on them by putting in place support mechanisms and at the same time identifying and removing blockages to individual and group learning.

About a quarter of the management groups we have worked with have given their own organizations ratings on the two dimensions which put them firmly in the 'frustrated' quadrant.

The frustrated organization has taken steps to provide opportunities and encouragement for learning and development within the organization. It may even have a detailed management and personal development strategy. It may have made generous provision for open learning access by means of learning centres and provided easy access to open or distance learning opportunities. However, there may be relatively little return on the investment because the workforce cannot see the point of undertaking the learning and is not actively supported and encouraged by supervisors and line managers, who see take-up of open learning as a luxury rather than seeing it as vital to the interests of the organization. People may also be under-confident in taking on learning and may feel relatively unskilled at learning. Employees may feel inhibited about taking advantage of the opportunities that are there, or their own supervisors and managers may inhibit or discourage them.

The 'frustrated organization' has made good provision for access to learning but will not get a return on the investment because the other half of the investment has not been made. This can include the development of a culture that values and supports learning, builds confidence and motivation to undertake self-development and uses other measures designed to sustain continuous learning.

Very few management groups place their organization in the 'frustrating' quadrant, but many shop-floor groups do. The 'frustrating organization' has a competent, intelligent and energetic workforce, but there is no structural provision for encouraging learning, nor access to open learning and sustained self-development in the longer term. In other words, the organization is living off short-term energy and vitality and is putting nothing in place to sustain and support learning and development in the longer term. This is the classic pattern of the newly created entrepreneurial organization where the relative newness of the organization and the directness and proximity of feedback on performance are themselves sufficient to ensure optimum natural learning and development. As the organization becomes larger, more complex and more structured there is a danger that the energy and vitality of the workforce becomes stifled and inhibited through increasingly bureaucratic processes and the structures required by a larger and more complex organization.

A common outcome of this exercise is a disparity between perceptions of the whole organization and of the participant's own function or department. A typical set of coordinates is shown in Figure 3.3.

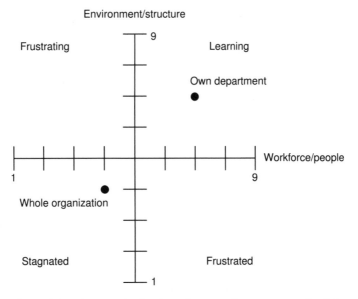

Figure 3.3 Contrasting ratings for own department and whole organization

In this analysis, the view is taken that the department is reasonably good on the two dimensions whereas the organization as a whole is rated much lower. This view tends to be common when a function or department is self-contained, does not communicate well with or understand other departments and maintains that it is the rest who have problems. When other departments have similar views, there is clearly a lack of agreed criteria or data for making the evaluation. Part of the difficulty arises from the catch-all quality of the two dimensions, which suggests the need for a more detailed look at the things learning organizations tend to do. Simple though this tool is, it can have a powerful effect on the thinking of participants.

A six-factor model: INVEST

Another way of looking at a learning organization is to expand the two dimensions (environment and people) into six:

- Inspired learners
- Nurturing culture
- Vision for the future
- Enhanced learning
- Supportive management
- Transforming structures.

The model (Figure 3.4) has been created out of a systematic review of the published literature on learning organizations (see the Annotated bibliography, page 203) and our own extensive experience of working with companies. A rating of one to nine on each of the factors, which are defined below, can be discussed by syndicate groups in a workshop and agreed using the 'anchors'. These 'anchors' are guidelines which give people criteria for deciding their ratings. The discussion may be based around both the broad definition of each factor, and the list of things to take into account.

Inspired learners
The extent to which the workforce as a whole is motivated to learn continuously, is confident to take on new learning and to seize opportunities for learning from experience, and is fully committed to self-development.

Things to take into account
- Does everyone feel the excitement and the necessity of continuous learning and development?

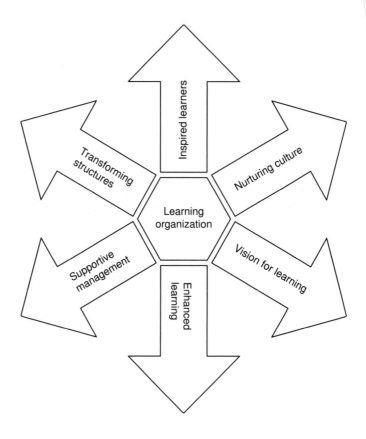

Figure 3.4   The INVEST model of a learning organization

- Does everyone take charge of their own learning?
- Does everyone identify and meet their personal and team development needs?
- Is continual learning and development an exciting part of everyone's role?
- Does everyone try to improve continuously the way things are done?
- Is everyone confident about acquiring new skills and knowledge?
- Does everyone make sure they learn from experience and from their mistakes?
- Is everyone good at learning? Has everyone had the opportunity to experience learning-to-learn sessions?
- Does everyone have an individual learning and development plan which is explicitly linked to performance objectives?
- Does everyone challenge the *status quo*, and ask questions?

Anchors

8 or 9 All employees learn continuously, are excited by learning and understand the significance of individual, group and organizational learning for the current and future viability of the organization.

6 or 7 Pockets of excellence only.

5   Rating not available (to discourage compromise).

3 or 4 Managers talk about these things but do not practise what they preach.

1 or 2 Most employees are passive, reluctant to take on new learning and are blocked by fears of not being able to cope.

Nurturing culture

The extent to which expressed values and displayed behaviour support continuous learning, encourage challenge to the *status quo*, questioning of assumptions, and established ways of doing things. Testing, experimenting, learning from mistakes, exploration and reasoned debate are valued activities.

Things to take into account

- Is individual, group and total organizational learning valued as a prime asset?
- Are there frequent opportunities to experiment without suffering serious consequences?
- Is there a general climate of mutual respect, openness and trust?
- Are incidental learning, or learning from everyday experience and reasoned debate, valued activities?
- Are people encouraged to learn from one another, by making their thinking explicit, and sharing this with colleagues?
- Is everyone always encouraged to question the way things are done?
- Are mistakes always treated as learning opportunities?
- Are reflection and review valued activities?
- Is continuous improvement a way of life? Is everyone encouraged to find new ways to do things better?

Anchors

8 or 9 There is universal support for continuous examination of established ways of thinking and doing at all levels in the organization, and processes for achieving learning at all levels are highly valued by everyone.

6 or 7 Pockets of excellence only.
5   Rating not available.
3 or 4 Managers benefit and/or talk about these things but they do not apply to the rest of the workforce.
1 or 2 There is active intolerance of questioning and challenge to the *status quo*. Mistakes are concealed, but when revealed are treated punitively. There is a fear of making mistakes.

Vision for learning
The extent to which there is a shared vision which includes the organization's capacity to identify, respond to, and benefit from future possibilities. Part of this vision recognizes the importance of learning at individual, group and system level to enable the organization to transform itself continuously and thus survive and thrive in an increasingly unpredictable world.

Things to take into account
- Is there a clear mission (i.e., what the organization is there to do) which is understood by everyone?
- Is everyone committed to the mission?
- Is there a clear and widely understood vision of where the organization is going?
- Does the vision emphasize the importance of learning to cope with whatever the future brings?
- Is a key component of the vision the ability to self-transform continuously?
- Does the vision emphasize the importance of creating capacity to shape the organization's future?
- Has an action plan or 'road map' to achieve the organization's vision of its future been put in place?
- Does everyone make sure that everything they do fits with the vision?
- Does the vision emphasize the importance of learning, at all levels, for continuous transformation?

Anchors
8 or 9 The vision is shared, fully articulated, communicated and understood by all members of the organization who are committed to it.
6 or 7 The vision has been created and communicated downwards but only in some parts of the organization.
5   Rating not available.

3 or 4 There is a vision but it is mainly confined to management levels.

1 or 2 The organization has no vision. It merely exists.

Enhanced learning

The extent to which the organization has put in place
processes and techniques to enhance, encourage and sustain
learning among all employees.

Things to take into account
- Is mentoring widely practised?
- Does everyone apply systems thinking?
- Is open or distance learning widely used?
- Is action learning used routinely through the whole organi-
zation?
- Is the organization part of a 'learning consortium', in which
it works closely with other non-competing organizations in
order to achieve best practice?
- Are methods routinely used for surfacing mental models?
- Are learning contracts widely used to make learning
objectives explicit?
- Does the organization make use of learning laboratories?
- Do trainers support and facilitate learning or do they merely
provide training?

Anchors
8 or 9 All employees benefit from practices and techniques to
enhance and enrich learning, e.g. learning contracts,
shadowing, networks, mentoring, personal development plans, systems thinking, learning laboratories.

6 or 7 Pockets of excellence only.

5   Rating not available.

3 or 4 The methods used to enhance learning are sporadic
and tend to be confined to management.

1 or 2 Methods to enhance learning are rarely, if ever, used.
Training is seen as the prime mechanism for achieving
learning.

Supportive management

The extent to which managers genuinely believe that encouraging and sustaining learning results in improved
performance by those who are much closer to the work

actually done and/or the customer. Managers see their role as facilitating and coaching rather than control and monitoring.

Things to take into account
• Are managers generally receptive to new ideas?
• Is the management team constantly helping the organization and everyone in it to achieve the vision of the future?
• Is everyone trusted to perform to the level of his or her competence with the minimum of supervision?
• Are managers actively involved in supporting employees to learn and develop continuously?
• Do managers genuinely believe organizational performance will be improved if decisions are pushed as far down the organizational hierarchy as possible?
• Is it the manager's prime role to coach and develop, rather than control and monitor?
• Are managers continually trying to empower others?
• Do managers reflect on their mental models and encourage others to do the same?
• Do managers encourage people to take time to reflect on and review their thinking as a valued activity?

Anchors
8 or 9   Managers in all parts of the organization actively support and encourage their own and other people's continuous learning.
6 or 7   Pockets of excellence only.
5   Rating not available.
3 or 4   Managers believe in and understand the importance of learning, but have not learned to change their behaviour to actually bring about learning in others. Top management are not generally walking the talk.
1 or 2   Managers behave and are rewarded for behaving in a way which results in the perpetuation of old ways of doing things and a passive and 'unthinking' workforce.

Transforming structure
The extent to which the organization has been designed and operates to facilitate learning between different levels, functions and sub-systems and permits rapid adaptation and

change. It is organized in a way that encourages and rewards innovation, learning and development.

Things to take into account
- Are there only as many managerial and supervisory layers as are necessary? Have unnecessary layers been stripped out?
- Is the encouragement of learning the responsibility of all managers?
- Is work organized into self-managed or self-directed teams (SDTs) with a high degree of autonomy and control over their immediate behaviour?
- Is work defined in terms of objectives and assignments rather than jobs, tasks and rules?
- Does the organization ensure that functional boundaries do not prevent continual sharing of knowledge and ideas across these boundaries?
- Are all parts of the organization customer-focused?
- Is centralized control only used where necessary? Is everyone given as much autonomy as possible?
- Is cross-functional working the norm?
- Is the top management team itself functionally diverse?

Anchors
8 or 9   The organization is designed to facilitate and encourage continuous learning. There is a strong emphasis on customer-focused business units, multi-functional team working and an avoidance of multi-level hierarchy and centralized control. There is great emphasis on sustained business partnership encouraged by a high degree of autonomy. The organization is as flat as possible.

6 or 7   Pockets of excellence only, some parts of the organization have enabling structures, but others do not.

5   Rating not available.

3 or 4   The organization is hierarchical and rigid. Individual careers tend to grow within functional 'chimneys', and there is little communication and mutual understanding between different parts and functions of the organization.

1 or 2   The organization does not even know it has got a problem with its structure and systems.

Ratings on the six dimensions when plotted on a radiating graph reveal distinctive profiles. Figure 3.5 shows the profile

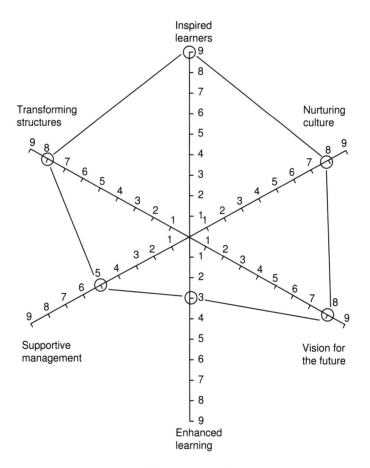

Figure 3.5 INVEST analysis: a manufacturing company

of a manufacturing plant in the north of England. It has a wide portfolio of products covering a range of manufacturing processes. On closer examination, it can be seen to be excelling on four dimensions, but not on the other two.

The company had a well-developed vision which included the development, and domination, of new markets which could benefit from the new communication technology which it was helping to create. The vision was widely understood by employees who benefited from a strong emphasis on high-quality training and development. The company had also set, and was working steadily towards, near-perfect quality standards in production and services. It also achieved a high rating for structure because it was decentralized, and was organized around technology and product groups which spanned the world. Communication between different operating companies was rapid. With regard to learning and the transfer of learning to where it was needed, the company had a facilitating rather than a restrictive structure.

The company also benefited from a supportive culture. The atmosphere was generally open and trusting. However, although the company was committed to empowerment and talked about it a great deal, many managers did not practise what they preached, either because they did not really believe in it or, more likely, because they did not know how to change patterns of behaviour which had become established over many years. Very often they did not achieve the response they wanted because their actions, or failure to act in a particular way, were more influential than their words. The workforce on the whole was very motivated to learn. They took pride in the company's performance and felt they were part of a successful team and that they contributed to it. There was a strong training culture: all employees were entitled to five days' training per year and a great deal of energy went into personal development.

Despite these strengths the company was comparatively weak in the area of enhanced learning. Although many senior managers were familiar with systems thinking and scenario-planning, especially at senior level, the use of such techniques was not widespread. It was also rare for specific measures to be taken to upgrade the learning skills of large numbers of people. The company was, however, strongly committed to distance and open learning.

The diagnosis was that the company already had in place the factors that took the longest time to develop and embed into the organization, and that the two remaining areas, supportive management and enhanced learning, would be relatively quick to develop and benefit from, especially in the fertile conditions created by the other four factors.

By comparison, another company in transition (Figure 3.6) produced a different profile. The company had undergone a recent merger with a company with a different working culture, and had become increasingly aware of the severely competitive environment in which it operated, to the extent that survival had become a dominating theme in its thinking. Rapid changes in production and information technology had caused a culture shock in what had been a very traditional industry. The company had a clear vision of its future, especially at senior management level, but this was not widely understood across the organization. The company had set out to become a learning organization as part of its overall

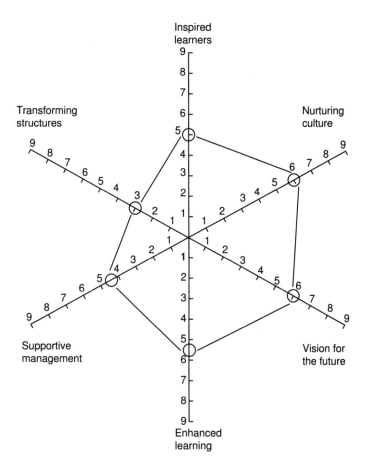

Figure 3.6   INVEST analysis: a company in transition

strategy. Its structure was traditional in that production was completely separated from marketing and sales, though cross-functional customer teams serving local markets had been introduced. The culture on the whole was supportive with a strong emphasis on learning new skills and on flexibility. However, many managers were not told what would be required of them in terms of empowering people in the organization at a time when senior management were planning to put considerable pressure on them to achieve results in ever more difficult market conditions: employee involvement was seen as a luxury that could not be indulged in when pressures were so great. It was not surprising to find that, on the whole, the workforce were demotivated. The one area in which the company excelled was in its range of measures to encourage and support learning. In addition to mentoring and personal development plans it had created several career development schemes to encourage employees to change career but, given its relative weakness in the other five areas, it is doubtful that this alone would achieve the changes in performance the company was seeking to make. Unless these five areas were also addressed, the company would end up as a frustrated organization (as defined by the two-dimensional model).

Finally, the profile of a public health organization (Figure 3.7) revealed its weaknesses as lack of shared vision and a disabling structure, despite its exemplary learning enhancements, and a supportive culture. The ratings show relative weakness in four out of the six dimensions. A vision had been created at senior management level, but it contained no reference to the significance of individual and organization level learning, nor had the vision been disseminated and accepted. The organization was very hierarchical and consisted of a large number of highly centralized power-bases coinciding with the main professional and technical specializations. It was these, rather than its vision or its customers (in this case actual or prospective patients), which essentially drove the organization.

Nonetheless, the organization did have a culture that supported learning, especially the acquisition of formal qualifications, though only those that were legally or professionally required. Management style tended to be authoritarian and traditional command-and-control. By contrast, people were generally highly committed and anxious to do a good job despite difficult conditions of growing demand, diminishing resources, and an atmosphere of uncertainty and continuous change. The organization also had a good record in enhancing learning including an exemplary shadowing scheme, but there was little take-up of this. Conducting an INVEST analysis can help an organization to build up a detailed picture fairly rapidly.

A process for conceptualizing learning organizations

The INVEST analyses can be achieved without formal commitment to a definition of a learning organization. However, a deeper understanding of the concept can be achieved by examining, contrasting and comparing different attempts to capture what is distinctive (indeed unique) about learning organizations. The conceptualizations of learning organizations presented below are all drawn from writers on learning organizations.

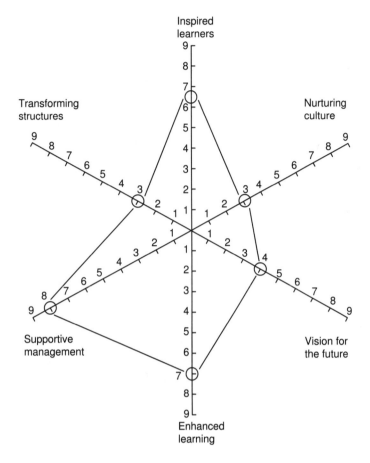

Figure 3.7   INVEST analysis: a health sector organization

A learning organization:

- Is continually expanding its capacity to create its future (Senge, 1990).
- Facilitates the learning of all its members and continuously transforms itself (Pedler *et al.*, 1992).
- Is a lot of people learning (Gaines, 1990).
- Facilitates participative and innovative development within and between people and institutions, commercially, technologically, and socially (Lessem, 1990).
- Forms the strategy, structure and culture of the enterprise itself into a learning system (Stahl *et al.*, 1992).
- Has the capabilities of capturing learning in its different parts, and incorporating that learning into the corporate knowledge base to generate new capability (Saint-Onge, 1993).

- Systematically gears the processes and everything in the organization to enhance its capability to capture market opportunities as they present themselves (Saint-Onge, 1993).
- Has a willingness to accept that learning occurs continuously at all levels of an organization and needs to flow freely to where it is needed (Garratt, 1990).
- Evolves in a very Darwinian way ... it is fostering its own mutation (Peters and Waterman, 1982).
- Has processes which can move knowledge around the organization easily to where it is needed (Ross, 1992).
- Must have an institutionalized procedure for identifying the managerial skills, behaviour and attitudes which will be needed in the future to support an organization's corporate plans (Beard, 1993).
- Encourages double-loop learning (Argyris, 1990).
- Responds to changes in the internal and external environments of the organization by detecting and correcting errors in organizational theory-in-use, and embedding the results of that inquiry in private images and shared maps of organization (Argyris and Schon, 1978).
- Is skilled at creating, acquiring and transferring knowledge, and at modifying its behaviour to reflect new knowledge and insights (Garvin, 1993).
- Makes intentional use of learning processes at the individual, group and system level to continually transform the organization in a direction that is increasingly satisfying to its stakeholders (Dixon, 1994).
- Is dedicated to knowledge creation, collection and control (Leonard-Barton, 1992).
- Makes many mistakes, but learns from them before others realize they have occurred ... it sees learning not as a confession of ignorance, but as the only way to live (Handy, 1992).
- Has as its primary aim rapid and continual regeneration of the total organization, and that depends on rapid and continual learning (Moss-Jones, 1993).
- Improves its knowledge and understanding of itself and its environment over time, by facilitating and making use of the learning of all its individual members (Thurbin, 1994).
- Aims to thrive by systematically using its learning to progress beyond mere adaptation; it purposefully develops strategies and structures to facilitate and co-ordinate learning in rapidly changing and conflictual circumstances (Dodgson, 1993).

It is probable that there are as many different definitions and conceptualizations of learning organizations as there are writers on the subject. However, four themes do emerge.

• Individual learning – organizational learning
• Elite learning – learning for all
• Current learning – future capability
• Oases of learning – irrigated learning

Individual learning –
organizational learning
One way to become a learning organization is to facilitate and enhance the learning of all the people who comprise the organization. The motive is to switch on the brains of all employees so that they are fully engaged. The argument is that a critical mass of challenging, developing, innovating people will result from the focus on individual learning. By contrast the definitions which focus mainly on organizational learning recognize that something else is required in addition to a critical mass of people learning and developing continuously. The whole organization approach recognizes the importance of the organization acquiring a new vision of itself which will include its own capacity to learn and self-transform. It will also recognize that some forms of learning are not available to it from the experience of its members and that it must therefore experiment and test hypotheses by means of techniques such as scenario-planning and/or the use of systems thinking. Too much focus on learning from experience can result in linear developments within accepted boundaries, and as a result an organization could become very efficient in the pursuit of the wrong, or already outdated, goals.

Optimizing individual learning at all levels of the organization is necessary but not sufficient. There must also be a desire, and suitable mechanisms, for testing perceptions and understanding of the external reality, both current and future, and processes for building this learning into the organization. On the other hand, too much emphasis on a macro-learning approach and a corresponding neglect of the development of learning capability of people within the organization could make it harder for the results of, say, systems thinking or scenario-planning to be understood, accepted and built upon by those whose task it is to make them work. In addition, neglect of the full development of the learning potential and brainpower available in all an organization's employees at all levels could allow competitive advantage to be gained by others.

*Elite learning –
learning for all*

Many approaches to learning organizations have concentrated on the significance and quality of managerial learning because of managers' role as leaders. There has been an understandable emphasis on discovering how these leaders learn or fail to learn, and on the creation of techniques and processes for overcoming, for example, organizational defence routines (Argyris, 1990). The focus tends to be on personal qualities and learning styles rather than on structures and systems for transferring the results of key learning to where it needs to be. Focusing on managers learning about long-term strategic issues can result in a top-down approach. The learning gained by managers is passed down the organization and possibly diluted, with compliance replacing internalization as it descends, possibly resulting in covert non-compliance or subversion.

A good example of elite learning is the leadership forum. Carefully selected young managers and professionals are brought together for a 12-month period, during which they attend seminars, regular review meetings and training sessions, and undertake action learning assignments supported by facilitators and personal mentors. Meanwhile, they carry out their normal jobs. The main objective is to create a critical mass of future leaders for the organization who will share a common understanding, common values and behaviour, and who will be capable of driving the organization to success in the next century when the external environment will be very different. The organization is creating a future elite to provide leadership.

The problem lies in the difficulty people experience when asked to accept learning by proxy—when they have not had an opportunity to go through all or part of the learning cycle which led to the conclusions with which they are being presented. In our experience of working with organizations, the tendency to pass on to others the results of senior management learning confirms the Tayloristic notion that management knows best and that the rest of the workforce merely needs to be told. It is a crucial feature of a learning organization that learning (rather than communication) processes are understood and intentionally used to secure commitment through understanding. Full understanding is best achieved by creating learning opportunities and learning cycles where the brains of everyone in the organization are actively engaged. Later in this book we will describe techniques for doing just that. If this approach is followed, learning is valued throughout the organization and not just at managerial levels.

*Current learning –
future capability*

Some conceptualizations of learning organizations place most emphasis on learning within accepted frameworks. The emphasis is on learning to do better what is already being done. Continuous improvement initiatives use the concept of Kaizen to relentlessly pursue incremental changes to process, but do not fundamentally attack or challenge the underlying assumptions which can lead to fundamental shifts of thinking. The *reactive* approach to learning organizations results in a quest to find ways to do better what has already been done before. One company the authors worked with captured this concept by creating the image of a dinosaur which had learned to balance its bulk on a small surfboard and had become highly skilled at surfing. The caption written underneath was: Wrong wave!

The *proactive* approach asks what we should be doing in the future and how we can equip ourselves to cope with situations and contexts that we can only guess at. How can we acquire a capability for influencing rather than merely reacting to future states?

*Oases of learning –
irrigated learning*

Many organizations can point to examples of good practice where there has been a reorganization of work by means of self-directed teams or high-commitment work groups. This is almost always associated with the introduction of advanced manufacturing technology within existing plants or in greenfield sites. The organization of the work has often been led by the need to work the new technology to its full potential rather than by a desire fully to exploit the intelligence available in the work group. As a result oases or isolated pockets of optimized learning can develop which leave other parts of the organization untouched. In the oases there may be a high level of empowerment, with devolved decision-making and team co-ordinators in place of regulatory supervisors. By contrast, the rest of the organization continues to function with multi-level supervision, somewhat autocratic management and little employee involvement. This contrasts with the irrigated approach, where the idea is to maximize the amount of learning in all parts of the organization and to allow a free flow of information and ideas across it.

One best way?

The question that presents itself is whether there is a preferred or a best approach that an organization should pursue. The answer is an unequivocal *no*. On balance it is our view that a whole organizational approach which embraces the need to inspire learners, create a nurturing culture, be guided by a vision of the future, systematically enhance different kinds of learning, support and encourage learning as a prime role of management and put in place transforming structures is more likely to succeed than an approach which does not cover all six aspects.

An initial focus on what we have called 'elite learning' may be necessary, but is not in itself sufficient to achieve sustained organizational improvement through learning unless everyone is subsequently energized and motivated to learn. In addition, an organization needs to have ways of testing out visions of the future, as it needs to be sure that it fully grasps and understands its present reality, both internally and externally. At the same time it needs to learn to do things better on a continuous basis lest it neglect its present while it gazes at the far horizon. Finally, oases of learning (involving new working practices associated with new technology) are opportunities for trials, and experiments, whose lessons can be transferred to other parts of the organization. If they are not, then they are nothing more than oases surrounded by desert as discussed in Chapter 2.

The key point is that the focus on individuals, oases, elite learning and present learning are all valuable in themselves, but only really contribute to a learning organization if they form part of an overall strategy for the *whole organization* to learn and adapt continuously and which itself is part of an overall vision of the future. The vision is the cohering framework. The order in which things are done cannot be prescribed in a way that meets the needs of and constraints on every organization. It is important that the significance of learning for an organization is fully internalized rather than maintained solely on the surface.

Internalized vs surface learning   Surface learning occurs when an individual or an organization has acquired the ability to describe to others the importance of, say, empowerment or organizational learning, and perhaps even provide a neat definition. By contrast, internalized learning occurs when the individual's values, feelings and expressed behaviour also change. Each individual might or might not be able to provide a neat definition of a learning organization, but their priorities and their behaviour have changed in accordance with a newly developed understanding.

We believe that much of the learning that is supposed to be taking place about learning organizations is surface rather than internalized learning. Consider the following examples:

- The expert on learning who gives a 45-minute uninterrupted lecture about the need for new learning (revealing that he or she understands little about learning).

- The senior manager who says 'we are all learning together', but who reacts emotionally and defensively to any challenge to his or her judgements.
- The manager who says, of empowerment, 'I don't care who makes the decision, so long as it's the right one', i.e. one that she would have made herself.
- The organization that says we must learn from our mistakes, but nevertheless reacts punitively when they happen.
- The organization that values learning for everyone, but where the board routinely plays power games and does not see itself as needing to learn.
- The organization that challenges everything except its own assumptions, and its tacit beliefs.

It is possible to believe that an organization as a whole is committed to learning and yet does not behave or function in a way that is consistent with that belief. In our view, it is best not to encourage senior managers to sign up to a specific view of 'the' learning organization by means of a prescriptive definition. Definitions can be used powerfully to help create an understanding of the significance of organizational learning but they can also be used to restrict and inhibit change.

Summary of steps for conceptualizing a learning organization

Step 1 Present to a group open-ended questions about possible Purposes, Consequences, Contrasts, and Checks without first defining learning or learning organizations.

Step 2 Collect in all ideas without evaluation or comment.

Step 3 Discuss broad implications for learning.

Step 4 Analyse the organization using the INVEST model.

Step 5 Present 20 different definitions or concepts of the learning organization on cards and ask participants to group them into three to five piles according to underlying themes and to label each of the themes which emerge.

Step 6 Collate all the themes on to a flipchart and discuss them.

Step 7 Identify which themes are most relevant and use them to create their own vision or conceptualization of a learning organization.

Step 8 If several groups have carried out step 7 the different versions can be displayed for all the groups to examine, and allowing all the individual participants to cast votes using self-adhesive dots.

The aim here is not to achieve a definition of a learning organization as it would apply to their own organization, but rather to take the participants through a learning cycle (or thinking process) which expands and stimulates their thinking in a way that internalizes and develops understanding rather than one that requires acceptance of, and compliance with, an externally proffered definition.

In the next chapter we

• describe a collection of tools that can be used on a 'pick and mix' basis to help an organization move towards becoming a learning organization.

References

ARGYRIS, C. (1990) *Overcoming Organizational Defences: Facilitating Organizational Learning*, Boston: Allyn and Bacon.

ARGYRIS, C. and SCHON, D. (1978) *Organizational Learning*, Reading, Massachusetts: Addison-Wesley.

BEARD, D. (1993) 'Learning to change organizations', *Personnel Management*, January, 32–35.

DIXON, N. (1994) *The Organizational Learning Cycle: How we Can Learn Collectively*, Maidenhead: McGraw-Hill.

DODGSON, M. (1993) 'Organizational learning: A review of some literatures', *Organization Studies*, 14, 3.

GAINES, G. (1990) 'Introducing the concept of self-managed personal development: One company's experience'. Paper presented at Economist Conference Unit Conference. *Creating the Learning Organisation*, London, 5 November.

GARRATT, R. (1990) *Creating a Learning Organization: A Guide to Leadership, Learning and Development*, Cambridge: Director Books.

GARVIN, D. A. (1993) 'Building a learning organization', *Harvard Business Review*, July–August, 78–91.

HANDY, C. (1992) *Managing the Dream: The Learning Organization*, London: Gemini Consulting.

LEONARD-BARTON, D. (1992) 'The factory as a learning laboratory', *Sloan Management Review*, Fall, 23–35.

LESSEM, R. (1990) *Developmental Management: Principles of Holistic Business*, Oxford: Basil Blackwell.

MOSS-JONES, (1993) *Learning Organizations: An Emerging Paradigm?*, Milton Keynes: Open University.

PEDLER, M., BURGOYNE, J. and BOYDELL, T. (1992) *The Learning Company*, Maidenhead: McGraw-Hill.

PETERS, T. and WATERMAN, R. (1982) *In Search of Excellence*, New York: Harper and Row.

ROSS, K. (1992) 'The learning company', *Training and Development,* July, 19-22.

SAINT-ONGE (1993) 'Towards Implementation'. *Valuing the Learning Organization: A Symposium to Investigate the Concepts, Language and Metrics for Measuring Human Capital in the Knowledge Era,* London: Ernst and Young.

SENGE, P. M. (1990) *The Fifth Discipline: The Art and Practice of the Learning Organization,* New York: Doubleday.

STAHL, T., NYHAN, B. and D'ALOJA, P. (1992) *The Learning Organization: A Vision for Human Resource Development,* Brussels: Commission of the European Communities.

THURBIN, P. J. (1994) *Implementing the Learning Organization: The 17-Day Programme,* London: FT/Pitman.

4   Tools for a learning organization

In this chapter we

- describe how to develop employees as more skilful learners
- present a working approach to becoming a learning organization
- distinguish between inhibitors and enhancers to learning at
individual and organizational levels
- use a hot-air balloon as an analogue for a learning organization
- describe 10 actions as a flexible programme for becoming a
learning organization
- describe the experience of one organization in using the tools.

Writers on learning organizations tend to be strong on ideas
but noticeably weak when it comes to practical tools which
organizations can actually use to promote learning. Over the
years we have spent working with clients we have created a
range of practical tools, instruments and processes to help
organizations progress towards a self-defined (in our terms,
conceptualized and internalized) idea of a learning organization.

Our work began with the creation of practical tools and
instruments for improving the skills of learning for both
young people (aged 16–18) and for adults (Downs and Perry,
1984, 1987). Much of this work was commissioned by government agencies in the UK. The tools included the Learning
Blockages Questionnaire and the Job-Learning Analysis, as
well as specific exercises designed to improve people's ability
to learn. These exercises were designed to increase confidence
to learn, to help people understand that there are different
kinds of learning which require different approaches from the
learner, to help learners grapple with learning blocks and

develop effective questioning techniques, and to teach new ways of memorizing, learning practical activities and increasing understanding of concepts and ideas.

Principles for developing skilled learners

The principles presented here were originally devised by Sylvia Downs and Pat Perry. The techniques, and the general approach, were labelled developing skilled learners (DSL) and the main characteristics are described below:

- Learning is the relationship between the processes used in order to learn and the material to be learned.
- Core skills of learning can be identified, made explicit to the learner, and practised, so that they can be improved, e.g. memorizing strategies, and questioning techniques to increase understanding.
- Learning skills have to be made overt to the learner in order to be used appropriately and deliberately.
- For learning skills to be improved, people have to take responsibility for their own learning, which involves pursuing actively and consciously the learning skills associated with a particular outcome.
- The processes, or skills of learning, can be grouped in terms of differences in the material to be learned. These differences can be categorized as factual material to be memorized, concepts to be understood, and activities, skills or processes to be carried out.
- The learning environment must be supportive and encouraging. People have to be encouraged to ask questions and check for themselves. Feedback should be both relevant and realistic.
- While error should be avoided in relation to memorizing facts or learning physical skills, it can be a valuable aid to the development of understanding.
- There are blockages which hinder learning. It is necessary to identify the blockages inside the individual learner, as well as those blockages created by external circumstances so that remedies can be applied and learning improved.

In addition the DSL approach specifies 12 characteristics of *skilled learners.*

Skilled learners:

- take responsibility for their learning and generally adopt an active role;

- can distinguish between things they have to memorize, things they need to understand, and things that are best learned by doing;
- use all the ways of learning available to them and choose between them according to the material to be learned and their preferred way of learning;
- do not fall back on trying to memorize things that they should be trying to understand;
- make conscious decisions on how, when and where they will learn something;
- make sure they learn despite poor teaching;
- ask more questions and ask particular kinds of questions to ensure that they learn properly;
- seek feedback on their own performance;
- realize that difficulties in learning something are not always due to their own inability to learn but frequently lie in inadequacies in the delivery system;
- understand what can block their learning and how to act accordingly;
- realize that they learn best in particular ways that may suit them but not others;
- are confident about new learning opportunities.

A learning culture in a green-field site

In one application, the DSL principles and techniques were applied to an induction programme designed to create a culture that was conducive to learning in a newly created computer-integrated oil-blending plant belonging to the oil company Shell Oils UK (Pearn and Downs, 1991).

The company had built a computer-integrated lubricant blending, packaging and distribution centre. In the application of manufacturing and systems-control technology the plant represented a quantum leap for the company. It was very complex, handling a total of 2500 product variations. The whole process was to be automated from receipt of an order, through calling up raw materials, scheduling the manufacture and packaging, planning storage or direct delivery, including positioning of product on pallets, and planning itineraries for the delivery of the products. All this was to be completed within 48 hours of the receipt of an order. It was an ambitious project and over the three-year planning period a great deal of time and energy had gone into the specification of the technology and manufacturing hardware to be used. Unfortunately, it was only during the last six months of the project that serious thought was given to the kind of people that would be needed to run such a plant. At the time the company had little experience to draw on from any of its operations anywhere in the world.

Some thinking had gone into the culture of the new organization that would be needed to make the plant effective, as the plant was designed to run on about one-fifth of the number of people that the previous plant had needed. The transition from the established ways of working to the culture of the new plant was summarized as shown in Table 4.1.

Table 4.1   Transition from established to new ways of working

	From	To
Organization of work	• defined jobs and demarcations • hierarchical structure • separate functions • working groups	• tasks, roles, responsibilities • flat organization • multi-functional working • team working
Job performance	• heavy physical work • concrete, repetitive work • direct feedback on actions • localized impact • local information	• keyboards and VDUs • application of principles and understanding • remote indirect feedback • system-wide impact • system-wide information
Job demands	• working in fixed groups • safety in numbers • close supervision • restricted decision-making • static, learned environment	• dispersed teams • isolation, vulnerability • autonomy • devolved decision-making • constantly changing
Problem-solving	• proven, familiar technology • stable environment • predictable • familiar problems	• state of the art, unproven • dynamic, interdependent • uncertain • past experience won't help
Values	• imposed/acquiesced to • implicit, taken for granted • production-orientated • do what you are told • sell what we make	• shared, internalized • examined, discussed • market driven • use understanding and initiative • make only to order

The company had located the new plant within a marketing rather than a production company which in itself was a break with tradition. The whole approach was to use new technology to make and supply only what was ordered and to be able to deliver any of its 2500 products within two days of receipt of order to any location in the country. Associated with the change from a production to a marketing environment was a commitment to a new culture expressed through shared values based on more open management, increased individual responsibility, commercial awareness in all employees, greater flexibility and a flatter and more friendly working environment.

The workforce for the new plant was to be drawn from two existing plants both using manufacturing technology that had not changed for decades and with little experience of computer-assisted manufacturing. Many of the new employees had no experience of working with VDUs, keyboards or PCs.

A selection process was designed in order to assess suitability for working in the new plant with its new culture. The selection process was based on generic work competencies such as team working, autonomy and readiness to learn rather specific job-related skills and experience. The new employees then underwent a three-week induction programme which had four main objectives:

- To develop an understanding of the new culture and why it was necessary and a commitment to it.
- To develop an understanding of the business environment which made the new plant necessary.
- To learn the basic concepts underlying the design and operation of the new plant.
- To acquire confidence and ability to learn more effectively.

The induction was in part to prepare the new employees for the considerable amount of training that would be required to operate the new plant. About one-third of the induction process was devoted to each of the last three objectives. The design and running of the induction was an embodiment of the first objective, though a few sessions were specifically designed to develop an appreciation of the new culture and the shared values. In particular, the induction was designed to allay workers' fears that they could not cope with the new technology, and to show that by improving their learning skills they could take on new learning, not only in the induction itself, and in the technical training to follow, but also on a continuing basis.

The sections of the induction that specifically focused on improving confidence and the skills of learning dealt with:

- overcoming fears and learning blockages
- making learning active rather than passive
- increasing personal repertoires of ways to learn
- learning through effective questioning
- improving observation skills
- learning to take notes
- learning to memorize
- getting the best out of instructors
- acquiring a habit of review and reflection
- coping with poor-quality instruction
- using techniques to aid understanding
- learning techniques to improve learning how to do things
- using others to help you learn.

A follow-up study to evaluate the induction process asked the new employees to identify the most important thing they personally had learned. Over a quarter said that improving learning skills was the most important. About a quarter said that understanding the business realities of the new plant was most important. The rest were divided between teamworking, the new technology, and other factors such as safety and familiarization. The induction process had developed in the new employees high expectations of effective training. Most of the induction had been run by the new line managers and team leaders who had themselves gone through the same induction. The line managers ran the induction with energy and enthusiasm, and although they were not professional trainers they understood enough about learning processes to deliver the induction in a way that secured commitment and learning from the new employees.

By way of illustration of the raised expectations, a group of trainees complained to the plant manager that an external trainer who had been contracted to deliver one of the technology training modules was not abiding by the agreed quality standards for effective learning. The trainees felt that he was sticking to a timetable that was convenient to him as a trainer and that he was moving on to new topics before the group of trainees as a whole was ready. After a request to the trainer from the plant manager that he should ensure that all the trainees learned, the trainer still adhered to his own timetable, and as a result he was dismissed. As one trainee put it: 'We need to ensure that we have *all* understood—otherwise we cannot run this plant effectively. Their job is to provide training but we are the people who have to learn.'

A later study of how the new culture was developing revealed that a strong concern for personal fulfilment, responsiveness to individual needs, a general understanding of the business environment of the new plant and a desire to help the plant succeed were more prominent than concerns with individual status and rewards, even though they were of course considered important. Despite the greater than expected commissioning problems which caused considerable strain on the new system and the new culture, it was widely recognized that the learning culture that had been created meant that the expected and unexpected problems were handled better than would otherwise have been the case.

From skilled learners to learning organizations

It became increasingly apparent that, although the DSL tools were of proven effectiveness in improving the learning skills of individuals, and sometimes groups, employees' capacity to learn and adapt was restricted or inhibited by the wider environment. This included such factors as the attitude and behaviour of their immediate supervisors, the prevailing culture of the organization which did not encourage questioning and challenge, low value being placed on individual development, and lack of opportunity to learn.

It was recognized that the tools and exercises which had been developed to improve learning skills would be more effective if placed within a coherent framework which allowed, or better still encouraged them to be used as part of a strategy for organizational change and development. One advantage of the framework would be that gaps would be revealed suggesting where further tools might be needed which did not yet exist.

Another concern was that most of the available practical material was orientated to individual learners and, occasionally, groups. Organizational or cultural factors were not being addressed in practically orientated material designed to improve learning. By contrast, the growing literature on learning organizations seemed to concentrate mainly on concepts, ideas and aspirations: although some writers such as Peter Senge identified practical tools, there was a general dearth of practical aids and tools which could be used within a coherent organizational framework.

A project to create a set of tools

In 1990 we initiated a project to develop a range of practical tools within a coherent framework that could be used by trainers and line managers in organizations of all kinds which wanted to improve learning at organizational, group or individual level.

The formal aims of the project were:

1. To create a working approach for learning organizations that was non-prescriptive but which none the less could be used to guide action and achieve measurable change and performance improvement.
2. To create a simple but robust framework within which a set of practical tools could be located.
3. To identify existing tools (based on the earlier work of the Pearn Kandola team) which could be incorporated within the framework.
4. To design and trial new tools to complete the framework where gaps were identified.

The first part of the project was carried out through an informal partnership with a Paris-based consultancy. A series of meetings took place early in 1991 and an approach to the learning organization evolved, an early version of which was incorporated in the book published in Paris by Carré and Pearn (1992). The Pearn Kandola team continued with the development of a practical working approach to learning organizations and with the development and trialling of tools, exercises and instruments that could be used by companies and other employers.

Eight organizations decided to sponsor the work. They were the BBC, Colgate-Palmolive Ltd, Courage Ltd, Glaxo Manufacturing Services Ltd, Marks & Spencer plc, National Health Service Training Division (formerly the Training Directorate), National Westminster Bank plc and Shell UK Ltd. Over a period of time the sponsors gradually changed into partners in the project. Several of them also offered opportunities to carry out trials and initial evaluations of the new material that was being developed. It was fascinating to discover that these very disparate organizations were interested in the concept of learning organizations. They were all undergoing significant organizational change, and for broadly similar reasons which they articulated as:

- down-sizing, achieving more with less
- delayering, removing unnecessary layers of management
- changing organizational culture
- empowering the workforce
- decentralizing, working cross-functionally
- becoming more customer-focused
- introducing advanced manufacturing, information, and other technologies
- working towards total quality, and world-class standards
- overcoming traditional demarcations and introducing flexible working
- developing high-commitment, cross-functional, customer-focused work teams.

In general all the organizations were moving away from Tayloristic concepts of scientific management, where production is separated from decision-making, and were seeking to move away from a command-and-control style of management towards increased involvement and empowerment of everyone in the organization (Figure 4.1). Several of the sponsors talked about survival and the fact that their 'predictability horizons' were closing in at an alarming rate. The sponsors had not, at the outset, developed their own understanding of, or commitment to, the idea of a learning organization. However, they had all recognized the critical importance of maximizing learning in all parts of the organization.

The group of sponsors/partners played a crucial role in advising and supporting the project team in the design and

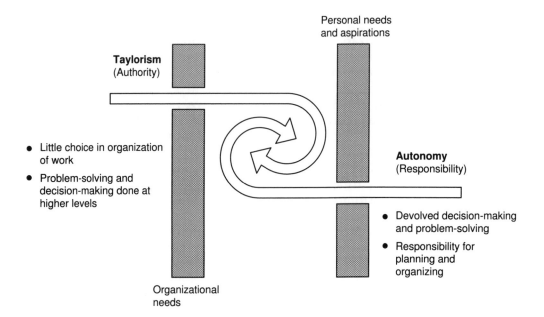

Personal needs
and aspirations

Taylorism
(Authority)

- Little choice in organization of work
- Problem-solving and decision-making done at higher levels

Autonomy
(Responsibility)

- Devolved decision-making and problem-solving
- Responsibility for planning and organizing

Organizational
needs

Figure 4.1 Taylorism and complete autonomy as opposite ends of a spectrum (from Carré and Pearn (1992), reproduced with permission)

development of a range of practical instruments, which was published as a toolkit (Pearn Kandola, 1993) and has since been revised and enlarged (Pearn and Mulrooney, 1995).

For two years the project was an approved member of the Eurotecnet network of innovative training and development projects across the European Union. Eurotecnet is co-ordinated, but not funded, by the Eurotecnet Technical Assistance Unit in Brussels. The Unit is itself active in this area, notably Nyhan's study of 'self-learning competency' (1991) and the more recent analysis of learning organizations (Stahl *et al.*, 1992). Involvement in Eurotecnet meetings of experts and Eurotecnet conferences provided very significant support and stimulation for the project team. We will now go on to describe the working approach.

A working approach

One of our first tasks was the development of an implementation model to guide practical action. As we have noted, it was felt that a prescriptive definition of the learning organization should be avoided. Instead a *working approach* was developed that could be adapted or used as a springboard by organizations. The working approach has five components (see Figure 4.2).

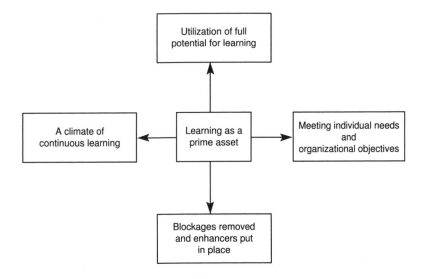

Figure 4.2 Five components of the working approach for a learning organization

- *A learning organization places high value on individual and organizational learning as a prime asset.* For an organization to regard something as a prime asset it must take stock of the asset, invest in it, and capitalize on it. Many organizations are accustomed to doing this with tangible assets such as stock, buildings and land, and also with less tangible assets such as brands, patents, and even goodwill. If the mobilization of the brainpower of all employees is critical to the achievement of sustained competitive edge, then it follows that the learning potential and learning achievements of the organization should be a highly valued asset which needs to be monitored, fertilized and harnessed.
- *It is working towards full utilization of all individual and group potential for learning and adapting in the interests of meeting (and eventually setting and renewing) organizational objectives (mission and vision).* Not only is the full learning potential of all employees being cultivated and harnessed in order to meet current and foreseeable needs in terms of currently understood mission and vision, but also in a way that challenges the *status quo*, and is eventually built into the processes for reviewing and creating its mission and vision. Continuous learning is not only something that needs to go on at lower levels of an organization (a notion which tends to be reinforced by traditional approaches to training) but at

every level, including those responsible for overall strategy and policy formulation.

- *It does this in a way that also satisfies the needs and aspirations of the people involved.* It is self-evident that an organization which attempts to meet its own objectives in a way that is not also acceptable or indeed satisfying to the members of that organization will eventually fail because the motivation, goodwill, and potential contribution of its members have not been fully engaged. Even if the organization does not fail (it may even be dying so slowly that it has not become aware of its critical condition) its competitors may be achieving more and in a sustainable way because they have successfully engaged the hearts and minds of *all* their employees.

- *Inhibitors or blocks to learning are being identified and removed and strong enhancers and structural support for sustained continuous learning are being put in place.* The notion that learning at an individual level can be blocked was critical to the learning-to-learn approach described above. The notion that such blockages can also exist in the environment and at the organizational level has not received as much attention in learning organization theory, though Argyris has described 'organizational defence routines', and Senge has drawn attention to mind-sets and mental models that impede creative thinking. The systematic identification of learning blockages both in individuals and in the structure and systems of the organization, coupled with the introduction of individual and structural enhancers to learning, is critical to the process of becoming a learning organization.

- *A climate of continuous learning and improvement is being created.* For sustained continuous learning to occur in an organization, its mission, vision and corporate values must support the quest, as indeed must the behaviour of its leaders. Supportive management and a nurturing culture, together with the values that flow from the vision, combine to form a climate conducive to continuous learning.

Enhancers and inhibitors

Our working approach to becoming a learning organization places great emphasis on *enhancers* to learning as well as *inhibitors* of learning. These inhibitors and enhancers can operate at an individual or group level, but they can also function structurally or organizationally (Figure 4.3). In order to exploit the potential for learning which exists within an organization, it is necessary to be able to identify what would enhance as well as what would inhibit individual, group or whole organizational learning. On the other hand, it is also necessary to identify those things which would enhance as well as inhibit learning from a structural or organizational point of view.

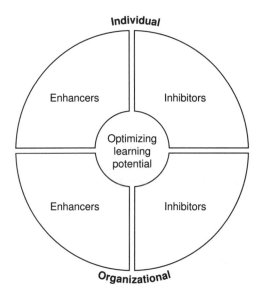

Figure 4.3 Individual and organizational enhancers to and inhibitors of organizational learning (from Carré and Pearn (1992), reproduced with permission)

An example of an organizational inhibitor of continuous learning within the organization would be a well-developed training function where training is designed and delivered by training specialists, and there is a loose match between learning/development needs of individuals and groups and the training provided. This training may meet some of the learning needs within the organization, but it is unlikely that it could satisfy all the rapidly changing and complex learning or development needs of work groups on an ongoing basis.

It is a common experience for people to return from training courses and say that the content of the training was interesting but not fully relevant to their needs. It is rare for work groups to identify their own learning needs and then choose ways in which these needs might be satisfied. As a result, it is possible that a well-developed training function or department could actually have an inhibiting effect on the achievement of effective learning.

Another structural inhibitor of organizational learning would be the not uncommon belief on the part of management that the workforce has little intelligence of its own to use in terms of problem-solving, prioritizing, planning and organizing, and that these are best done on their behalf by managers and supervisors. This mode of managing engenders a passivity in work groups as well as an alienation from the workplace, which encourages inertia and as a result fails to stimulate flexibility and creativity.

The formal introduction of autonomous working groups (AWGs) or self-directed teams (SDTs) (cf. Lawler, 1986) would be a good structural 'enhancer' of organizational learning. To equip and then allow a group to regulate itself, to plan and prioritize its activities, and to identify its learning and other resource needs provides a powerful incentive for self-development within the group. As noted above, there is a danger that autonomous work groups or self-directed teams become oases of autonomy and self-learning which are relatively isolated from the rest of the organization.

An open style of management which encourages two-way communication and the development of autonomy within subordinates is also an important structural or organizational enhancer. For a true learning organization to develop, the principles of the learning-orientated organization should operate across the whole organization, though they might manifest themselves in different ways in different parts of the organization. From a structural or organizational point of view, inhibitors need to be removed or neutralized and enhancers need to be put in place at all six levels of organizational learning.

More examples of enhancers and inhibitors, individual and organizational, are shown in Table 4.2.

Our working approach used a hot-air balloon as a simple but evocative analogy of a learning organization (Figure 4.4). If the objective of the organization is to maximize opportunities for learning at all levels and to exploit the potential for learning and adaptation of all the people who make up the organization, then this can be likened to the air within a hot-air balloon. In order for the balloon to rise, it is necessary to expand the volume of this air. This is done by means of the flame, which can be likened to individual or organizational enhancers to learning. The implication is that nothing at all will happen if enhancers are not put in place at individual, group and organizational level.

Table 4.2   Individual and organizational enhancers and inhibitors

	Enhancers	Inhibitors
Individual	• recognition of personal learning achievements • opportunities to learn from mistakes • highly developed personal learning skills • empowerment processes • accurate feedback on performance • coaching • mentoring • self-development • self-directed learning • a sense of purpose (doing something worth while)	• learned helplessness • managers believe they know all the answers • managers hooked on status and traditional 'us' and 'them' role • unwillingness to take responsibility • entrenched view that learning stops in the classroom • couldn't care less about standards • imbued with 'not invented here' syndrome • fear • lack of confidence to learn
Organizational	• cross-functional work teams • everything permitted not actually banned • redesigning jobs to include dialogue and problem-solving • quality reflection time • inter-company consortia • open learning • widespread use of systems thinking • scenario planning • systematic examination of mental models • learning laboratories • action learning • managers as facilitators	• too many management levels • design and manufacturing separate (functional separatism) • workers confined to narrowly defined tasks • equipment specialized and inflexible • individuals treated as brain-dead • too hierarchical • centralized decision-making • bureaucratic culture • preoccupation with getting it done • only do what is permitted • belief that workforce is lazy and stupid

Even if the enhancers are put in place, it is possible that the balloon will not rise because of the individual inhibitors represented by the sandbags. The sandbags have to be removed in order for the enhancers to have the maximum effect. Even then it is still possible that the balloon will not rise from the ground because of organizational or structural inhibitors, which are represented by the ropes. In consequence, it may be necessary to put enabling structures in place to provide support for sustained learning and development at individual and organizational level, represented by the temporary scaffolding to hold the balloon until it is ready to rise.

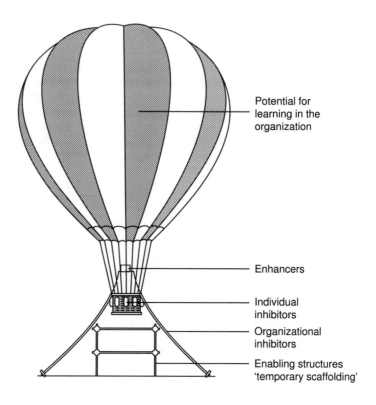

Potential for
learning in the
organization

Enhancers

Individual
inhibitors

Organizational
inhibitors

Enabling structures
'temporary scaffolding'

Figure 4.4   Hot-air balloon as an analogy of a learning organization (from Carré and Pearn (1992), reproduced with permission)

The value of the analogy of the hot-air balloon is the way it makes plain that all contributing forces need to be taken into account in order to optimize the learning opportunities within the organization. In order to become a learning organization it is necessary to identify and remove, over a period of time, the unjustifiable organizational inhibitors or constraints and also to remove individual or group constraints to sustained continuous learning.

One apparent disadvantage of the balloon analogy is that the balloonist has little control over the direction of travel and eventual destination of the balloon. The balloon is very dependent on the prevailing winds at any time. By contrast an organization which regards itself as a learning organization needs to have a very clear idea of its overall objectives and what it is trying to achieve (its mission and vision), as well as how it will know when it is succeeding. While this is true, it is also true that a learning organization recognizes that it cannot predict a rapidly changing future and that part of its vision must be readiness to cope with and respond to whatever the future brings. There is, of course, a great danger in having a too-clear, too-confident and unchallenged view of the future. In this sense the hot-air balloon is not inappropriate, as an organization must be prepared and able to change and transform itself to reflect not wholly predictable changes in markets, technologies, and in socio-economic, political and environmental conditions. The hot-air balloon is a useful reminder that if you can see the destination too clearly you may be looking in the wrong direction. The recent near collapse of IBM with its stranglehold on the world market for mainframe computers is a salutary reminder that past success and market domination are no guarantee of success in the future, or as Pascale (1990) put it: 'Whom the gods wish to punish they first give forty years of success.' Put another way, in the future, nothing will fail like success in the past.

Another useful viewpoint is that an organization may not be equally successful in capitalizing on the learning potential available to it in all its activities and functions. The organization can move from small areas of already exploited learning potential towards the almost limitless possibilities that lie within the area of unexploited learning potential. If, at the same time, it identifies and puts in place support mechanisms for continuous individual and group learning the development of learning potential eventually becomes part of the self-sustaining and dynamic culture of the organization.

It cannot be stressed strongly enough that learning organizations are not achieved overnight, nor are they an end-state. Senge (1994) expressed it succinctly: 'The learning organization exists primarily as a vision in our collective imagination.' The whole point of a learning organization is that you never get there. That is why they should never be regarded as 'flavour of the month'. It is evolutionary or it is nothing. The goal of learning organizations is to generate a process of continuous change and self-transformation from within the organization.

Ten actions for a learning organization

The working approach was built around 10 actions (see Figure 4.5) or building-blocks for a learning organization. The actions were not designed to be a complete programme. Instead they serve as a framework for tools to support the process of becoming a learning organization. The 10 actions are briefly reviewed in the following pages.

Examine the concept at top management level   Learning organizations reach into all aspects of organizational behaviour and thinking. Workshops for senior or top management are necessary to develop an understanding of the significance of learning for organizational success and the links with corporate objectives and values. If the characteristic culture of the organization is not addressed, there will be less chance for optimum learning to occur at all levels throughout the organization and the risk of isolated 'pockets' of learning will increase.

Having developed an understanding of the idea of learning organizations, as it applies to the particular enterprise, and identified the strengths, weaknesses, opportunities and threats existing within the *status quo*, it is then important for the top management team to create a vision of the kind of organization they want to work towards. An important part of this process is the examination of the organization's current mission and vision. The mission may be clear but the vision may fall short of the inspirational quality that will motivate all members of the organization. If the vision is not shared by everyone in the organization it is likely to be greeted with cynicism, which itself is a significant inhibitor to learning.

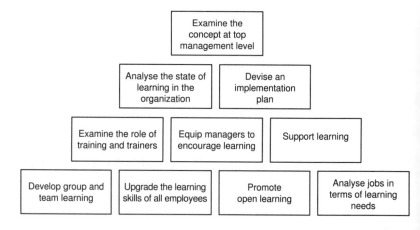

Figure 4.5   Building-blocks for a learning organization

Analyse the state of learning   A key step towards becoming a learning organization is a survey of the current situation and the identification of areas that require change. An audit of employees at all levels which identifies inhibitors and enhancers of learning, at both individual and organizational level, is essential for detailed planning. The state of learning in the organization can be assessed by means of quantitative survey instruments which yield scores on a number of dimensions (e.g. the Learning Climate Questionnaire which is described in detail in Chapter 5). Alternatively, the state of learning can be assessed by means of focus groups.

Devise an implementation plan

Becoming a learning organization is a journey which requires careful planning. In order to set the process in motion an implementation plan is necessary. This plan should take into account the vision and strategy created by the top management group and needs to encompass the whole organization, if not all at one go, then in a series of planned stages. The implementation group should take part in discussions about the benefits of effective organizational learning, the possible consequences of failure to achieve it, and the means by which a company can measure its own performance and progress.

An important aspect of the implementation planning phase is to identify where to start, who to involve, time-frames, resources required, measures of success and the actions and measures which would stimulate as well as sustain the desired changes. For example, this could include a review of the role definition of managers within the organization. This might be both in terms of how the role is perceived and the skills and competencies that are considered necessary for effective management, or a review of the role and the operation of the training function within the company, in the light of a decision to move towards being a learning organization.

Examine the role of training and trainers

The learning organization is likely to move away from heavy reliance on formal training by a centralized training function which often satisfies the short-term needs of the workforce, to a training function which supports, facilitates and sustains learning and autonomy at all levels. It follows that the role of training and trainers, and the boundaries between work, learning and training, will change.

The very nature of a developed training function has necessitated the establishment of professional staff and a long-term commitment to resources and personnel. There is a risk that 'the trainers' become separate and detached from the 'real work' of the organization and as a result the provision of training meets the trainers' perception of need. Consequently, only a tiny part of the true learning need is satisfied, or the need is met in a way which cannot easily be adapted and used in work.

Equip managers to encourage learning

A 'command-and-control' style of management can inhibit individual learning. For a variety of reasons, many organizations are developing coaching and facilitating skills in managers as part of a more open and consultative style of management. Making the processes of learning clearer to managers leads to them increasing their competence as learners.

An important part of the manager's role within a learning organization is to develop an understanding of how he/she learns as an individual, as well as how others learn. This includes a knowledge and understanding of the things which inhibit or enhance learning in others.

Managers can also be taught simple techniques for encouraging quality contributions in discussions, stimulating problem-solving in groups and reviewing progress towards learning objectives both at individual and group levels. If managers and supervisors do not learn and practise these simple techniques and realize that they actually work (a realization that is also shared with the work group), there is a danger that, although they understand what is being said to them in terms of adopting a more open and facilitative style of management, they may lack the repertoire of behaviours which enable them to act in accordance with the new style.

Support learning

Learning should be supported at all times wherever it occurs in as many different ways as possible. A learning organization is a continuous dynamic process rather than an end-state to be achieved. However, it may be necessary to introduce both temporary and permanent support mechanisms to ensure that the new forms of behaviour which are necessary to stimulate and support continuous adaptive learning are developed. These can include the encouragement of networking and the provision of personal development plans, quality circles, mentoring, learning contracts, and so on.

Another support mechanism is the formation of focus groups which can meet periodically to take an overview of learning and development within specific areas of the organization. One group could be nominated to review continuous learning within the organization as a whole and other groups could be nominated to review specific areas and to recommend changes. This was the approach adopted in one of the case studies described in Chapter 10.

Upgrade learning skills of all employees

One of the paradoxes of learning organizations is, as Argyris (1991) has pointed out, that the senior managers and professionals may find it hardest of all to learn. Professionals and

managers in organizations can be enthusiastic about continuous improvement in others but are often the biggest obstacle
to its achievement because they have little understanding of
how it applies to themselves and how people really learn. Top
managers have instinctively built on their successes and have
rarely experienced failure. Moreover, they often feel that they
cannot be seen to be learning because acknowledging the
need to learn implies a lack of knowledge which would
undermine their credibility as leaders. Accordingly, they have
not acquired learning strategies which enable them to make
more positive use of errors and to learn to reason produc-
tively, as opposed to defensively or negatively.

The learning skills of everyone in the organization can be
enhanced and developed by means of special learning-to-
learn exercises. We have devised exercises which are designed
to develop an appreciation of learning blockages; to reveal
that different kinds of learning are needed in different
situations; to show that there are many different ways of
memorizing factual information; to demonstrate that asking
the right kinds of question enhances learning enormously, but
that failing to ask can seriously inhibit learning. In addition,
the exercises seem to develop in the learner a systematic
approach to understanding conceptual or theoretical material
which can be used time and time again and a self-awareness
about learning which gives them confidence to undertake new
learning where previously they may have felt inhibited.

Develop group and
team learning

Learning organizations mobilize individual talent through
team-working. Workers can be organized into self-directed
teams (SDTs), high-commitment teams (HCTs) or autonomous work groups (AWGs), giving them a potentially high
degree of autonomy and control over their work patterns and
accountabilities. Companies that have gone down this route
have not always found it easy, but perseverance has produced
results. In general it is easier to establish teams in green-field
sites or in oases or pockets of the organization where new or
advanced technology has been introduced. It is much harder
to introduce them across a whole site, hence the importance of
the integrated approach underlying the concept of a learning
organization (cf. Buchanan and McCalman, 1989).

First, individuals need to learn how to work in a team.
There are several well-established techniques for project or
group-based learning. 'Action learning' is probably the best
known of the techniques. One of the most important objectives
of these techniques is to persuade individual learners that a
co-operative group approach to learning is both more enjoy-

able and more productive than an individually based, competitive approach to learning.

The skills to be acquired are as much social as intellectual. The most common problem with teams is failure by team members to understand the feelings and needs of their colleagues. Learning how to talk constructively to others in the team is imperative; these are skills which have become known as 'dialogueing' (Senge, 1994). Much depends on inspiring a sense of confidence and trust so that people feel free to express themselves without the fear that they will be attacked.

Promote open learning   It is observed of open learning, as of much else, that the mere provision of opportunity does not ensure adequate take-up.

Helping employees to get the most out of open learning material and distance learning resources is critical to the success of open learning strategies. Too many open learning materials are not used, or not used properly.

For open learners the most valuable development exercises in the workplace will be those which facilitate the exchange of theory and practice, which strengthen the transferability of learning, which enable the practising of those skills which need contact (interpersonal, communication, negotiating skills), which stimulate discovery and experimental and problem-solving approaches, and which permit the execution of work-based projects at a practical level.

Analyse jobs in terms   Most job analysis or training needs analysis methods focusing
of learning needs   either on the content of particular jobs (i.e., tasks that needed to be performed), or the skills, knowledge and other attributes that are needed to perform them. This tends to result in training that focuses on the development of specific skills, but which neglects the learning processes that are needed to acquire and develop them. We describe in Chapter 8 an instrument, the Job Learning Analysis (JLA), which is specifically designed to analyse jobs in terms of nine different kinds of learning that might be required in order to learn to perform specific jobs.

Building-blocks not a   The 10 actions are proposed essentially as options for
complete programme   organizations to consider. Most will wish to undertake some but not necessarily all of them. The order is not laid down, although some will tend to be undertaken before others. The actions were chosen for their usefulness and effectiveness, but are not intended to be a comprehensive programme or system for building a learning organization.

There are other actions which might be regarded as advanced versions of some of the actions here. For example, the 10 actions above do not offer practical guidance or tools to support the formation of self-directed teams or high-commitment work groups. Team learning is also a rather specialized action which may need separate attention.

This book does not describe processes for the implementation of World-Class Manufacturing, Total Quality Management, or Business Process Re-engineering, but the learning processes which we describe can contribute to the achievement of these goals.

The use of these interventions is best understood in the context of the real-life example which follows. Further examples can be found in Chapter 10.

A 100-year-old company in a dramatically changing socio-political climate

Southern Life Assurance had survived for a long time, but increasingly felt under pressure from competitors and a rapidly changing market-place. It had recently merged with another company but still had less than 10 per cent of the financial services market in South Africa. The initial concern was not to increase market share but to increase profitability, and being neither a giant nor a niche player the company felt vulnerable. At the time, South Africa was gradually moving towards democracy and there was widespread uncertainty, and in many quarters great fear, about the future. The challenge for the company was to respond to and prosper in what was an unpredictable environment.

A clear vision had been created for the company. It was expressed as follows:

In our orientation we aim
• to become a market-orientated and customer-driven company;
• to know who our customers are and to provide them with reliable, efficient service and profitable products which satisfy their needs;
• to value our customers and seek to build lasting relationships with them.

In all our dealings with them to try
• to be helpful, friendly and courteous;
• to encourage all our staff to contribute to the company's marketing success.

In our way of work we aim
• to look to and plan for the future with purpose, focus and drive;
• to be known as enthusiastic professionals;

- to have dignity and quality as our standards;
- to make the company a challenging and enjoyable place to work where encouragement is actively given to participate in the development of our company and its objectives;
- to care for the environment in which we live and work.

In our business ethics we aim
- to deal honestly and fairly in our business relationships;
- to behave at all times in a manner befitting a respected leader in our business;
- to be informed, business-like and protective of our position when dealing with our competitors.

The company had identified 11 critical success factors to support its vision to become South Africa's most customer-focused and successful financial services company. A key to the achievement of the vision was organizational renewal. The critical success factors were labelled the 'vision elements'.

- Financial strength which targeted an improvement in dividend yield.
- AIDS — developing strategies to overcome the threat to profitability posed by AIDS in Africa.
- Improvement in investment performance.
- Becoming significantly more market-orientated.
- Improved performance in key service indicators.
- Highly motivated and skilled staff dedicated to serving the customer.
- Affirmative action and cultural change to create a supportive environment.
- Systems technologies that are the most cost-effective relative to customer service requirements.
- The maintenance and development of strong family connections to contribute to the generation of new business.
- To be a leader as a forward-thinking liberal company in the context of socio-political developments in South Africa.
- A structure in place that will enhance rather than inhibit the achievement of the overall strategy.

For each of the vision elements there was a plan of action and associated accountabilities. A number of HR initiatives were put in place to support the achievement of the vision elements. These included:

- a management of change programme
- development centres and the creation of a development-orientated competency framework
- a performance management system across the company
- a new job evaluation programme
- performance-related pay

- an employees' assistance programme
- intercultural sensitivity training
- strong support for personal education and development
- a leadership forum.

Several of these initiatives were in the early stages of implementation, but the leadership forum was already in its second year. For the company, the forum represented the embodiment of a learning organization.

The objective was to create an environment and a framework for young and not-so-young middle managers to develop high-level leadership skills. In other words, to learn to lead and to manage effectively in the fast-changing South African environment. In so doing they would acquire the potential to play a key role in the company in the future. Each forum lasted for 12 months and consisted of four workshops or blocks lasting about 5 days each, run by a combination of internal and external tutors. There was a strong emphasis on both individual development and on team learning.

The introductory block (the start-up block), covered team-building, learning styles, learning organizations, leadership, vision, and systems thinking. The later blocks covered business leadership, followed by a people skills block which covered negotiation, conflict management, communication, development and coaching.

During the first 6 months each forum participant creates a learning contract and maintains a learning log. The next 6 months are devoted to action learning by means of agreed group projects which are negotiated and implemented in a client department. The ongoing assessment of the team's progress also contributes to each individual's own learning and development. Finally, the participants 'graduate' at the end of 12 months and become members of the growing leadership forum in the company.

The overall objective of the forum was to create a critical mass of new leaders through learning, learners who were holistic and reflective and who would both support and challenge other key processes such as the restructuring and flattening of the organization, and the culture change that would be required for the new South Africa.

Despite the significant and growing contribution of the leadership forum to change within the company there was an unease among several members of the top management team that a learning organization was just one of many factors that could contribute to success in the future. They agreed that may be there was enough interest in the idea to justify a closer examination.

At this point an 'awareness workshop' was run for some members of the top management team. The objectives were to arrive at an understanding of the learning organization concept and to examine the role it could play in achieving the vision and the new culture of the organization.

The approach required management groups to work out for themselves the significance of learning for the organization as a whole (using the Understanding Organizational Learning exercise, described in Chapter 2), rather than to become pre-occupied with premature definitions of either learning or the learning organization. The approach also required that the managers experience learning (by trying to learn something new) and also that they experience and understand the significance of blocks to learning, both individual and organizational.

The initial workshop had a powerful effect on the team. They noted:

- the need for a longer-term vision and the role of continuous learning within it;
- the need for change to be 'internalized' through learning and understanding;
- that team learning and not just individual learning was critical;
- that the various initiatives needed to be linked and integrated by a common theme;
- that a learning culture or a learning organization could be the lubricant through which the 'initiatives' could deliver the desired benefits for the organization;
- that learning could be a more conscious activity in many activities and processes in the organization.

The senior management team of the largest division within the company (which contained two-thirds of the total workforce) decided that learning was the 'lubricant' they were looking for to ensure that the various initiatives already in place actually worked. The division did not want to wait until a corporate initiative got off the ground. It would go ahead with the knowledge of the other divisions, some of whom were supportive, though others were less so because they felt they had other priorities. A further workshop was run for the management team of the division to develop a deeper understanding of learning organizations as it might apply to the division. Senior managers in some of the other divisions were also invited. One of the exercises in the workshop was a SWOT analysis (Strengths, Weaknesses, Opportunities and Threats) of the company in terms of its capacity to encourage and sustain learning in all employees. The results were both encouraging and disquieting.

Altogether over 30 strengths were identified, but these were outnumbered by the weaknesses. Too many were identified to list them all here, but the following sample gives a flavour. The organization was seen as having a clear vision and effective leadership from the board, its values were clearly stated, there were many opportunities and vehicles for management debate. In addition a wide range of progressive HR initiatives had been undertaken, in the context of careful strategic planning. Finally it was recognized that the company possessed well-educated employees which positioned them well to thrive in the new South Africa. The strengths were clearly impressive but the identified weaknesses were worrying. They included narrow functionally specific careers, managers being too autocratic, a lack of challenge and experimentation, complacency, fear and a habit of 'chasing rabbits'!

Despite the many valuable initiatives there was seen to be a cultural 'sludge' of attitudes and behaviour which would seriously undermine the organization or inhibit it from really changing in line with its vision. The group identified many opportunities both in existing initiatives and also in possibilities that could be tapped into in order to generate benefit at

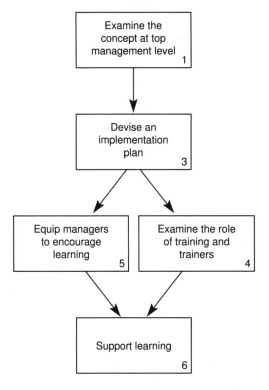

Figure 4.6   Southern Life's route through the actions of the working approach

individual, group, or organizational level. It was decided to run workshops for all the managers in the division, followed by some training workshops to teach a group of managers to run various exercises and processes from the Toolkit. A workshop was also held to introduce the company's HR specialists to the tools, techniques and instruments in the Toolkit.

The management team of the division also recommended that the central personnel function should attend an adapted version of the workshop that they had already attended, so that the HR specialists in the company would understand and support what they were trying to achieve. One of the division's objectives was to take responsibility for their own training and development rather than respond to initiatives from the HR function. In addition, some of the tools and techniques were incorporated into the leadership forum with the idea that, gradually, the number of future leaders of the organization would grow to share a common language and common expectations in terms of their understanding of, and commitment to, the importance of encouraging and sustaining learning in the company.

The independence of the division in creating a new learning culture for itself was supported by the chairman of the executive board as an example of the empowerment the company was seeking to create. The company did not formally commit itself to becoming a learning organization, because it felt that its array of 'initiatives' was designed to achieve the desired organizational and cultural change, but by becoming a more learning-orientated organization it felt it would ensure the success of its change and renewal programme.

The example described above illustrates the way in which one organization adopted an evolving programme that combined instruments and tools in a way that met its own needs. The company's route through the actions of the *working approach* are summarized in Figure 4.6.

In the next chapters we

- consider further techniques and processes to help achieve the goal of becoming a learning organization.

References

ARGYRIS, C. (1991) 'Teaching smart people how to learn', *Harvard Business Review*, May–June, 99–109.

CARRÉ, P. and PEARN, M. (1992) *L'Autoformation dans l'Entreprise*, Paris: Editions Entente.

COLLINS, J. C. and PORRAS, J. I. (1991) 'Organizational vision and visionary organizations', *California Management Review*, Fall, 30–52.

DOWNS, S. and PERRY, P. (1984) *Developing Skilled Learners: Learning to learn in YTS*, Research and Development Report 22, London: Manpower Services Commission.

DOWNS, S. and PERRY, P. (1987) *Developing Skilled Learners: Helping Adults to Become Better Learners*, Research and Development Report 40, London: Manpower Services Commission.

LAWLER, E.E. (1986) *High Involvement Management: Participative Strategies for Improving Organizational Performance*, London: Jossey-Bass.

NYHAN, B. (1991) *Developing People's Ability to Learn: A European*

Perspective on Self-Learning Competency and Technological Change, Brussels: Technical Assistance Office, Interuniversity Press.

PASCALE, R. T. (1990) *Managing on the Edge*, London: Viking.

PEARN, M. A. and DOWNS, S. (1991) 'Developing Skilled Learners', in Nyhan, B., *Developing People's Ability to Learn*, Brussels: Eurotecnet Technical Assistance Office, Interuniversity Press.

PEARN KANDOLA (1993) *A Toolkit for the Learning Organization*, Marlow: Institute for Training and Development.

PEARN, M. A. and MULROONEY, C. (1995) *Tools for a Learning Organization*, London: Institute for Personnel and Development.

SENGE, P. M. (1994) *The Fifth Discipline Fieldbook*, London: Nicholas Brealey.

STAHL, T., NYHAN, B. and D'ALOJA, P. (1992) *The Learning Organization: A Vision for Human Resource Development*, Brussels: Commission of the European Communities: Eurotecnet Programme.

5 Analysing the state of learning in the organization

In this chapter we

- describe several techniques, each with different strengths and weaknesses, for gaining a more systematic assessment of the state of learning in the organization
- describe and present in full the Learning Audit, a focus or group discussion-based instrument designed to give insight to the operation of individual and organizational blocks to learning
- describe The Learning Climate Questionnaire, a quantitative survey instrument.

 As we have noted earlier, a key step towards becoming a learning organization is to study the current state of learning and to identify areas that require change. This chapter is mainly devoted to two instruments which have been designed to gather data in a systematic way on the state of learning in the organization. The Learning Audit is a checklist to focus group discussions on identifying inhibitors and enhancers of learning at both individual and organizational level; it can also be used for individual interviews and adapted to operate as an initial survey instrument. The Learning Climate Questionnaire is a quantitative instrument yielding scores on a number of dimensions which can be used both for initial diagnosis and for before-and-after measurement once changes have been put in place.

The Learning Audit

The Learning Audit was developed by the authors and is designed to be used in a number of ways to provide insight into how individuals or teams perceive the state of learning in their organizations. Information from the audit can then be used either in a process to establish top management commitment or as a starting-point in the formulation of an organization-wide implementation plan.

The Learning Audit has a five-part structure designed to assess individual and group ability to encourage and sustain learning:

• in the organization as a whole;
• in the individual's department or function;
• by the individual's own line manager or supervisor;
• by the training and/or HR function;
• by inviting more general comments from the participants about the sorts of things which either hinder or prevent them learning at work, and also the things which they think would encourage or support them learning at work.

The Learning Audit can easily be adapted for use in different contexts. For example, it can be used as a syndicate exercise in a workshop, as the basis of a one-to-one interview or focus group on the current state of learning in the organization, and as a survey instrument for a large sample of the organization. Quantitative measures can be obtained by analysing the frequencies of agree/disagree statements and comparing between departments or over a period of time.

The Learning Audit is reproduced in full on the following pages.

LEARNING AUDIT

Part 1

Please rate your *organization as a whole* in terms of its ability to encourage and foster learning in all employees.

For each item ring the 2, 1, or 0. Add up the scores and then indicate your overall satisfaction by ticking one of the boxes at the bottom of the page.

	Generally true	*True to some extent*	*Not true*
• Top management is committed to fostering learning in all employees	2	1	0
• There is strong management support for self-development in all employees	2	1	0
• There are many opportunities for gaining access to education, training, open learning	2	1	0
• This organization has made good provision for individual access to learning opportunities	2	1	0
• This organization encourages questioning of and challenges to assumptions	2	1	0
• This organization believes in empowering people, not just telling them what to do	2	1	0
• This organization makes good use of teamwork for decision-making and problem-solving	2	1	0
• Management here does not believe it has all the answers and recognizes that good ideas can come from others	2	1	0

Total score [   ] + [   ]   = [   ]

Please rate your overall satisfaction with the organization as a whole in its encouragement of continuous learning and development in all employees.

[   ]   [   ]   [   ]   [   ]

Excellent   Satisfactory   Marginal   Poor

Part 2

Now consider your *department/function's* ability to encourage and foster learning in all employees.

For each item ring the 2, 1, or 0. Add up the scores and then indicate your overall satisfaction by ticking one of the boxes at the bottom of the page.

	Generally true	True to some extent	Not true
• The managers in my department are committed to fostering learning and development in all employees	2	1	0
• In my department there is strong management support for self-development in all employees	2	1	0
• I feel I have many opportunities for gaining access to education, training, open learning	2	1	0
• In my department, there is a strong emphasis on always finding ways to do things better	2	1	0
• I feel I personally have good access to learning opportunities	2	1	0
• I feel I am free to ask questions and challenge assumptions	2	1	0
• I feel I have the scope to take important decisions and solve problems for myself which affect my work group	2	1	0
• We make good use of teams for decision-making and problem-solving	2	1	0
• My manager does not believe he/she knows all the answers	2	1	0

Total score ☐ + ☐ = ☐

Consider your overall satisfaction with the department/function as a whole in its encouragement of continuous learning and development in all employees.

☐   ☐   ☐   ☐

Excellent   Satisfactory   Marginal   Poor

Part 3

Consider *your manager's* capacity to encourage and foster learning in the workplace.
For each item ring the 2, 1, or 0. Add up the scores and then indicate your overall satisfaction by ticking one of the boxes at the bottom of the page.

My manager/supervisor:	Generally true	True to some extent	Not true
• Has an open and accessible management style	2	1	0
• Encourages questions about and challenges to assumptions	2	1	0
• Uses coaching and mentoring as a means of development	2	1	0
• Uses teams well to achieve decision-making and problem-solving	2	1	0
• Encourages the group to adopt different viewpoints	2	1	0
• Allows us to develop solutions to problems instead of telling us his/her view	2	1	0
• Allows time for reflection on how to do things better and learn from experience	2	1	0
• Has agreed Personal Development Plans and takes appropriate action	2	1	0
• Listens to and takes heed of our views and opinions	2	1	0
• Believes in the value of developing all his/her subordinates	2	1	0

Total score ☐ + ☐ = ☐

Consider your satisfaction with your manager in their encouragement of continuous learning and development in all employees.

☐   ☐   ☐   ☐
Excellent   Satisfactory   Marginal   Poor

Part 4

Now consider the *training/HR function's* ability to encourage and support learning in all employees.

For each item ring the 2, 1, or 0. Add up the scores and then indicate your overall satisfaction by ticking one of the boxes at the bottom of the page.

The training/HR function:	Generally true	True to some extent	Not true
• Understands the real learning and training needs of my work group	2	1	0
• Provides the training/development we really need	2	1	0
• Provides access to open learning (e.g. packages we can do at home or away from the workplace)	2	1	0
• Helps us become better or more confident learners	2	1	0
• Uses methods to analyse training and development needs	2	1	0
• Provides flexible and adaptive responses to our learning needs	2	1	0
• Makes good use of modern methods (e.g. computer-based training, interactive video, etc.)	2	1	0
• Provides a range of development options, not just courses	2	1	0
• Encourages feedback and constructive criticism	2	1	0
• Works in a consultative, supportive manner	2	1	0

Total score   [   ]   +   [   ]   =   [   ]

Consider your overall satisfaction with the training/HR function as a whole in its encouragement of continuous learning and development in all employees.

[   ]   [   ]   [   ]   [   ]
Excellent   Satisfactory   Marginal   Poor

Part 5
In general, what kinds of things do you think hinder or prevent you from learning to do things better at work?

In general what do you think would help you or encourage you to learn to do things better or acquire new skills and knowledge?

**Using the
Learning Audit**

The following examples illustrate practical applications of learning audit methods.

The Learning Audit in a manufacturing plant

The plant was one of three 3M manufacturing sites in the UK. The factory manufactured a variety of breathing masks, electronic components, and chemical solvents. The company specialized in innovative products and frequently created whole new markets for products which it had invented.

The company was very quick to introduce initiatives to improve quality and output. Many of these had produced measured improvements, but there was a strong feeling in the management team that more could be achieved if everyone in the factory could be stimulated to become 'masters of their own jobs' who could develop and improve their jobs day-by-day. It was also recognized that managers and supervisors would need to change from being primarily controllers and become facilitators and coaches.

A project team of managers, supervisors and operators was formed. In the past the workforce had been 'involved' by means of questionnaires which were sent out, filled in, and then, in the eyes of the workforce, 'nothing was done'. As one operator put it: 'We've heard it all before, done it all, nothing will come of it'. It became clear to the management team that the workforce had never really been consulted and involved in the formulation of a change process before. For over 25 years the managers had been telling the workforce what was good for them. This time they were going to ask them.

The Learning Audit was adapted and the whole site participated in focus groups run by members of the project team who had been trained specifically for the purpose. The key blocks to learning were identified as being a general lack of support for and recognition of the importance of learning; lack of time and opportunities for learning; resistance to change in general, coupled with fear and distrust; lack of resources, both time and money and facilities to help bring about necessary learning; and a perceived lack of commitment from management, linked to poor communication within the site and a culture that did not support and encourage true challenge and experimentation, especially on the shop-floor. Many good things were said, but the site clearly fell into the *frustrated* category (see page 36).

In the light of the data obtained and wider consultation, the project team developed an action plan which was approved by the whole site. Further details of the action taken can be found in Chapter 10.

The Learning Audit in a Health Service Trust

In another example, the Learning Audit was used by a Health Service Trust to both explore the state of learning in the organization and to help 'condition' senior managers to the change processes implied in a move towards becoming a learning organization.

The Trust encompassed diverse health services across a number of different sites within the city. After an introduction to both the learning organization as a whole and specific diagnostic tools, a steering group was established to conduct early investigations of the state of learning in the organization. As was the case in earlier examples, this group was composed of a mix of staff including ward managers and nurses, rather than solely comprising human resource professionals. The group chose to use the Learning Audit as the mechanism for both exploring current perceptions of learning within the organization, and then, at a later stage, using data generated as a means for gaining senior management commitment to other learning orientated initiatives.

Focus groups at unit and ward level were established by members of the steering group in order to gather data using the Learning Audit. Their experience was that the headings provided by the Audit provided both a stimulating base for general discussion as well as quantifiable data for later reporting.

At a later meeting with the directors of the Trust, the steering group members were able to report their findings with an authority and credibility that would have been difficult for an outsider to achieve. At the same meeting, the directors completed the Audit themselves to give still further insight into enhancers and inhibitors of learning within the organization and to provide another point of comparison.

Used in this way the Audit produced findings which were both counter-intuitive and challenging and which are now forming the foundation on which future initiatives will be built. Typical findings in relation to opportunities for personal development were as follows:

- Development was perceived as in the 'gift' of particular managers.
- Individuals' personal relationships with their managers were frequently the basis of access to development opportunities (in other words it was often unsystematic and arbitrary).
- There was little perceived linkage between individual develop-ment and organizational goals.
- The training function was seen as the means by which access to development opportunities was 'rationed'.

The steering group then planned a series of initiatives to address these and other issues. The key to successful implementation was the involvement both in the steering group and in the data-gathering of the people directly affected, giving them the equip-ment with which to conduct an investigation and, finally, empowering them to use the results of their investigations to formulate solutions to the problems they identified.

In both these cases the Learning Audit was used as a tool for equipping groups to explore the state of learning in the organization, and to disseminate the findings.

The Learning Climate Questionnaire

Whereas the Learning Audit is primarily designed to provide qualitative data and anecdotal insights, the Learning Climate Questionnaire (LCQ) is a standardized psychometric instru-ment. The questionnaire was developed by Newland Park Associates (Bartram *et al.*, 1993a, 1993b) in collaboration with the UK Employment Service. As a standardized psychometric instrument, the LCQ has been shown to be both reliable and valid (cf. Kline, 1993). It has been tested on a large number of people. A total of 1344 people completed the trial question-naires during the development phase.

According to the User's Manual, the LCQ was designed to help organizations find answers to four key questions, namely:

- How well are we, as an organization, helping to support workplace learning and development?

- What practical things can we do immediately to increase learning and development?
- What are the longer-term implications?
- How should we aim to change in the long term, to further support learning and development?

In practice, the LCQ only achieves the first of these objectives, as the manual does not provide any guidance under the remaining three headings. It does, however, provide the statistical information with which to attempt addressing the remaining questions.

The LCQ provides organizations with a useful starting-point from which to understand their learning climate. The LCQ can be used in three different ways. First, it can be used to provide an assessment of the relative strengths and weaknesses of a particular workplace or team environment, in terms of seven dimensions of the learning climate outlined below. This assessment provides organizations with a firm foundation from which to generate ideas on how the learning climate might be improved. Second, the LCQ can be used to compare different workplaces, or workteams, to assess how perceptions of the learning climate differ in different parts of the organization. This might be used, for instance, to provide a basis for making decisions on how to prioritize resource allocation across the different workplaces, or workteams. The third way in which the LCQ can be used is to conduct before-and-after assessments of the learning climate. Such comparisons help organizations to evaluate in quantitative terms the effects of organizational change and development.

The model of learning climates which underpins the LCQ is a useful one for organizations who wish to enhance and harness learning. Developing a learning climate conducive to efficient and effective learning is a goal which benefits the organization, as well as its individual members. Understanding the dimensions of the learning climate is important for people who want their organization to become more of a learning organization, irrespective of whether or not they intend to use the LCQ to quantify the climate.

The LCQ is based on seven dimensions which comprise the learning climate:

- Management relations and style
- Time available for learning effectively
- Autonomy and responsibility
- Team style

- Opportunities for development
- Guidance available
- Contentedness.

The following definitions are reproduced from the *User's Guide*.

1. Management relations and style
High scores reflect perceptions of management as being supportive, caring and willing to help their staff. Managers are seen as honest but constructive in their appraisal of staff. They are involved and co-operate with staff, and understand their staff's various working styles. Examples of items which measure this dimension of the learning climate are: 'My immediate manager makes me feel like a valuable member of the team', and, 'I can discuss work with my immediate manager and get constructive comments'.

2. Time available for learning
High scorers see themselves as being allowed to do their job properly and to learn effectively. They see themselves as having time to think, practise and keep up with changes; time to talk things through with colleagues and their line manager. Two items from this dimension are: ' In some parts of my job there is not enough time to keep up with changes', and, 'There is no time to practise the things I need to know how to do'.

3. Autonomy and responsibility
High scores are associated with perceptions of control over how one organizes one's work, and the opportunities given for making decisions and initiating action. High scorers see themselves as encouraged to take responsibility for learning and as being given the freedom to experiment and take risks. Examples of items which examine this dimension of the learning climate are: 'The day-to-day running of the job is left to me', and, 'I feel free to organize my work the way I want to'.

4. Team style
High scorers see the workplace as providing an environment in which there are opportunities to learn from colleagues with expertise who are supportive, caring and willing to help each other and share information and work. Team members are seen as knowing their own limitations, and as being willing to admit them. Examples of items which examine this dimension are: 'If we ask each other for help it is given', and, 'If I have a question about my job there is someone available to answer it'.

5. Opportunities to develop
People producing high scores see the workplace as providing

opportunities to learn new jobs and do a variety of work; they see scope for creativity and opportunities for learning about issues outside their immediate work. They have an awareness of what learning materials and options exist and are involved in discussion of plans and policies for change. Two items which measure this dimension are: 'There are lots of different ways to learn new jobs here', and, 'I have the opportunity to do a variety of work over and above my normal duties'.

6. *Guidance available*
High scores indicate ready access to written information and guidelines relevant to the job and the availability of help from relevant others for coaching, and both formal and informal training. Two items measuring this dimension are: 'Information is kept up-to-date', and, 'There is written guidance on how to do my job available for me to refer to'.

7. *Contentedness*
A general feeling of satisfaction with the workplace climate in terms of there being a lack of complaints, moans and negative attitudes from colleagues. A low score would arise when colleagues do not get on well, when they tend to blame each other if things go wrong, when people perceive that they are not given credit for the work they do and where people are resistant to trying new ways of doing things. Examples of items measuring this dimension are: 'Some people here don't put themselves out to do the job well', and, 'Some people here are always complaining about things'.

In addition to the seven dimension scores a composite *General Climate Score* can also be obtained: high scores indicate a generally positive view of the learning climate, while low scores indicate a generally negative one. This scale is the mean of the raw scores from the seven scales. Variations in the general climate score between people in the same work group are influenced by general individual differences in how the same learning climate is perceived or rated. Variations in the profiles of scores of the seven scales reflect individual differences in the perception of the relative strengths of different aspects of the learning climate.

   The LCQ is a good starting-point for beginning to understand the learning climate. The next section provides examples of the information gathered by using the questionnaire in practice. This is intended to provide an overview of how organizations have used the Learning Climate Questionnaire; it is not exhaustive, and it is certainly not the only recipe for interpreting LCQ data.

Using the LCQ in a hospital

The LCQ was administered to 62 nursing staff within an NHS trust hospital. The results are illustrated in Figure 5.1.

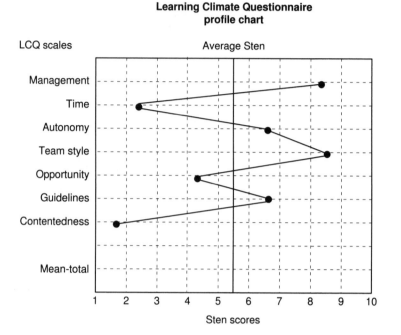

Figure 5.1 Nursing staff LCQ scores (The LCQ profile chart is reproduced with permission of the Employment Service and Newland Park Associates Limited)

The two dimensions which were rated particularly highly were Management relations and style, and Team style, suggesting that nursing staff felt colleagues and managers were generally supportive. Two areas which received particularly low ratings were Time available for learning effectively, and Contentedness. These quantitative results were summed up by a full-time member of the nursing staff, who commented on the questionnaire: 'The problems are not with the most immediate managers, they are with the system, meaning too much work between too few people.' So the LCQ analysis gives the organization a point of leverage for improving the learning climate. By adopting a strategic approach and focusing resources on the weaker areas identified, organizations can expect to see tangible improvements more quickly than if they were to take a broad-based approach to improving the learning climate.

The NHS trust hospital assessed its learning climate across two occupational groups: nursing staff and administrative staff (see Figure 5.2).

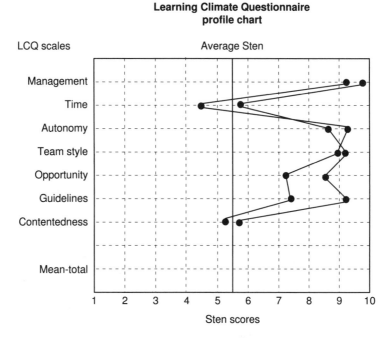

Learning Climate Questionnaire profile chart

LCQ scales   Average Sten

Management
Time
Autonomy
Team style
Opportunity
Guidelines
Contentedness

Mean-total

1   2   3   4   5   6   7   8   9   10

Sten scores

Figure 5.2 Sub-sample of an NHS Directorate—normative scores (The LCQ profile chart is reproduced with permission of the Employment Service and Newland Park Associates Limited)

Some clear differences emerge between the two groups. Overall, the nursing staff rated their general learning climate more positively than the administrative staff. Looking at the data more closely, nursing staff rated the learning climate more positively on three dimensions: Time available for learning effectively, opportunities for development, and Guidance available. On the other hand, the administrative staff rated their Autonomy and responsibility more positively than the nursing staff.

A word of warning   The LCQ is a valuable tool, but one which should not be accepted uncritically. It has been extensively tested in the course of its development, and it is psychometrically valid. However, the tool has not yet been used extensively in other contexts, although its use is increasing all the time as companies become more and more concerned about organizational learning. At the time of writing we are unaware of any organization that has yet used the LCQ to assess the impact of organizational change programmes over a period of time. This is not surprising, given that the questionnaire was only published in 1993. More importantly though, the questionnaire was piloted on a sample drawn from two public sector organizations: the Employment Service and the NHS. How well this sample compares to private sector organizations is not yet known. Only when the Learning Climate Questionnaire is used more extensively by private sector organizations will it be possible to evaluate the utility of the public sector-based norm-tables.

In order to make best use of LCQ data we would advise against averaging the data derived from different groups because this will reduce the sensitivity of the instrument, and make interpretation more difficult. It is important that people know whether they are being asked to rate their immediate working environment or the organization as a whole. Only in the latter case is it meaningful to overlap data from different groups.

While it might seem self-evident that some form of objective diagnosis should precede action, it is often the case that change and improvement initiatives are based on little more than the 'gut feel' of an individual. The type of tool described above gives the opportunity for a more rigorous approach to action planning based on a fuller understanding of what people in the organization actually perceive to be the issues as far as organizational learning is concerned. Whether used as insight tools, or as psychometric data gathering mechanisms that allow detailed comparisons to be made, or as a combination of these, diagnostic tools such as those described in this chapter are valuable in building interventions that are rooted in the reality of organizational life. The actions that grow from this information base also come from a wider organizational understanding of what is happening and greater commitment because of the involvement of larger numbers of people within the organization. We have now diagnosed the state of learning within the organization, using the Learning Audit, the LCQ, or indeed the INVEST process discussed in Chapter 3.

In the next chapter we

• go on to consider implementation planning.

References

BARTRAM , D., FOSTER, J., LINDLEY, P. A., BROWN, A. J. and NIXON, S. (1993a) *Learning Climate Questionnaire (LCQ): Background and Technical Information*, Hull: Newland Park Associates.

BARTRAM , D., FOSTER, J., LINDLEY, P. A., BROWN, A. J. and NIXON, S. (1993b), *Learning Climate Questionnaire (LCQ): A User's Guide*, Hull: Newland Park Associates.

KLINE, P. (1993), *The Handbook of Psychological Testing*, London: Routledge.

6 Devising an implementation plan

In this chapter we

- describe a group-based process for creating an implementation plan
- provide a list of options for action
- briefly introduce metaplanning.

Ideally, the implementation plan should stem directly from the vision and strategy created by the top management group. The plan needs to encompass the whole organization, if not all at one go, then in a series of planned stages. As we show in Chapter 10, it is not always possible to adopt a timed linear process and inevitably compromise becomes part of the planning equation. The implementation group should develop their understanding of learning organizations by taking part in discussions about the benefits, the possible consequences of failure to achieve effective organizational learning, and the means by which its own performance and progress could be measured.

This is the Understanding Organizational Learning technique which we discussed in Chapter 3. Exercises to conceptualize the nature of learning organizations, together with techniques to explore, diagnose or even evaluate the current state of the organization (such as SWOT, the INVEST process, or the Learning Audit), equip the group to devise an implementation plan.

It is important that the project team experiences at least part of the learning cycle which the top management team went through, in order that they develop the same understanding of and commitment to being a learning organization. It is also important that the project team uses words and concepts that have evolved from their shared understanding rather than to rely on terms and language imposed from outside. An implementation planning workshop should focus in more depth on the nature of learning and learning blockages at personal and organizational level, and on the options for action. It should conclude with a metaplanning session.

Where to start

An important aspect of the implementation planning phase is to identify where to start, who to involve, appropriate time-frames, the resources required, the identification of performance indicators, and the actions and interventions which would stimulate, as well as sustain, the desired changes.

Options for action

The options or actions that can be considered as part of the planning process include those described below.

A management awareness programme
Clarification and realignment of the organization's vision in line with a new understanding of the significance of individual, group and systemic learning for the organization is a step towards becoming a learning organization. This is best achieved through a series of senior-level workshops to create and expand the vision of a learning organization. Further workshops may be necessary to consolidate and develop shared understanding of the organization's evolved conceptualization of a learning organization, and why it is necessary.

A learning audit or survey
A systematic exploration of the changes in behaviour, values, structures and policies that are needed to take the organization from where it is now to where it wants to be (as a learning organization) should lead to the identification of performance indicators. This can be achieved by means of the Learning Audit or the Learning Climate Questionnaire as described in Chapter 5. Other avenues for data-gathering are inter-company consortia to share learning, and the development of competency frameworks which emphasize the importance of encouraging and sustaining learning and which are defined in precise behavioural terms.

A programme of awareness-raising and skill development in relation to the critical importance of learning

The objective of the programme is to change the way managers and team leaders see and carry out their role, especially in relation to how they can enhance learning in themselves and others. This is best achieved by means of awareness-raising workshops coupled with skill development modules where managers learn the importance of facilitating learning. The focus is on how to change from being primarily controllers and regulators, based on authority and sometimes intimidation, towards being coaches and facilitators using motivation and challenge as the means for achieving results. We discuss the appropriate role of line managers in a learning organization in Chapter 7.

A review of the training and development function

A commitment to becoming a learning organization must result in a radical review and realignment of the human resources training and development function. This function has traditionally been seen as the source of planned formal learning which is delivered by means of courses and development programmes. A learning organization places increased responsibility for learning with the individual learner, the team, and with line managers, and raises the question of whether the training function should be solely customer driven or should pursue a mixed economy which also includes proactive interventions. A key issue to be considered is whether an organization actually needs a training function and people in the dedicated role of trainers. These issues are discussed further in Chapter 9.

Helping everyone to learn more effectively

Some of the methods we have used to enhance learning skills have already been referred to above, but more detailed descriptions of the actual processes can be found in Chapter 8. If managers and supervisors can be blocked in their learning and can learn to improve their skills at learning then it is even more likely to prove beneficial to people who are less well educated formally and who may, as a result, be under-confident about their ability to cope with the learning. Learning to learn, and gaining the motivation, if not the inspiration, for everyone to learn continuously, should be one of the main goals of a learning organization.

Helping managers, supervisors and team leaders learn how to encourage learning in others
Managers need to understand how they learn and how to avoid unconsciously blocking others from learning. Simple techniques can be learned which will enable managers to run problem-solving sessions with work groups in ways that encourage creativity and ensure that everyone contributes equally. Managers need to learn that their behaviour, even unconsciously, can inhibit others from learning. An important part of this process is self-examination of a manager's personal style in dealing with others as a manager or team leader (see Chapter 7).

Creation of task groups to plan and implement change
The objective of task groups is to create and implement a programme of change. This can best be achieved by planning workshops after the members of the task groups have had an opportunity to examine for themselves the critical significance of individual, group and systemic learning for the organization, and have internalized their commitment to a learning organization. An important role for the task group is to carry out or initiate audits and to use the findings to help create action plans. In addition, the task groups will need to identify performance indicators of all kinds to show not only that individual behaviour is changing but that results are being translated into quality indicators as well as medium- and long-term organizational performance.

Examine the design of jobs and role definitions
The design and structuring of jobs should be examined in order to open them up to learning opportunities and to avoid organizational learning blocks and unconscious stagnation. The possibilities for learning about customer needs quickly and more directly can be examined, as can opportunities for cross-functional working. Role definitions should be examined and revised to ensure that they emphasize the value and importance of encouraging continuous learning and adaptation, and to ensure that they are goal-orientated rather than task-orientated. They should also ensure that learning is translated into improved processes and outcomes for the organization on a continuous and sustainable basis.

Reorganize jobs and teamworking to maximize continuous and flexible learning

Many organizations have introduced customer-focused teams and self-directed teamworking, and found considerable benefits in terms of flexibility, quality and speed of response, as well as the creation of a more motivated and energized workforce. A critical activity of such teams should be to monitor their own learning processes and find ways of continuously improving how the team learns to perform better. This action and the one described above, examining the design and structuring of jobs, are close to the goals of business process re-engineering (Hammer and Champy, 1993).

Provide maximum supported opportunity for distance and open learning and self-development

Much has been written on the subject of open and distance learning as a flexible and adaptive means of creating desired learning in an organization. The provision of open learning resource centres is only the first step. This provision will have little impact if there is not also a change in the organization's culture and values to actively encourage and support learning by means of open and other forms of learning. We later describe some tools that have been developed to help open learners to learn more effectively from open learning material (see Chapter 8).

Reassess the design and delivery of training to make it more learner-centred and optimally efficient in achieving learning goals

Not only should the role of the training and development function be reviewed in a learning organization, but also the way in which formal training is designed and delivered. In an organization that is committed to learning at all levels there needs to be a review of training from the learner's point of view. The principles for reviewing training material in terms of learning efficiency are presented in Chapter 9.

Develop key groups to use systems thinking with a strategic focus

Systems thinking is not only a powerful problem-solving tool to apply to specific issues and problems, but also a language and a way of thinking that can be used naturally on a day-by-day basis. The key features of systems thinking are to distinguish the patterns that lie behind events, and to look at the relationships between events. A key message is that the situation will worsen unless the whole system is dealt with rather than just the symptoms. Managers and other key people who are developed as natural systems thinkers can embody the principles in their decision-making and problem-solving processes, which can also be linked to other strategic thinking techniques such as scenario-planning.

Train everyone as systems thinkers
This is an option which would allow everyone in an organization to think beyond the immediate symptoms of a problem, understand the interdependence of key factors, and look for systemic solutions to problems whether or not they lie outside their immediate sphere of influence. It would also encourage everyone to think in a long-term way, rather than having only short-term reactions.

Metaplanning

Finally, we look at a practical method to assist the planning process. *Metaplanning* (Eurotecnet Technical Assistance Office, 1993) is a set of tools and techniques, based on the work of Hermann Will and Ulrich Lipp in Germany, which can be used in order to facilitate and enhance group discussions and meetings by improving the exchange of views in the group. It is designed to help groups achieve consensus, while taking individual needs and concerns into account.

Metaplanning requires supporting equipment: a board and small cards that can be fixed to, and moved around, the board. Equipment can be purchased that is designed specifically for use in metaplanning sessions, although a whiteboard and post-it notes can also be used.

There are four strands to the metaplanning process, each of which is appropriate in different situations—card questions; clustering; dots procedure; and flashlight.

Card questions

Card questions can be used to gather a group's views on problems, possible solutions, or ideas. It is a technique which gives everyone an equal opportunity to express their view, independent of their confidence to speak in public. The procedure is a simple one. The discussion leader prepares the board with questions and materials, and explains the question which the group have come together to address, and what prompted it. The ground rules for the meeting are explained.

The participants respond to the question by writing down ideas on small cards. This process can be done individually, or in small groups of two or three people. In responding to the question, people can write only one idea on each card; the writing on the card must be legible from the back of the room; each person may write as many cards as he or she has ideas; and each person puts up their own cards on the board. The cards are placed in any order on the board.

There are a number of possible variations to this approach. Each participant may be given only a restricted number of cards; the discussion leader may put categories on the board, and cards are then pinned under relevant headings. As an alternative to participants writing the cards themselves, two 'scribes' can be used to write down the responses called out by participants.

Clustering

The second strand of the process is clustering. The aim of clustering is for the group to order the ideas generated by the card question. This ordering is a useful step between idea generation and subsequent follow-up work on the question or issue that led to the discussion.

Initially, participants read all the cards on the board. Any unclear cards are identified, and the group discusses each one and comes to a view on how it should be interpreted. Then, the facilitator takes one card at a time and transfers it to a second board, so that the cards are grouped. Finally, each grouping of similar cards is given a name.

There are a number of ground rules to be observed in conducting such a session. First, participants define where each card belongs. If, however, there is any doubt about how a card should properly be classified, the author of the card has the final decision. It is possible that statements may be repeated; these cards should be put on the board next to one another, because repeated ideas are likely to be more important. A final guideline is that no cards should be discarded. Again, there are possible variations that might be useful in running this kind of session. The cards can be placed into groups or fields rather than columns, as this helps to illuminate the relationship between the different clusters. Also, instead of working through card by card, the discussion leader may begin the clustering exercise by asking participants whether they can see a number of cards that cluster naturally together.

Dots procedure

The dots procedure follows naturally from the clustering. Here, participants vote with stickers. This technique can be an effective way to prioritize statements, select ideas, make decisions, and express views, providing participants are given a clear set of alternatives that have been well thought out.

First, the original question and a number of choice possibilities from the cards are put on the board by the facilitator, who explains each of the possibilities. The aims and consequences of the procedure are also explained to the participants. Each participant then receives an adhesive dot, and sticks it to the board to indicate their preferred choice. Then the votes are counted, and the different options are ranked in order of the group's preference.

There are a number of alternative ways to approach this kind of session, depending on the aims of the process. Participants might receive more than one dot each, which may have to be placed in different categories, or they may be allowed to distribute their votes how they choose. A rating scale might be used in order to weight the votes, which can then be expanded on by asking participants to explain why they gave the rating they did. Also, different coloured dots could be used to differentiate between groups, or to permit a before–after comparison.

Flashlight

The final strand is flashlight, which might be used at any point in group discussions. This process creates an overview, or snapshot, of the group's feelings on an issue. The facilitator begins by explaining why he or she would like to have a flashlight at this particular point in time. He or she then presents the discussion stimulus, allows the group time to reflect, and then selects the first speaker.

The process itself is very straightforward. All participants state in one or two sentences their position on the question or issue before the group. There is no evaluation; the flashlight process is intended to illuminate the views of the group, not to develop them. Participants may also temporarily 'pass', in which case the facilitator moves on to get the views of the next person.

Like the other strands of the metaplan process, there are some variations on this process which might be useful in different contexts—the justified flashlight, the documented flashlight, and the advice flashlight.

First, using the *justified flashlight* each person explains the rationale behind their position. The *documented flashlight* requires the responses to be written down. This can be useful in identifying the diversity of views on an issue, or for before–after comparisons. Finally, using the *advice flashlight* a member of the group with a problem situation provides the background for the rest of the group. The group members then prompt for further information on the problem. This is used as the discussion stimulus and all the group members flash-light their views on this problem, and, finally, the problem-owner is given the opportunity to respond to these views.

Techniques such as metaplanning are valuable in assisting the implementation planning process. As we have noted, however, perhaps the key success factor at this stage is not to attempt implementation planning until a shared under-standing has been developed. While the US Marine Corps is reputed to believe that 'A piss-poor plan violently executed is better than no plan at all', for most practical purposes the better the level of shared understanding of the issues, the better the chances of success.

We have described a detailed process for ensuring efficient and effective group planning sessions. The Keys to Under-standing technique (described in detail in Chapter 7) has also been extensively used to equip groups for planning and problem-solving activities.

In the next chapter we

- look at ways in which managers can be helped to support their own learning and that of their teams.

References

EUROTECNET, Technical Assistance Office (1993) *Metaplan: A Method to Assist the Planning Process: Practical Guidelines*, Brussels: Commission of the European Communities.

HAMMER, M. and CHAMPY, J. (1993) *Re-engineering the Corporation: A Manifesto for Business Revolution*, New York: Harper Business.

7   Helping managers to manage learning

In this chapter we

- examine the role of managers in a learning organization
- describe a workshop which is designed to help managers understand how they can support learning
- analyse the role of managers as leaders of learning, as facilitators, and as individual learners
- describe and explain the Keys to Understanding technique
- describe a self-assessment instrument to reveal the extent to which the manager naturally adopts a coaching rather than a controlling style.

The role of managers

In working towards becoming a learning organization, there are key activities required from the management role. These can include the creation of a shared vision for the organization and the role that learning plays within it; gaining commitment to the vision and values of the organization; and embodying the values of the organization in their own behaviour. In addition, the management team should scrutinize structures and systems within the organization to ensure that they do not directly or indirectly inhibit learning and self-development, and should establish accountabilities and the performance indicators which are necessary for achieving continuous learning for the whole organization.

Managers should also empower people in the organization to act upon rather than merely respond to received instructions, and provide the resources for initiatives and techniques to encourage and enhance learning, such as methods to break traditional moulds of thinking, mind-sets and paradigms. Finally, managers need to examine their own learning and what blocks it, not only to enable them to learn more effectively but also to enable them to encourage team learning where greater output and innovation would result.

In effect, there are three key roles for managers in a learning organization:

- as a leader
- as a facilitator of learning
- as an individual learner.

The *leadership role* involves the examination of the concept of the organization and the critical role learning should play in ensuring enduring and sustainable success for the organization. It also involves initiating a process by means of which others in the organization can develop a similar awareness and understanding so that they can be involved in diagnosing and implementing change programmes. It is not possible to be prescriptive about how the leadership role should be carried out, as each organization needs to work out its own routes to change (and it is not the purpose of this book to prescribe change management processes). Instead we describe below a learning process which enables senior managers to examine the learning organization concept and commit to action.

The *facilitator role* is also crucial. The point has been made earlier that it is a common experience for managers to espouse the ideals of empowerment and yet by their behaviour, their interpretation of and response to problems, and their day-to-day actions disable rather than empower. Confusing signals are emitted by a manager who talks about the critical value of learning but does not allow enough time for reflection, reacts punitively to mistakes, does not admit when he or she does not understand something, and thinks people are stupid if they do not pick up something at first or, at worst, second attempt. In order to encourage learning in others, the manager needs to understand how people need to learn, what helps, and what hinders, and to realize that his or her own behaviour can create obstacles to learning, just as the use of simple techniques, and day-to-day actions as a manager can greatly enhance learning in others. In this chapter we describe a workshop process and a diagnostic instrument designed to help managers change their behaviour so that they facilitate learning in others as a conscious and important aspect of their role.

Finally, the manager is an *individual learner*, who may need help in understanding how learning occurs, that people have different learning styles, and that their own learning can be enhanced by use of the techniques we describe in Chapter 8.

Managers as leaders of learning

In order to understand their role in a learning organization, senior managers need to understand the critical significance of learning for their organization. This can first be achieved by a systematic examination of the concept by means of a special workshop.

Having developed an understanding of the significance of learning, and a conceptualization of a learning organization as it applies to their own organization (see Chapter 3), an analysis of the strengths, weaknesses, opportunities and challenges existing within the *status quo* can be undertaken. It is important for the top management team to create or enlarge their vision and strategy for achieving the kind of organization they are working towards. The next stage would be to communicate, consult and share this vision more widely and to initiate an implementation planning team (see Schein, 1993).

The workshop can be run for top managers, preferably involving all major functions. It can also be run with participants from all levels in the organization. The key outcomes of the workshop process are:

- A conceptualization of a learning organization that fits the needs and circumstances of the organization
- A commitment to becoming a learning organization
- A decision to gather more data and/or create an implementation plan, possibly by means of a special project team.

A workshop of this kind usually requires one to one-and-a-half days. After a brief introduction to workshop objectives, the participants are asked to speculate freely about the possible purposes of stimulating and sustaining the learning of *all* employees; the consequences for the organization if this is not done or not done well; and the signs that would indicate that the organization was succeeding in stimulating learning. The participants work in pairs using specially prepared worksheets. All their thoughts are collated using the procedure described in Chapter 2, which ensures that all ideas are expressed and recorded without judgement or evaluation. The group then discusses the output.

Following discussion of the implications and a review of key learning points the group is then in a position to examine the output from a *survey* of the state of learning in the organization, using instruments such as the Learning Audit or the Learning Climate Questionnaire, both of which are described in Chapter 5. The group then carries out a SWOT analysis (Strengths/Successes-Weaknesses/Opportunities-Challenges/Threats) based on their previous analyses and discussions and supported by a checklist of performance indicators.

Several of the exercises used in the top management awareness-raising workshop should also be used in other workshops which are designed for use with other groups, for example the implementation planning team, or a workshop to review the role of trainers and the training function in a learning organization. This approach avoids 'handing down' learning from one group to another. Each group 'creates' its own understanding by going through a similar or related sequence of exercises.

Finally, it is most important that managers analyse the aspects of their own behaviour which inhibit learning or are not consistent with the goal of optimizing learning in others; these can be listed under the heading of 'stop doing/do less'. Similarly a collective as well as an individual list of 'start doing/do more' behaviours can be created, but a separate learning process is needed to help managers understand and practise the new behaviours and techniques to enhance learning.

Managers as facilitators of learning

In a learning organization managers and team leaders need to understand, absorb and communicate the learning-orientated values of the organization so that they can encourage and support continuous learning within work functions and work groups. They need to be able to identify the conditions in the workplace which enhance and sustain continuous learning and exploit wherever possible all opportunities for adaptive learning and development. They need to learn and use the skills of coaching and facilitation with reduced reliance on the use of authority. In an empowering role they should encourage and support increased autonomy in decision-making and problem-solving within work groups, and actively support individual and group self-development. They also need to function as a two-way channel of communication and information between the rest of the workforce and senior management in order to maximize the potential for learning and adaptation.

Below we describe a process that enables managers to understand how they themselves learn, and which also allows them to learn to use some simple techniques to encourage and support learning in their teams. The objective is to develop in managers an understanding of the importance of encouraging and sustaining learning in all employees, to give experience of how learning (their own and that of others) can be blocked, and also to learn some practical techniques for encouraging learning in others.

The workshop again begins with the Understanding Organizational Learning exercise which asks the participants to speculate freely about the possible purposes of encouraging and sustaining learning in all employees, as well as the consequences of not succeeding in doing so. Finally they are asked to think of possible ways in which one could tell whether learning was in fact being encouraged and sustained.

Practical applications

A series of exercises follows which reveal the extent and nature of blocks to learning which can exist both in the individual or the organization itself. The managers then examine how different material needs to be learned in different ways. This is achieved by a card-sorting exercise and a series of follow-on exercises. These exercises form part of the Tools for a Learning Organization (Pearn and Mulrooney, 1995). Here we describe two of the exercises: *Learning to ask questions* and *The Keys to Understanding*.

Learning to ask questions

The exercise involves learning to carry out a task from a demonstration in which the facilitator only answers the questions asked, but otherwise says nothing. The exercise typically begins by the participants asking: What are we going to learn?, Why are we doing it this way?, etc. At this point the exercise has begun and all the questions that are asked are recorded on a flipchart. The participants continue asking questions and the tutor answers as helpfully as possible until the group is ready to start the demonstration. They go on asking questions during the demonstration (or repeated demonstrations, if they ask for them) until they are satisfied that they can carry out the task unaided. They then carry out the task and in most cases find that they can do it without difficulty because they have had complete control over the information they needed in order to learn how to carry out the task. For the purpose of the exercise any practical task will do, e.g. folding a piece of paper into a ball using origami techniques, or dismantling and reassembling a PC.

The real point of the exercise is to analyse the questions that were most helpful to the learners. The exercise with the paper ball can generate as many as 60 questions, about two-thirds of them before the demonstration actually starts. The participants highlight the questions which they felt helped them most. These tend to fall into a distinct pattern:

- Questions that relate to the *purpose* of the exercise, for example:
  What are we going to do?
  Why are we doing it this way?
- Questions that anticipate or focus on potential *problems*, for example:
  How many folds are there?
  Is there a test at the end?
  Does everyone manage to learn the task?
- Questions that make *comparisons* and contrast one thing with another, for example:
  Is it like origami?
  Is it the same as?
- Questions that *check* understanding, or progress, or achievement, for example:
  Are the folds symmetrical?
  Is there a model for us to look at?
  How precise do the folds need to be ?
  How can I tell if I have got it right?

Occasionally questions are asked about how something is seen from someone else's *viewpoint*, for example: Have other people refused to do this exercise?, What did ... think of this exercise?

Other helpful questions emerge, and their value to the learning process can be analysed by the group. Another kind of question is significant only by not being asked. For example, participants in this exercise often say that it would have been easier if they had taken notes. The facilitator's response is that if they had asked he/she would have said yes. Sometimes the participants complain after the demonstration is finished that they could not see properly. The facilitator replies that they did not ask if they could come closer. In other words by not asking these questions they had unconsciously imposed *constraints* on their own learning. When questions of this type are asked, e.g. Can we come closer?, Can you repeat that?, they function by influencing or exercising control over the facilitator. Not asking them can result in inhibitors to learning whereas asking them gives more control to the learner.

The key points which arise from this exercise are that some kinds of questions are more helpful than others; not asking questions can limit learning; questioning can be actively encouraged, and if necessary taught as a technique; and finally that managers should be ready to encourage and respond to questioning by giving helpful answers.

Using the Keys to Understanding

A simple framework for asking questions can be constructed by the participants themselves by noting the questions which helped most during the demonstration and fitting them into a simple model:

- purpose
- contrasts
- problems
- viewpoints
- checks.

If they pose questions using the model as a framework, they can enhance their understanding. Alternatively one can pose the questions to oneself and then seek the answers. The skilled questioner can ask:

1. The purpose or possible purposes of something, for example:
   What possible purposes can be served by encouraging and sustaining learning in all employees?
2. How it compares and contrasts with something that is already familiar, for example:
   In what ways do you think a learning organization is similar to and different from a bureaucratic organization?
3. What problems might arise, for example:
   What problems might arise if we do not succeed in encouraging and sustaining the learning of all employees, both short-term and long-term?
4. How it might look or be seen from the viewpoint of a specified group, for example:
   What would a learning organization look like from the viewpoint of customers? (or a supplier?)
5. How you can check that you have understood or got something right, for example:
   How could you tell if an organization is actually encouraging and sustaining the learning of all employees?

We call these questions the *Keys to Understanding*. They can also be used to structure brainstorming or problem-solving sessions which are designed to open up people's minds to the complexity and diverse manifestations of a set of ideas, such as the learning organization or the management of diversity, or to deepen understanding of issues such as quality or safety. We have worked frequently with this model and have run many exercises to allow a wide range of people to work out the model for themselves, including brewery operatives, managers in a retail organization, oil refinery managers, factory operatives and health service workers. Although the set of five keys works well and is easy to remember, other categories of questions can be added, such as:

- *What if? questions*, for example:
  What if our competitors doubled capacity and halved their prices overnight?
- *Consequence questions*, for example:
  What would be the consequences if we did not assure quality in everything we did?

What if? and consequence questions could be seen as special instances of *Problem* questions. One advantage of confining the Keys to only five is that they are easily remembered and retained as an informal model.

The diagrams in Figure 7.1 attempt to explain how the Keys to Understanding work. The *purposes* question draws into the open all the thoughts the group has about possible purposes without evaluation, editing or other constraints. Looking at the issue from the (specified) viewpoints of others, and comparing and contrasting the issue with things with which the group is already familiar, further expands the range of ideas which are brought to the surface in the group. All of the ideas are logged without evaluation on a flipchart. When the group begins to think about problems that might occur, it begins to focus more on reality and possibilities. Finally, the group generates ideas about signs and indicators for successful resolution of the problem, or the level of learning to be achieved. The Keys to Understanding can be used to develop a deeper understanding of an issue by drawing together the collective thoughts of the group. This is particularly helpful when the newly developed shared understanding in the group is applied to the resolution of a problem, or is used to help make a complex decision.

As a structured discussion technique in which the contributions are handled according to the procedure described earlier, the Keys to Understanding can be very powerful. It is not necessary to ask all the questions; usually a purpose question, followed by a problem and a checking question, are sufficient. However, if more depth is needed then one or more comparison and/or viewpoint

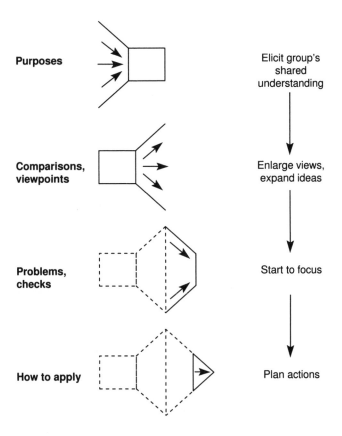

Purposes		Elicit group's shared understanding
Comparisons, viewpoints		Enlarge views, expand ideas
Problems, checks		Start to focus
How to apply		Plan actions

Figure 7.1   How the Keys to Understanding work

questions can be added. The sequencing of questions is important with a purpose question nearly always coming first, if necessary followed by viewpoint and comparison questions.

The technique can easily be taught to line managers, who can use it to structure and run discussion groups and problem-solving sessions. It can also be taught to work groups as an informal model to use when trying to understand something either by asking the questions about purpose, viewpoint, comparisons, etc. or by thinking systematically in these terms. If both team managers and members of a team use the same model to guide and structure discussions then synergy is created.

To use the technique more formally, especially when the questions are written down for examination by a group, requires gaining insight into the form of words that work best for each type of question:

- *Purpose questions* take the form:
  - What possible reasons ...?
  - What possible purposes could be served ...?
  - Why does ...?
- *Viewpoint questions* take the form:
  - How is A seen by B?
  - How would A be viewed by B?
  - How does A look to B?
- *Comparison questions* take the form:
  - In what ways is A similar to and different from B?
  - How does A contrast with B?
  - What are the differences between A and B? What are the similarities?
- *Problem questions* take the form:
  - What could go wrong?
  - What would happen if we were not successful?
  - What could prevent us being successful?
  - What are the possible consequences of not succeeding?
- *Check questions* take the form:
  - How could we tell if we were succeeding?
  - How could we tell if we were getting it right?
  - How could we tell if we were making progress?

The Keys to Understanding technique has been widely used in a range of different contexts. These include opening up *free-ranging examination of issues* such as equal opportunities, change programmes, quality, or safety; *examining problems* such as absenteeism, poor safety performance, difficult working relationships, with a view to finding solutions; *building understanding* from within the group's experience rather than imposing a theory, e.g. interviewing skills, team working; as *preparation* for planning and organizing a complex event such as a team visit to another site, an induction course; and *overcoming fears* and resistance to new ideas being imposed from outside, new working practices, computerization. In some organizations in which we have worked the Keys to Understanding have been internalized to the extent that they are routinely used to structure meetings, formulate agendas and solve problems.

The manager as coach or enabler

Much has been written on the subject of managers changing their style from authority-based control and regulation, towards empowering and encouraging autonomy and self-development in others (Moss Kanter, 1989; Belasco, 1990). The thinking behind the approach is that better results are obtained when staff have responsibility for and involvement in their work because they have been developed and supported to function effectively at a higher level of performance that requires less direct supervision, monitoring and control. In a learning organization managers are more likely to see their role in terms of coaching and facilitating rather than a command-and-control style of management. The problem for many managers is that, in terms of how they personally operate and behave, they do not know how to position themselves on a spectrum ranging from the autocratic to the enabling. It is one thing to know that a less authority-based style of managing is wanted, but it is often difficult to translate this into changes in one's own behaviour.

Below we describe a self-assessment instrument (developed by Peter Moxon working in collaboration with Glaxo Manufacturing Services Ltd and forming part of the Learning Organization Toolkit) which was designed to enable managers to position themselves in relation to nine aspects of managerial functioning:

- objective-setting
- change management
- leadership style
- decision-making
- performance management
- training and development
- communication
- self-awareness
- external relationships.

Managers are asked to examine the descriptions of behaviours relating to these nine aspects, and identify the behaviour most typical of them. Table 7.1 gives examples of some of the behaviours described. Completion of the self-rating under the nine headings results in an individual profile which can then form the basis of a personal development plan. In addition, subordinates as well as peers can draw up a profile of the manager using the same headings so that similarities and disparities can be examined in more detail.

We used the profile as part of a process to improve the learning skills of line managers in a large retail organization. The objective was to increase their understanding of the nature of learning and to help them develop skills as facilitators rather than as directors or controllers of people. The workshop comprised a range of exercises designed to reveal the importance of learning, and included learning to

Table 7.1 Nine aspects of managerial functioning: typical items at the disabling/ enabling extremes

Function	Disabling	Enabling
Objective-setting	manager determines objectives and communicates to the team	individuals develop personal objectives for agreement with manager
Change management	manager draws up plans and communicates to the team	manager initiates the process but works closely with the team to refine and develop
Leadership style	manager provides close direction and supervision in all situations	manager creates a vision but day-to-day control and monitoring of results resides with the team
Decision-making	manager decides both what needs to be done and how	manager provides broad framework in which the team should work and gives individual responsibility for decisions
Performance management	monitors performance closely and is quick to intervene and take over	maintains overview of progress and identifies areas where the individual may need help
Training and development	manager determines and organizes all training	helps the individual determine own learning programmes
Communication	passes on only information needed to complete tasks	is consistently open and honest in dealing with others
Self-awareness	seeks little or no feedback on own style	openly shares own feelings and concerns where it will help the individual or group
External relationships	focuses solely on effectiveness of own patch	develops close working relationships with other areas to support own area

use the Keys to Understanding, and profiling on the Manager as Coach/Enabler instrument.

At the end of the workshop the implications for their role as line managers were identified. The managers' evaluation was very positive. Their main conclusion was that they needed to create more time for what they now saw as their real job, that is, enhancing learning. They felt empowered to influence and facilitate learning processes. They also recognized the importance of identifying blocks to learning and of putting enhancers to learning in place. The group realized the demotivating effects of not gearing learning to individual differences and the importance of having tools and techniques to help overcome what they saw as a play-safe environment where people did not ask challenging questions.

A follow-up to the workshop identified what had been achieved. Comments made by the managers included: 'I realized for the first time that with every pair of hands you get a free brain'; 'We need to learn to switch on the brains of our 52 000 employees'; 'Helping others to learn is the best way to improve company performance'; 'Supervisors need to learn how to encourage learning in others'; and 'Good learners encourage other learners to learn'. There was a strongly held view in the group that the facilitation of learning was critical to the company's long-term success.

In the next chapter we

- look at a wide range of techniques and processes for enhancing and improving the quality of learning in the organization.

References

BELASCO, J. A. (1990) *Teaching the Elephant to Dance: Empowering Change in Your Organization*, London: Hutchinson Business Books.

MOSS KANTER, R. (1989) *When Giants Learn to Dance: Mastering the Challenges of Strategy, Management and Careers in the 1990s*, New York: Simon and Schuster.

PEARN, M. and MULROONEY, C. (1995) *Tools for a Learning Organization*, London: Institute of Personnel and Development.

SCHEIN, E. (1993) 'How can organizations learn faster?: The challenge of entering the green room', *Sloan Management Review*, Winter, 85–92.

8   Tools for enhancing learning

In this chapter we

- describe 10 ways to enhance learning and provide practical guidance on each
- outline some processes to upgrade the learning skills of all employees
- describe two instruments to help develop learning from experience and to identify personal learning blocks
- present a selection of exercises for developing group and team learning
- summarize three instruments designed to improve the quality of open learning, and a fourth which enables the user to analyse jobs in terms of the types of learning involved.

Learning organizations do not leave learning to chance. In terms of our hot-air balloon analogy, learning organizations support learning by putting in place individual and organizational enhancers to learning, as well as temporary scaffolding, which together optimize the quantity and quality of learning opportunities within the organization. In practice this means supporting learning at all times and wherever it occurs, in as many different ways as possible.

Ten ways to support learning

The 10 different ways of supporting learning covered in this section are:

1. Learning contracts
2. Mentoring
3. Shadowing
4. Self-directed learning
5. Self-development

6. Personal development plans
7. Networks and learning communities
8. Learning logs
9. Learning accomplishment audits
10. Learning albums

Each of the support mechanisms has the goal of enhancing learning. There is some overlap between them, but each has something distinct to offer to people in organizations who want to support learning.

Learning contracts
A learning contract is a signed or formal agreement drawn up by the learner, his or her trainer and manager, which sets out a clear set of specific learning objectives, how these will be achieved, within what time period and what the criteria of evaluation will be (Boak and Joy, 1990).

The foundations for the development of learning contracts lie in a number of principles of learning and development. First, the learner's participation is increased, and this active role makes learning more effective. Second, the learning objectives should be work-related, thus making the learning highly relevant to the learner. Third, learning contracts have a sound theoretical basis: the concept of the learning cycle (Kolb, 1984; Honey and Mumford, 1986). Learning contracts help the learner to move successively between reflection, knowledge, planning and action. The continual movement between these different learning activities is the key to effective learning. For a learning contract to be successful, two activities must be undertaken before it is negotiated: preparation and auditing.

It is essential that the learner is adequately prepared, and the facilitator must make sure the learner understands three things at this stage. First, the objectives are very specifically *learning* objectives; they are not project-based, although these learning objectives will be achieved through project activity. Second, the rationale for using learning contracts: namely to accelerate the process of moving through the learning cycle. Third, the learner's responsibilities. The initiative lies with the learner; he or she leads the process of negotiation. The learner must conduct a self-audit, or assessment of learning needs, to provide a clear focus for the learning contract. The learner may not be equipped to conduct this self-assessment, and the role of the trainer and manager at this stage is to help the learner develop the skills required to do this. For example, this could involve input from the learner's manager, or exposure to a model of good practice. The aim of the audit is for the learner to make his or her learning needs explicit.

Once learning needs have been identified, the learning contract can be negotiated. This process is led by the learner. The role of the manager and the trainer is to clarify the needs and wants of the learner, and to help the learner develop a plan of action to carry out the learning contract within the time-frame specified. Good learning contracts set realistic objectives, which means the self-assessment must be accurate. They also 'belong' to the learner, because she/he very clearly leads the negotiation process. Finally, and most importantly, good learning contracts are explicit. It is absolutely critical that all three parties have a shared understanding of the objectives, activities, deadlines and assessment criteria contained within the contract.

Mentoring

Mentoring relationships have been found to be critically important to the developing individual. A mentor takes particular care and responsibility for providing advice and guidance, often in the context of a specific project, to someone junior in the organization in order to make the best of their abilities. This is a special role which is undertaken by someone other than the individual's direct boss. A successful mentoring relationship results in benefits not only for the individual (Smith, 1990) but also for the mentor and the organization. Below we summarize the issues to consider in implementing a mentoring programme; the characteristics to seek and to avoid in a mentor, the things a good mentor will often do, the success factors, and finally the benefits to the individual and to the organization.

A skilful mentor has a good record for developing other people and has a wide range of current skills to pass on; has a good understanding of the organization, how it works and where it is going; has sufficient time to devote to the relationship; can command an individual's respect; and has their own network of contacts and influence within the organization.

By contrast the mentor to avoid is heavily engaged in corporate politics; has recently been appointed to a new position; is involved in activities which carry little weight in the organization: or is obviously on the way down in the organization and has a consistently high turnover of staff. Thus it can be seen that a good mentor often becomes a model that the individual can follow whenever he/she is unsure how to approach a problem; instructs and provides the subordinate with a chance to try his/her hand while making sure he/she does not make crucial errors; suggests specific strategies for accomplishing work objectives, gaining recognition and achieving career aspirations; tells the individual when they are doing a good or a poor job; and can help the individual achieve major life goals.

Factors for a successful mentoring relationship are acceptance and commitment from participants and non-participants alike; preparation of employees at all levels for the introduction of the mentoring programme; and careful identification and selection of the mentoring pairs. Smith (1990) has identified the benefits of mentoring to the individual. He sees them as the creation of a carefully planned and organized development programme aimed specifically at the needs of the individual; the possibility of accelerated learning/work experience/promotion; recognition of individual effort and worth, providing satisfaction and/or motivation; and priority introduction into existing organizational networks and power centres.

The kinds of thing people can learn learn from their mentors include:

• risk-taking behaviours
• communication skills
• survival in the organization
• skills of their professions
• respect for people
• setting high standards and not compromising them
• how to be a good listener
• how to get along with all kinds of people
• leadership qualities
• what it means to be a professional.

Equally there are benefits both to the mentor and to the organization. Organizational benefits include employees working better as a result of all they have learned; more effective use of human resources; a powerful development tool; and improved communications. As far as benefits to the mentor are concerned, these include developing leadership skills in the mentor; fostering teamwork, openness and trust; improving communication through shared values; and can of course be satisfying to the mentor.

Shadowing

Shadowing involves learning from colleagues at work by observing these skilled and experienced colleagues in action. Shadowing can be used in two ways, depending on the characteristics of the task being performed by the experienced colleague. The first, and most common, way of shadowing a colleague involves observing the tasks being performed. This is appropriate for a range of activities, from learning how to process cheques to negotiating contracts with clients. The key learning point for the person doing the shadowing is to identify and reflect on the tasks which are performed and how these are done. This allows the learner to increase his or her knowledge of the set of tasks, and plan how to transfer the knowledge gained into action.

A second form of shadowing, less obvious than the first, is very similar to project-based mentoring (Smith, 1990). For some tasks, there is simply no clearly defined opportunity to shadow and observe a colleague. An example of this might be a design project. During the initial meeting to clarify the objectives and constraints of the project, the learner could observe his or her colleague; but the work resulting from the meeting cannot be observed so easily. To shadow this type of task, the learner might be shown the design at various stages, and would take the opportunity to discuss the work with the experienced colleague. Alternatively, some of the work may be given to the learner, who, with the support of a colleague, actually contributes to the project, and in this way gains first-hand experience of what is involved, but in a supportive environment which is conducive to learning.

In both these ways shadowing can be an effective technique for developing new or existing employees. The likelihood of learning effectively can be increased by providing the learner with support and opportunities to reflect on what has been learned, for instance by discussing key learning points with a colleague, or by putting the new learning into practice in some way.

It is important to note that shadowing is *not* enough on its own. Effective learning demands that the learner continually moves between reflective observation, conceptualization, active experimentation and concrete experience (Kolb, 1984). This suggests that shadowing should ideally be combined with other approaches, such as a learning log, or a more formal learning forum such as a workshop. A second caveat on the shadowing of procedural tasks is also necessary. Shadowing must not be used instead of writing down formal procedures, as this tends to propagate errors and make it difficult to question 'the way things are done around here'. Shadowing might help some people learn procedural tasks, and so could be used *in addition* to providing the learner with the formalized procedures.

Self-directed learning   The self-directed approach (Ravid, 1987) to learning involves individuals taking the initiative and responsibility for their own learning rather than waiting for their organization to guide or 'tell' them what to learn and how to learn it. Self-directed learning has much in common with flexible learning. There are three core elements to the approach. First, the learner has major responsibility for day-to-day decision-making on learning needs, information-gathering, resource selection and ways of learning. Second, someone takes responsibility for helping the learner to reach the level of competence he or she wants, and to acquire the skills necessary to access learning resources and, third, the evaluation of learning is done mutually by the learner and someone else, such as the learner's direct manager, or learning facilitator.

An important factor for the successful introduction of self-directed learning is the support role, that of the development adviser. It is the adviser's responsibility to provide access to a range of learning opportunities to allow the learner to meet his or her own development needs. The adviser must also provide assistance in the learning process *as and when it is needed*; further assistance changes the adviser's support to a more traditional directing role. Underpinning these activities is the need to shift to a new mind-set. People must question the way their organizations do things; successful self-directed learning requires that everyone in the organization rethinks what they mean by training and development, and how they see their roles in such activities. However, the key point is that, while training is clearly a part of learning, learning is very much more than training.

The self-directed learning approach confers two main advantages. First, because self-directed learning is individually based, it can be a useful approach to developing people at all levels of the organization. Second, the learner's ownership of the process ensures that the learning is personally relevant to his or her role in the organization. This tends to enhance both the quantity and quality of learning that takes place, and allows learners to make better use of their new knowledge and skills.

A very powerful limitation to the impact of self-directed learning can be the organizational climate. An 'open climate', one which emphasizes the individual's independence, and devolves responsibility for decision-making as far down the organization hierarchy as possible, is conducive to the successful implementation of a self-directed learning programme. On the other hand, a 'closed' climate, which operates on a hierarchical, command-and-control basis is not conducive to effective self-directed learning programmes.

This last point highlights a very important caveat to this entire chapter. Different ways of enhancing learning have been discussed and, while the value of these support mechanisms is great, it must not be forgotten that they are no more than superficial structures. If the underlying foundations are weak, then the structures built on them will quickly collapse. The mechanisms for enhancing learning presented in this chapter will be most effective where the foundations of the learning organization—inspired learners in a structure, culture and a management approach that supports and rewards learning and the transfer of new knowledge—have been thoroughly prepared.

Self-development

The self-development approach involves helping individuals to understand their own personal learning and development processes and thus to take more control of, and responsibility for, their own development (Pedler *et al.*, 1986). In this way learning and development are driven by the learner and negotiated and agreed with them before a plan is developed.

Self-development is a broad term which encompasses self-directed and flexible learning approaches. It is difficult to pin down as it is more an approach than a technique. At its core are two ideas:

- The learner must be given the power to learn autonomously.
- The trainer's role should not be directive, but facilitatory.

The recent emphasis on *self*-development fits in with the contemporary context of organizations. It is almost self-evident that 'where work organizations rely increasingly on self-motivated, self-starting, entrepreneurial, resourceful, responsible members ... the means of equipping people with the necessary skills and abilities must also reflect these self-directing values' (Pedler, 1988). Self-development is an approach which is congruent with the contemporary view that organizations must empower individuals and provide increased autonomy at work. Within the broad framework of the approach, there are examples of techniques that help learners to manage their own learning, such as learning to learn and *learning communities*. Learning communities are discussed later in this chapter in relation to networks.

Personal development plans

Personal Development Plans (PDPs) are a contract between the individual and the organization which specifies mutually agreed learning and development needs and targets of performance and behaviour. The organization then encourages the individual's development through regular appraisals and revisions of the PDP.

PDPs can have different objectives in different contexts, but by way of illustration here are three different objectives that can be identified:

- To link development needs to aspirations and plans for current and future roles and jobs, rather than to performance in current job alone.
- To help individuals take a more structured and broader approach to their development.
- To encourage a climate where individuals have greater responsibility for developing themselves.

A major source of information for the development of a PDP will clearly be the individual's performance appraisal, and a PDP can be a useful developmental adjunct to the performance appraisal process. Although PDPs and performance appraisal are clearly very closely linked, it is important to recognize the differences between them, in terms of both process and outcome, as shown in Table 8.1.

Table 8.1   Appraisal and PDPs: process and outcome differences

Appraisal	PDPs
Process: • Evaluation of current and past performance • Review of objectives • Review of individual's abilities, strengths and weaknesses • Link development to current business needs, manager's objectives and department requirements	Process: • Review of likes and dislikes • Review by individuals of their competencies and areas for development • Review of possible directions and objectives to pursue in individual's career • Review of business objectives against individual requirements
Results: • Appraisal grading and merit review • Objective-setting for next 12 months against business objectives • Training for the current role • Training for performance shortfalls/to fulfil development needs	Results: • Individual action plan • Pursuit of activities to improve satisfaction in current or future roles • Actions to broaden horizons • Individually focused objectives may not always be in line with company, directorate, department or manager's objectives.

PDPs will complement appraisals and the information from both sources can be used to develop action plans. These action plans will identify:

- the *activities* to be carried out;
- who will be *responsible* for ensuring they occur;
- where the learner has *authority* for carrying out an action autonomously.

For individuals assessing themselves in order to develop a PDP, the process can be helpful in a number of different ways. It can be a chance to sit down and think about what they really like doing at work; an opportunity to get their likes and dislikes taken into account when their careers are being planned; a help in shaping their futures; an opportunity to look at their job and career in a non-threatening environment; a chance to get people other than their managers involved in helping them to structure what they want out of their job.

Similarly, for individuals who have a management role, the PDP process confers a number of benefits. It can be a non-threatening device which can provide additional information about their staff to help in appraisals and planning for the future; a chance to find out what people really want to do; a facilitator of job satisfaction among staff; a chance for staff to take a more active role in their development; and an opportunity for staff to feel more responsible for their development. The offer of a PDP to all staff was a key element in the Rover Learning Business's initiative to enhance learning throughout Rover Group companies.

Networks and learning communities   Networks are one form of mutual learning that comes from the direct exchange of practical ideas within a group of people. At a general level, networks consist of a wide selection of people brought together because of a common interest. They provide the individual with many opportunities to learn from the range of ideas and information that stems from varied interests and experience within the network.

Hastings (1993) argues that the contemporary organization depends fundamentally on its networking processes for success, and identifies four different core networking processes:

- networking within the organization, internally driven, which focuses on spanning functional boundaries.
- networking between organizations, which is externally driven, and centres on developing successful partnerships.

• hard networks, which are technology-driven and used to connect computers.
• soft networking, which is people-driven and used as a means of connecting people.

The term 'networking' is often used to refer to soft networking, which is generally an unstructured process, although there are steps organizations can take to facilitate it (see Hastings, 1993). Networking within and between organizations can be more easily structured, and these approaches are therefore more useful for people who want to enhance learning in their organizations.

Networking within the organization
Groups can be brought together for the express purpose of learning; these groups can take several forms, for example, learning sets and learning communities. Learning sets are discussed in detail elsewhere (e.g. Cunningham, 1994), so the focus here will be on learning communities.

The label 'learning communities' is perhaps a misleading one; despite its monastic tone, it applies to a learning event which has fixed time limits, and exists for a more or less specific purpose. There are two major principles which underpin learning communities (Pedler, 1988). First, each individual must take prime responsibility for identifying and meeting their own learning needs. Second, each individual is responsible for helping others to identify their needs and for offering themselves as a flexible resource within the learning community.

Canning and Martin (1990) describe a workshop approach to learning community events. A learning community event will typically address a specific theme, which must be relevant to all the participants; there will also be limited resources available to support the event. The aim is to provide a group of people with an opportunity to work together as a community of learners. Once individuals in small groups have identified what they need to learn, and how they want to learn it, then the whole group comes together to set an agenda for learning workshops with the support of the event facilitators. The facilitators may provide the group with a map of possible ways in which people could learn, but participants would be encouraged to find and develop ways of learning outside of this map which matched their individual needs more closely.

Essentially, learning community events employ a self-directed learning approach. The difference is that the focus is at the group, rather than the individual, level; consequently learning community events are able to harness the group dynamic, and use it to drive learning.

Networking between organizations

A further example of a way of establishing a learning network is through *inter-company consortia* (Tobin, 1993; Hastings, 1993). Inter-company consortia promote learning in two ways: first, they enable companies to learn from one another and, second, they enable them to learn together. Such a consortium combines the bench-marking philosophy of best proven practice with the spirit of co-operative learning and partnership.

Three different patterns of partnership can be identified:

- research and development partnership
- values-based partnership
- bench-marking.

Joint *research and development* ventures are becoming increasingly common as technology increases in sophistication, and individual organizations can no longer afford to take on the risk of research and development alone. An example of such a partnership is the recently discussed potential collaboration between Boeing and Airbus on the 'Superjumbo project'. The ECLO (European Consortium for the Learning Organization) based in Brussels represents another example of such a multi-company, multi-institution collaboration.

A second form of partnership is one based on an organization's *value chain*. Increasingly, close links between suppliers and manufacturers, and manufacturers and distributors is becoming an essential component of organizational strategy for increasing quality. The new philosophy is that by learning together, and jointly solving problems, the partnership will generate higher levels of quality for the customer.

The third form of partnership is based on *bench-marking*. People from a number of non-competitive organizations meet to address specific issues. The meeting provides a forum for the sharing of approaches and knowledge with the goal of all the participating organizations ultimately being able to achieve best practice in each of the areas addressed by the consortium.

Inter-company relationships and collaboration in order to learn from each other are becoming an increasingly important business asset. The ability to nurture and benefit from such relationships will increasingly become a critical success factor (Moss Kanter, 1994).

Learning logs

Learning logs consist of writing up significant learning experiences from everyday incidents in a way that increases the probability of doing things better in the future. Effective learning logs should include specific statements about the learning experience and conclusions and action plans arising from them.

Honey and Mumford (1989) suggest that for learning logs to be most effective they should be integrated into an overall development of learning competencies and skills.

Benefits of using learning logs

- Learning becomes a more deliberate and conscious process.
- Learning logs facilitate the monitoring and consolidation of learning and thus enhance and maximize learning from everyday experience.
- Keeping a learning log provides the individual with unique and valuable insights into their own learning processes.
- The process of keeping a learning log ensures that learning results from successes as well as from mistakes.

Points to remember when filling in a learning log

- Learning logs may be adapted to suit individual style, but on no account should any section be omitted.
- Experiences should be written up as soon as possible after the event.
- To avoid getting overwhelmed it is advisable to select the most significant learning experience from a particular day or event.
- Entries should be quite brief as this ensures that logs are written up without delay.
- When writing your detailed account of the experience, avoid attempting to write what you have learned, but instead write exactly what happened.
- When drawing up your action plan be as realistic and as clear as possible.
- The 'when' section of the action plan is very important and does not have to refer to a date or time, but can be a situation in which the learning points could be implemented.

• Regular reviews of your learning log are vital as they highlight any weak areas that need to be overcome.

Learning accomplishment audits   A learning accomplishment audit is a tool which can be used to promote the idea that learning at work is very important for everybody. 'Learning' is often associated with school, and 'work' is what people do once they have finished school. Consequently, work and learning are often seen as very distinct activities, separated in time and space. This separation may lead some people to feel uncomfortable with learning at work; some people may feel they are not good at learning. This is the second benefit of conducting a learning accomplishment audit; it can also help to overcome a lack of confidence in learning, because the process leads to a broader understanding of learning. A learning accomplishment audit can help to break the association between learning and school.

The audit itself can take several forms; workshops or questionnaires can be equally well used. The core of the audit is a simple question: 'What skills have you learned?' The responses are then aggregated, and this represents the learning accomplishments of the individuals in the organization. One of the key outcomes of this process is the recognition that people in organizations are generally very energetic and capable learners. This leads to the question, 'Why is everyone an energetic learner outside the organization, but not inside?' The next step is to provide an environment in which this high-energy learning can be harnessed.

Learning albums   The learning album provides a method to support self-directed learning. It is a technique which has been developed in Germany, and which uses some simple pieces of equipment to provide the learner with a structure which is completely flexible, and very clearly driven by the learner. The core of the method is a photograph album: the type which has two sides of overlapping clear plastic pockets into which photographs and/or cards can be inserted. The learner is encouraged to use a Polaroid camera to take photographs of stages in the evolution of a piece of work or of flipcharts summarizing a discussion. The learner inserts a photograph, and/or writes out a card containing words that explain its most important aspects, and inserts it in the plastic wallet opposite the photograph. In addition notes can be written on cards and inserted in the album near the photographs. The bottom line of the cards is reserved for labelling or classifying the learning points summarized on the card. When inserted in the wallets, the bottom line is not covered. The cards can be rearranged and displayed according to the bottom-line summary or links between different key points. Using this method, learners can build up a compendium of knowledge which is personally relevant.

Learning albums can be used to support a learning event, making it easier for participants to capture the most personally relevant learning for themselves. Alternatively, they can be used to support on-the-job learning. Used in this way, someone learning a new aspect of a manufacturing process may take photographs of different machine states, then write in what each one represents.

By way of illustration, we developed this idea by creating a learning log, incorporating components of the photographic album and structuring it according to phases of the learning cycle. In one version, we divided the learning album into three sections: lift-off (analysis and diagnosis), orbiting (creative thinking) and re-entry (implications and planning). It consisted of review and reflection forms, and various means of recording key learning points. The album was specially created as a tool to enhance and capture both personal and shared learning over the course of the annual conference of an international company.

Upgrading the learning skills of all employees

One of the paradoxes of the learning organization is that its senior managers and professionals may find it hardest of all to learn. Human resource professionals and senior managers are often enthusiastic about continuous improvement in others, but can in fact be a serious obstacle to its achievement because they have little understanding of how it applies to themselves and of how people really learn.

Some characteristics of individuals in a learning organization are that they:

- take greater responsibility for their learning both as individuals and as group or team members, in terms of identifying learning needs, as well as discussing and identifying ways of achieving desired learning;
- are given more opportunity to solve their own problems and become involved in group processes to make decisions and resolve problems without automatic reference to supervisors or 'experts';
- develop an understanding of respective roles within a team and how to ensure maximum output of a team;
- acquire the skills and tools for monitoring, evaluating and improving their own performance;

• ask questions to challenge existing practices, experiment and find new ways of achieving desired results;
• understand how to learn and progressively become more skilled at learning.

To achieve these, people must be equipped as well as empowered to learn more effectively. The learning skills of everyone can be enhanced and developed by means of special learning-to-learn exercises designed to:

• develop in the individual an appreciation of personal and organizational learning blockages and what can be done about them;
• reveal that different kinds of learning are needed in different situations;
• show that there are many different ways of memorizing factual information;
• show that asking the right kinds of question enhances learning enormously, but that failing to ask can seriously inhibit learning;
• develop in the learner a systematic approach to understanding conceptual or theoretical material which can be used time and time again;
• develop in individuals a self-awareness about learning which gives them confidence to undertake new learning where previously they may have felt inhibited.

Some of these processes are discussed in previous chapters, but here we describe two instruments that can help learners to learn more effectively with two techniques for encouraging team or group learning.

Everyday Learning *Everyday Learning* is a practical guide, intended for supervisors and managers, which draws on the personal experience of people who have achieved significant learning without formal training. (The guide was developed by Sylvia Downs, and forms a part of the Pearn Kandola Toolkit for a Learning Organization.) Designed as a distance learning booklet, it describes in their own words the methods and techniques used by people who have successfully learned from experience. The original research was based on interviews with people who were successfully doing jobs for which there is normally no formal training, e.g. running a small business, radio broadcasting, being a self-employed artist. The guide covers:

- Knowing when to learn: how successful learners realize that they need to learn something and ask the user to link what they say to his or her own experiences.
- Knowing what to learn and getting started: how successful learners decide what they need to learn and how they set about it.
- Keeping going reviewing and checking: how successful learners keep going once they have started, and how they review and check progress.
- Deciding when you have learned: how successful learners understand that they have learned something.

Everyday Learning offers lists of ideas and practical tips used by successful learners and invites the user to compare the list with their own repertoire of techniques and methods. The guide draws heavily on actual quotes from the successful learners in the original study. It takes 2–3 hours to work through and can be used as part of a workshop to improve learning skills or on a stand-alone basis. A typical section is given below.

More ways to get started
Tick those which you have used before.
Put an asterisk (*) by those which you could use in the future.

- ☐ watch other people's style
- ☐ reflect on what you have seen or heard
- ☐ get feedback when you can use it and not too soon
- ☐ listen to people's arguments and logic
- ☐ learn from other people's mistakes
- ☐ insist on understanding the answers to questions
- ☐ go beyond the first answers to a question
- ☐ ask questions to check your understanding
- ☐ go back to basics if you do not understand
- ☐ assess what you do know and draw upon this knowledge
- ☐ find gaps in your knowledge which need to be filled
- ☐ talk to people to find out information
- ☐ talk to people to check out ideas
- ☐ read relevant materials
- ☐ listen to advice
- ☐ collect and build on other people's ideas
- ☐ tell yourself that the important thing is to get started—however you do it

---

The Learning Blockages Questionnaire   The Learning Blockages Questionnaire (LBQ) was designed to help people gain an understanding of what might be hindering their learning. (The questionnaire was developed by Newland Park Associates and is a part of the Pearn Kandola Toolkit for a Learning Organization.) It is designed primarily for use at lower levels of an organization, and can be used as part of a course on learning skills or on a stand-alone basis with the support of a supervisor or HR specialist. The LBQ takes about half an hour to complete. The original research identified over 200 ways in which people interviewed said that their learning could be blocked. Statistical analysis reduced this to 60 different blocks to learning, divided into four broad categories:

- lack of appropriate learning skills
- problems with distractions and concentration
- worries and fears about learning
- inability to learn from others.

A representative sample of items in the LBQ is given below:

☐ When I have to learn something by heart I just sit and stare at it
☐ I can't keep things in my head for long
☐ I find it difficult to follow written instructions
☐ I find it hard to know whether I have understood something
☐ Unless I can see something working I have difficulty understanding it
☐ I'm easily distracted by people around me
☐ My attention wanders after a heavy lunch
☐ I'm embarrassed when I'm asked a question in a group
☐ I can't learn anything to do with computers
☐ People get impatient with me if I don't understand
☐ I miss things when the instructor goes too fast.

The LBQ also offers advice to the user on how to deal with the four categories of blockage, but this is best done with the assistance of a supervisor or a support group.

Exercises for developing group and team learning

Below we describe two processes which are designed to encourage an understanding of team learning as distinct from individuals learning in teams.

Team learning

Much of the thrust of our work has focused on the idea that learning can and should take place anywhere. It is not something that is confined to the classroom or something to be accorded 'special event' status, but, rather, an everyday experience. Harnessing such everyday learning and putting it to conscious use at work is one of the characteristics of a learning organization.

It is self-evidently the case that since much work now takes place in teams or groups then these everyday settings should be explored and used for their learning potential. It is also clear that work-group and team settings provide a rich context for some types of learning that are overtly social, for example, learning from others, sharing experience, brainstorming, and so on. It is also the case that for some groups, social learning provides distinct benefits, and there is evidence to suggest that, for example, older people are better placed to take advantage of team-based learning activities. Once again the key to liberating the potential of such learning settings is explicit consideration of learning processes and the conscious positioning of learning as a key item on the agenda for the team or group.

Many of the facilitatory techniques that have been explored so far depend on a group context for their effectiveness. As we have seen, such techniques allow individuals to contribute in a less threatening environment, ensure that groups share their experience and allow people to build understanding by considering the viewpoints of others. In some situations, however, it is appropriate to consider the team learning process itself and to this end a number of interventions can be used to focus on how the group itself is functioning. Consideration of teamworking processes is well explored territory, with techniques from Belbin (team types) perhaps being the most commonly used. At a level above that of team structure, however, any team can usefully explore its processes and particularly its learning processes. At its most basic this could simply involve asking the question 'what have we learned?' at the end of any team activity, thus exposing team processes to scrutiny. At a more fundamental level, teams/ groups can consciously explore their learning and build processes that capture the group's potential for learning, problem-solving and continuously improving the way they work. Four interventions designed to achieve this are described below.

The knots exercise
For any group, one of the challenges of work is the development of new skills. As we have seen, however, the most

common reaction to learning something new is to focus on the content and to ignore the process until it is clear that something is going wrong. The knots exercise helps to reveal this tendency and enables a group to consider ways of countering it. At its most basic, the exercise demonstrates the worth of asking the question—'how shall we learn this?', as well as the more common—'what must we learn?'

In the exercise a group is invited to learn a new skill, namely, tying knots of varying complexity. Any number of different skills could be used; knots have the advantage of being interesting, sufficiently complex and portable. Either as a single group or as two teams (which introduces the distraction and reality of competition), people are given rope and diagrams describing how to tie a range of knots. Knots of different complexity attract different points and the idea is to get as many points as possible at the end of the exercise. However, the team only gets points for those knots that *all* the team members can tie when the time comes to demonstrate their newly acquired skill. At this stage no mention is made of learning processes and typically the teams will leap straight into the task of deciding which knots to learn. At the end of the allowed time (usually 20–30 minutes) the teams demonstrate their knot-tying ability with the facilitator as judge.

Clearly, outcomes of the exercise vary in terms of how effectively the team has learned together but the key learning points are always demonstrated. When asked to review the process by which they learned, groups consistently identify the same issues:

- We should have spent more time considering our strategy at the outset; the knots we chose to tie were too easy (not enough points)/too difficult (we couldn't tie them).
- Once we got the rope in our hands we all went straight into learning different knots; we wasted half of our time before we realized that we all had to be able to tie the same knots.
- We didn't spend enough time understanding the key elements of particular knots so we learned imperfectly.
- We assumed that learning by rote/learning by observation/learning by pictures/learning by verbal description would work for everyone; it didn't!
- We didn't build on existing experience; it turned out that Joe (or Mary or Chris) knew how to tie one of the difficult knots because they were keen sailors, but we didn't hear them or think of a way of capturing their experience.

At the end of this review process it is seldom necessary to

point out that a failure to put learning on the agenda is at the root of most of the difficulties described. There is always agreement that a few minutes spent on considering how they might learn most effectively as a team would have been well spent.

If the exercise is repeated (with a different task) it is noticeable that groups spend more time on process issues and are less seduced by the task itself. While this doesn't guarantee faster learning, it does ensure better understanding, more consistent/more enduring learning, and learning that is transferable to other tasks/situations. Once again this group process is built on the premise that learning about learning is better than being taught about learning.

Learning skills exercise
A number of the interventions used to promote organiza-tional learning are designed to help people to consider learning as a skill and to develop their abilities as learners. An important adjunct to these interventions can be explicit attention to developing learning skills in a group context. The learning skills exercise has been used as a stand-alone method of exposing some key elements of learning and as a support to exercises which consider different types of learning, for example Memorizing, Understanding and Doing. Once again the exercise is experiential, with partici-pants being asked to review processes at the end of the session. The exercise is also deliberately designed to be fun and to contain an element of 'performance' which helps to position social learning as something which is intrinsically enjoyable. As in earlier examples, the precise nature of the tasks is less important than the processes that people go through in learning them, though the ones quoted here have been tried and tested as suitable vehicles for some key messages about learning in teams.

The process involves splitting a group into three teams, each team being given the task of learning something and then reporting back to the group as a whole on their experience. As well as being asked to demonstrate their new learning they are asked to review how they learned, under headings such as:

• What helped you to learn, what hindered you?
• How did you go about learning?
• How did learning in a team influence how you learned?
• Next time, what would you do differently?

The tasks
A number of different tasks have been used, each one focusing on a different type of learning (though inevitably involving others as well).

Juggling
The team is given three balls or bean bags and asked to learn how to juggle. While this task emphasizes the physical skills involved in terms of hand-eye co-ordination, team members must first understand the principles of juggling, which balls are in the air at the same time, and so on. Other options include darts, indoor bowls, the sleight of hand needed for a magic trick. In all cases the need for practice, feedback and knowledge of results becomes apparent.

Recitation
The team is given a passage of prose or poetry (one of Hamlet's soliloquies works well) and are asked to learn it 'by heart' so that they can recite it to the group. While the task emphasizes memorizing as a key learning skill, the performance element forces consideration of how to accomplish the recitation physically as well as demanding that understanding is considered in terms of conveying the meaning of the passage.

Explaining
The team is given a problem to solve or a concept to understand which must then be conveyed to the rest of the group so that they understand it as well. Concepts used have included Einstein's theory of relativity (a short one- or two-page description being given to the group and used as a basis for finding ways of making it more understandable), and Newton's laws of motion (acceleration being explored from first principles using a stop-watch to time balls being rolled down a sloping table). While the task emphasizes understanding of principles, the need to share understanding with the rest of the group forces attention on how key points can be remembered and sometimes on the physical skills of organizing a demonstration of the principles.

After the fun of demonstrating these tasks the teams share their experience of learning and, with the help of the facilitator, list key learning points to emerge. With groups at all levels it is common for this output to encapsulate most of what is known about the basics of learning without the need for the facilitator to provide a 'lecture' on memory, experimentation, hypothesis testing or physical skill acquisition. It is also common for the group to recognize the benefits that came from learning in teams in terms of shared experience, willingness to make mistakes, synergy and enjoyment.

Group problem-solving

There are a number of group problem-solving tasks which can be used to elicit key points about learning in teams, the facilitatory processes being the same as those described above. Many of these are billed as team-building exercises, for example, the well-known Desert Survival task, and are in the public domain. These are all usable for the purpose of exploring how the group learns while solving a problem by including a suitable review at the end of the exercise. The example given here is a modification of one such exercise and has proved effective in making key points such as:

- the value of considering learning processes at the outset of the task;
- the importance of regularly reviewing the process to realize the benefits of continuous learning;
- the benefit of ensuring that everyone contributes, with no 'isolates';
- the transferability of such learning to other group tasks.

In using such group problem-solving tasks it is often helpful to co-opt group members as process observers to monitor and record the group's activity rather than this task being accomplished by a facilitator. Again this serves to ensure ownership of learning by the whole group, and fosters learning as something that 'we do together and for ourselves' rather than as something that is done to the group by an outsider.

The companies problem

There are five companies with offices along a street. You must locate each company together with its 'characteristics'. You have all the information needed to do this.

1. There are five offices.
2. The British company is in the red office.
3. The Spanish company makes toys.

4. Coffee is the preferred drink in the green office.
5. In the Russian company they drink tea.
6. The green office is immediately to the right of the ivory office.
7. The company where they drive BMWs makes chairs.
8. Rovers are driven by employees in the yellow office.
9. Milk is the preferred drink in the middle office.
10. The American company is in the first office.
11. The company where they drive Fords is next to the company that makes soap.
12. Rovers are driven by employees in the office next to the office of the company that makes china.
13. The company where the employees drive Saabs has orange juice as a preferred drink.
14. Employees in the Japanese company drive Fiats.
15. The American company is in the office next door to the blue office.

For those without the patience to solve the problem for themselves, or who cannot find a convenient team to help them, the solution is given at the end of the chapter.

We now look at four tools for enhancing learning, three are related to the selection and use of open learning, the fourth is a technique to consider the learning demands as part of job analysis.

Four instruments for enhancing learning

Helping employees to get the most out of open learning material and distance learning resources is critical to the success of open learning strategies. Too many open learning materials are not used, or not used properly, and it is difficult to assess the quality of distance learning materials.

For open learners the most valuable development exercises in the workplace will be those which:

- facilitate the exchange of theory and practice;
- strengthen the transferability of learning;
- enable the practising of the skills that need contact (inter-personal, communication, negotiating skills);
- stimulate discovery, experimental and problem-solving approaches;
- permit the execution of work-based projects at a practical level.

We describe below four practical instruments designed to improve the effectiveness and impact of open learning in organizations already committed to open learning. (These instruments form a part of Tools for a Learning Organization, Pearn and Mulrooney, 1995.)

Instrument 1:
Guidelines on selecting
good open learning
material

The guidelines evaluate the effectiveness of open learning materials from the viewpoint of learning design. The main aim is to identify the usefulness of specific open learning products for the learner and to assess the degree to which the material actually aids the learning process. The guidelines are intended for anyone who is going to buy or use open learning materials, both individuals choosing between packages and companies purchasing for their employees.

The guidelines present an evaluation process and a pro forma for recording conclusions which can be filed for reference or attached to the open learning products to guide the choice of potential users.

The guidelines pose 24 questions in relation to the effectiveness of the open learning material which are divided into seven sections. The first section assesses the purpose and the limitations of the material. The remaining sections cover:

- Content and presentation.
- Does it keep learners mentally active?
- Does it allow for individual differences?
- Does it use the learners' experience?
- Does it provide a measure of learning?
- Does it suggest support?

There is a final summary section to record strengths and weaknesses of the material from a learner's point of view.

The following is an excerpt from guidelines for selecting good open learning material:

Does it keep learners mentally active?

- Are learners asked (not necessarily in the form of tests) to examine or solve problems in order to gain a better understanding of subject areas within the package?
- Are learners asked to compare and contrast the ideas presented in the package with other situations and see where else the ideas could apply?
- Are learners asked to seek information outside the open learning material? (This could be in the form of extensions, using other people or other sources to gain information.)
- Are there periods for reflection, review and consolidation?

Does it allow for individual differences?

- Are difficult areas revised using other approaches or other training media?
- Can learners obtain help on individual queries from their support tutor?
- Do sections contain pre-tests, enabling high scorers to take a fast lane through the material?

Does it use the learners' experience?

- Does it help learners to relate the contents to their past and present experiences?
- Does it help learners to relate the contents to anticipated future needs?

Instrument 2: Guidelines for designing open learning material which helps learners to learn

The guidelines cover six aspects of designing open learning material to help learners to learn, together with ways each of the aspects can be put into effect. The six aspects, together with illustrative items, are shown below:

- Providing a format which is easily understood by:
  - including a course map at the beginning indicating contents, approximate durations, and the media involved;
  - giving objectives for each section;
  - including cross-references to other parts of the material.
- Keeping learners mentally active by:
  - allowing learners to generate their own ideas before comparing them with suggested answers;
  - setting time aside for learners to reflect on and review their learning;
  - providing quizzes and learning checklists to enable learners to assess their own progress.
- Allowing for individual differences by:
  - where applicable, providing slow and fast routes through the material;
  - providing pre-tests to enable learners to assess where they should start;
  - when suggesting possible learning aids (such as memorizing strategies) providing a selection so that learners can choose those that best suit them.
- Using learners' experience by:
  - asking learners to think about how they might use the learning in the future;

    – requiring learners to find examples in their own lives that relate to what they are learning.
- Providing a measure for progress in learning by:
  - including a variety of tests and measures throughout the material;
  - providing feedback on the sorts of answers that other learners have given so that individuals can compare them with their own responses.
- Providing support for the learner by:
  - providing information on how to learn from others, including who might be of help and in what ways;
  - providing information on how to learn.

Instrument 3: 'Learning through open learning': a guide for open learners on how to get the most out of open learning materials

Learning Through Open Learning is designed to prepare an individual who needs to build confidence and improve learning skills before embarking on a significant open learning project. The pack can take three or more hours to work through, or significantly longer if done in a group. It is divided into five key sections:

1. What is open learning?
2. Problems in open learning and overcoming them.
3. Being organized.
4. Using resources.
5. Improving learning skills.

The pack is very practical, combining self-evaluation, checklists, and practical tips. It includes exercises which enable the user to identify different types of learning and the approaches that are effective and less effective from the point of view of the learner.

    An excerpt is given below.

Things a tutor could do to help you to learn

- Provide feedback to tell you how well you are doing.
- Help you work out why your score or grades were good or bad.
- Listen to your ideas.
- Answer your questions.
- Provide some information which enables you to work towards a solution.
- Give you encouragement.

- Suggest different ways of tackling a problem.
- Give you feedback on how you are doing compared with others.
- Introduce you to other learners.

Things you could do to get the most out of your tutor

- Ask your tutor to put you in touch with other learners.
- Get to know your tutor personally.
- Where possible check when it is convenient for your tutor to listen to your queries.
- Do some background work: this can put you in a better position to ask questions and may reduce the number of small queries you need to make.
- Be prepared to ask any question, no matter how small.
- Ask your tutor what he or she means by good work.
- Ask your tutor if you can give your own assessment of your performance first.

Instrument 4: Analyse jobs in terms of learning needs

The *Job-Learning Analysis* (JLA) is a specially devised job analysis method which has been designed to identify the different types of learning which are required in order to learn how to carry out a task or role (Pearn and Kandola, 1988). The results can be used to design learner-orientated training and/or development programmes specifically geared to produce the required forms of learning.

Although aimed primarily at operator, technician and supervisory roles, the JLA can be used successfully to analyse other jobs. Instead of focusing on analysing what has to be achieved in the job or role, the JLA differs from other analytical methods by concentrating on the forms of learning involved.

Most job analysis or training needs analysis methods focus either on the content of jobs (i.e., tasks that needed to be performed), or the skills, knowledge and other attributes that are needed to perform those tasks. This tends to result in learning designs and training that focus on the development of the skills, etc., needed to carry out a particular job, but which neglect the learning processes that are needed to acquire and develop those skills. The JLA is specifically designed to analyse jobs in terms of nine different kinds of learning that might be required in order to learn to perform specific jobs:

- physical or manual skills
- complex procedures or sequences
- checking, assessing or discriminating
- memorizing facts or information
- ordering, prioritizing, or planning
- looking ahead or anticipating
- diagnosing, analysing or solving
- interpreting written, pictorial or diagrammatic material
- adapting to new ideas or systems.

The nine categories of learning are:

Physical or manual skills
The activities which require practice and repetition in order to acquire competence (e.g. to become fast enough, to minimize errors). The category does not include activities which are really simple procedures that can easily be performed without practice.

Complex procedures or sequences
Procedures or sequences of actions which either need to be memorized or which can be performed by reference to check-lists and other aids to memory.

Checking, assessing or discriminating
This relates to non-verbal information which is received through the senses (sight, sound, etc.) and which is used to make judgements, or as a basis for action. It usually requires practice to achieve levels of competence in this area.

Memorizing facts or information
This relates to information that needs to be retained in the memory for short periods (usually minutes, occasionally hours) as well as information that needs to be committed to memory indefinitely.

Ordering, prioritizing or planning
The kind of learning necessary in order to devise plans or to make discretionary decisions about the order in which things are done.

Looking ahead or anticipating
The extent to which job holders need to think ahead and anticipate conditions and/or problems and take action accordingly.

Diagnosing, analysing or solving
The extent to which the job holders need to learn to interpret and solve problems either unaided or with the support of manuals, diagnostic devices, etc.

Interpreting written, pictorial or diagrammatic material
The extent to which written materials, manuals and other sources of information such as diagrams or charts need to be used or consulted in order to learn to perform the job.

Adapting to new ideas or systems
The extent to which the job holder is required to adapt to or learn new ideas, equipment, methods .

The advantage of the JLA is that it places primary focus on the learning needs associated with a particular job rather than on merely describing the tasks that are carried out. It also has other uses, for instance an NHS trust used the JLA to achieve two outcomes: first to increase understanding of the real learning involved in a particular support role, and second to develop a competency-based approach to delivering the role.

In this chapter we have described a wide range of tools for enhancing learning, some of them diagnostic, some of them aimed at increasing individual or team learning skills.

In the next chapter we

• consider the implications of these approaches for the training function.

Solution to the companies problem

Yellow	Blue	Red	Ivory	Green
American	Russian	British	Spanish	Japanese
Soap	China	Chairs	Toys	
Rover	Ford	BMW	Saab	Fiat
	Tea	Milk	Orange Juice	Coffee

References

ARGYRIS, C. (1991) 'Teaching smart people how to learn', *Harvard Business Review*, May–June, 99–109.

BOAK, G. and JOY, P. (1990) Management Learning Contracts: The training triangle, in Pedler, M., Burgoyne, J., Boydell, T. and Welshman, G. (eds), *Self-Development in Organizations*, Maidenhead: McGraw-Hill.

BUCHANAN, D. and McCALMAN, J. (1989) *High Performance Work Systems: The Digital Experience*, London: Routledge.

CANNING, R. and MARTIN, J. (1990) 'The learning community', in Pedler, M. *et al.* (eds), *Self-Development in Organizations*, Maidenhead: McGraw-Hill.

CLUTTERBUCK, D. (1985) *Everyone Needs a Mentor: How to Foster Talent Within the Organization*, London: Institute of Personnel Management.

CUNNINGHAM, I. (1994) *The Wisdom of Strategic Learning: The Self-Managed Learning Solution*, Maidenhead: McGraw-Hill.

HASTINGS, C. (1993) *The New Organization: Growing the Culture of Organizational Networking*, Maidenhead: McGraw-Hill.

HONEY, P. and MUMFORD, A. (1986) *The Manual of Learning Styles*, Maidenhead: Honey.

HONEY, P. and MUMFORD, A. (1989) *The Manual of Learning Opportunities*, Maidenhead: Honey.

KATZENBACH, J. R. and SMITH, J. R. (1993) *The Wisdom of Teams: Creating the High Performing Organization*, Boston: Harvard Business School Press.

KOLB, D. (1984) *Essential Learning*, New York: Prentice Hall.

MOSS KANTER, R. (1994) 'Collaborative advantage—the art of alliances', *Harvard Business Review*, July–August, 96–108.

PEARN, M. A. and KANDOLA, R. S. (1988) *Job Analysis: A Practical Guide for Managers*, London: Institute of Personnel Management.

PEARN, M. and MULROONEY, C. (1995) *Tools for a Learning Organization*, London: Institute for Personnel and Development.

PEDLER, M., BURGOYNE, J. and BOYDELL, T. (1986) *A Manager's Guide to Self-development*, Maidenhead: McGraw-Hill.

PEDLER, M. (1988) 'Applying self-development in organizations', *Industrial and Commercial Training*, March–April, 19–22.

RAVID, G. (1987) 'Self directed learning in industry', in Marsick V. J. (ed.), *Learning in the Workplace*, London: Croom Helm.

SHIPPER, F. and MANZ, C. C. (1992) 'Employee self-management without formally designated teams: An alternative road to empowerment', *Organizational Dynamics*, Winter, 48–61.

SMITH, B. (1990) 'Mutual mentoring on projects: A proposal to combine the advantages of several established management development methods', *Journal of Management Development*, 9, 1.

TOBIN, D. R. (1993) *Re-educating the Corporation: Foundations for the Learning Organization*, Vermont: Oliver Wight Publications.

9   From training to learning

In this chapter we

- examine the differences between a learning-orientated as opposed to a training-orientated approach to the development of people
- outline a process used to review the role of the training function in a major bank
- describe one company which is seeking to be a trainerless organization
- consider the shifting balance of power between trainees and learners.

In our view a learning organization is likely to move away from heavy reliance on formal training. There will be less dependence on a centralized training function which supports, facilitates and sustains learning, autonomy and self-development at all levels in the organization. It follows that the role of training and trainers, and the boundaries between work, learning and training will need to be examined.

The role of the training function

The very existence of a developed training function necessitates the establishment of professional staff and a long-term commitment to careers in training and supporting infrastructures. There is a risk that the trainers of the organization become separated and detached from the core business of the organization. As a result, training provision often meets the trainers' perception of needs rather than fundamental business needs. In addition, people see learning and development primarily in terms of what the training function has to offer, and achievement of learning and development in terms of attendance at courses and programmes.

In reality, only a tiny part of the true learning needs of an organization can be satisfied by means of formal training provision. In some organizations with which we have worked there has been minimal provision for formal training. Attending a training programme was seen as a luxury for the chosen few. Even then the courses tended to be chosen from a menu that sometimes had only marginal relevance to the individual's learning needs. In other organizations there has been extensive training provision, with all employees having an entitlement to a specified number of off-the-job training days each year. There is a closer match to the individual's needs but only in so far as they can be met through training provision. Most people would say that the most valuable things they have learned in their careers have come from experiences of one kind or another. These include the big mistake which made them rethink or radically change their approach, or a new experience which opened them up to new ways of thinking and doing. Sometimes training can have this effect, but in our view people learn most of what is important to them in spite of the training they receive rather than because of it.

This is not an argument against training as an activity of organizations, and there is a risk that we only caricature forms of training. The real point is that training is one way to achieve intended learning in an organization which tends to focus on the supply side of the equation, i.e. what is done to the learner. Meeting learning needs is the real objective and training is one among many means of achieving this goal. Training can only meet a small part of the total learning needs of the organization. Organizations with too little formal training and those which rely too heavily on training may both fail to achieve desired levels and types of learning.

The role of trainers and the training function within a learning organization needs to be reviewed. Based on a newly developed understanding of what a learning organization is, or can be, and using some of the exercises described earlier in this book, a deeper understanding of the difference between training and learning can be developed. Based on discussions with hundreds of people at all levels and functions in organizations, in dozens of workshops to examine the role of trainers in a learning organization, 10 key differences between learning and training emerge. They are summarized in Table 9.1.

Origins   It is evident that formal training by its very nature must be a planned and organized activity usually requiring substantial preparatory effort. Often an organization will take pride in

Table 9.1   Key differences between learning and training

	Characteristic of training	Characteristic of learning
Origins	planned, organized, programmed	organic, unfolding
Timeframe	sporadic	continuous, ongoing
Control	trainer	learner
Choice	predetermined	flexible, self-determined
Energy flow	trainer to trainee	from learner
Motivation	not always clear to learner	usually clear
Roles	learner often passive	learner active
Costs	add-on cost	integral to work
Impact	variable	often high, sometimes low
Focus	activities and delivery mechanisms	processes inside the person

the number and variety of training courses on offer. By contrast with training, learning can occur spontaneously and on an ongoing basis regardless of whether or not the individual believes he or she is learning. A learning culture will see continuous learning and development as a permanent priority. The training function as a separate activity within the organization could actually inhibit the evolution of a natural learning culture. On the other hand it could play a vital role in stimulating and supporting it. In a learning organization all employees have the confidence and skill to identify their learning needs, either as individuals or as teams, and as a result manage the satisfaction of those needs without necessarily relying on available training programmes. Clearly an effective human resource function would play an important role in supporting the identification and achievement of learning needs.

Time-frame

Just as most training programmes and courses have to be originated as a specific activity or series of events, the delivery of training also tends to be sporadic rather than continuous and ongoing; though multi-media and computer-assisted training, and open learning provision, make on-demand access to learning feasible. Frequently, specified amounts of time are allocated to training, usually away from an individual's normal workplace. Training events are usually one-offs and frequently relatively isolated from the everyday work of the learners. By contrast, learning is integral to the individual and happens continuously, regardless of the nature and relevance of the learning. A carefully nurtured learning culture would draw on the resources and inspiration available within a learning-orientated training and development function to ensure that learning occurred continuously, even though the rate and type of learning varied according to need.

Control

Because of the planning and organization involved in setting up training provision and the nature of delivery mechanisms there is a tendency for much of the control to lie with the trainer and not with the learner. This is not always undesirable, but a preoccupation with training delivery to justify the existence of a training function can lead to too much control staying with the provider and not with the customer. Even when careful training needs analyses are carried out, the effort involved in creating a response to the identified development needs, and the specialized knowledge and expertise needed in designing training provision, can gradually take control away from the learners, so that they feel they have less control or influence over how their needs are being met. Consequently, most formal training events, as distinct, for example, from open or distance learning, will be delivered at a time, in a place, at a pace, and in a manner that may not suit or meet the real needs of the individual. This is not to say that no learning would result from such training, but that it may not be optimally efficient or effective.

Choice

Because of the complex activity involved in setting up training the learner tends to be offered only what the training function puts on offer. In many organizations with low budgets this can be very little indeed. Even what is on offer may be far short of what is actually needed. In a training culture it will be assumed that if there is no training there is little formal learning. In a learning culture the choice of formal training on offer, even if extensive and varied, will be seen as only one source of learning opportunity. The relative lack of formal training provision is not a problem in an organization with a learning culture, but it is a serious handicap where only a weak training culture exists.

Energy flow

In a training-orientated culture most of the initiative lies with trainers, who try to identify, often by rigorous analytical methods, what the training and development needs of the organization are. They then decide the best means for delivering training to meet the identified needs. Learners play little part in the setting up of training provision or indeed the content of the training. As a result the learners tend to become passive, entering into a system designed for them by specialists. A 'learned helplessness' can develop, which accepts what is on offer, realizes that it is of only limited value, and becomes accustomed to this state of affairs. Busy line managers can end up seeing training as an inconvenience rather than as an aid. In a learning culture individuals not only demand training, they also are highly critical if it does not meet their needs, and become very proactive in shaping both content and delivery, as one mechanism for meeting learning needs.

Motivation

It is not an uncommon experience for people to attend a course and introduce themselves by saying: 'I don't know why I am here; I was told to come' or 'I know what this course is about but I'd much rather be dealing with my in-tray'. This is often the case when attendance at a course or programme is compulsory, though the cynics will often change their minds before the end of the course. Frequently, however, people will return from a course saying it was interesting but they cannot see how they can make use of what they have learned. Alternatively, they return from the course full of good intentions but within 24 hours have succumbed to the pressures of the job and their resolve to do things differently dissipates. A training culture does not worry too much about this, because it measures performance in terms of the number of courses provided, and establishes good value for money by calculating the number of people trained divided by the costs. A learning culture would be concerned that the learning and development needs of the individual are being met through a wide range of learning processes and that as far as possible these coincide with organizational needs. Motivation to learn is of prime importance in a learning culture.

Roles

It should be evident that the individual plays an important and proactive role in a learning culture, pursuing many learning goals through self-development, action learning and open learning where their role is active, and not that of the relatively passive recipient of organized training.

Costs

In many organizations training is seen as a cost to the organization. Training budgets are often cut during difficult times, communicating to all employees that it is a relatively low-status activity, only indulged in when it can be afforded. A learning culture sees formal budgeted training as crucial to overall success, but only as part of an overall strategy to ensure that learning of the right types and at the right levels is taking place and contributing to the organization's overall goals. In this sense the commitment to learning and development is integral to organizational success and not an optional cost. In addition, learning on a continuous basis is seen as integral to the work of the organization on a day-by-day basis, just as quality is. Just as quality must be built into the organization's processes rather than being assumed, or in extreme cases hoped for, the achievement of desired learning must also be assured. Commitment to extensive training programmes may or may not be an option for an organization, but sustained learning is indispensable.

Impact

Some training programmes, especially those geared towards achieving culture change or attitude change across an organization, such as 'Customer First' programmes or quality programmes, can have a high impact because of their intensity and because they form part of an integrated organization change programme. However, as noted above, many training programmes have little impact because they are not in a form that is flexible and relevant to individual needs. In a learning culture formal training is seen as one among many ways of achieving the learning required. There are many high-impact processes for enhancing learning which can be harnessed to ensure that individual needs are being met in the most effective way. Many of these techniques for enhancing learning are described in Chapter 8. Because the techniques and processes for enhancing learning are flexibly geared to individual learning needs in ways that can be directly related to performance, they are likely to have higher impact than isolated, sporadic training provision.

Focus

Finally training is an activity external to the individual. Trainers in many organizations provide training or information about available training. In a learning culture there is a recognition that learning essentially goes on inside the individual. The objective is to provide support, guidance and opportunities for the learning to occur in ways that meet the needs of the individual as identified by the individual, or as a member of a team, or in conjunction with a line manager, supported by processes such as development centres. Although the focus is learning that takes place within the individual rather than activities that are engaged in, the ultimate test is improved performance. This can be measured by appropriate indicators that apply to the individual, the team, the function, or the organization as a whole.

Much of the comparison made above between a learning culture and a training culture has caricatured the training function as a mere provider of courses, some compulsory, some company-wide, and some optional; some highly specific, some arbitrary and some as part of an organizational change strategy. While it is true that some organizations see training in this way, many are also committed to development activities. However, there is still a danger that development is seen as something that is done to others. In other words, 'development' is offered to people rather than being built into the day-to-day activities and culture of the organization. In a learning culture the objective is to integrate continuous learning into all activities of the organization on an ongoing basis, so that training and specific development activities are seen as supporting that end rather than being ends in themselves.

Practical applications

Examining the role of training in a major bank

Forty-five training managers and training advisers from the National Westminster Bank attended a workshop to examine their role in a learning-orientated organization. At that point the bank had not decided formally to become a learning organization, by any definition, but it had already recognized the need to achieve more with its 40 000 employees and had initiated a major culture change strategy.

The training managers had no difficulty in identifying the benefits to the bank of encouraging and sustaining learning in all employees. Using the Understanding Organizational Learning exercise, described in Chapter 3, the managers identified eight main potential benefits:

- increased competitiveness, greater output and profitability through increased motivation, self-esteem of all our employees;
- unlocking potential, greater skills, more flexibility;
- increased innovation, creativity, and willingness to experiment and challenge;
- greater responsiveness to change;
- lower staff turnover, better people attracted;
- ability to manage diverse objectives, learning in different ways;
- synergy from teamwork, and empowerment;
- better planning.

They were equally quick to identify the consequences of not succeeding in sustaining the learning of all employees. The main groupings were:

- stagnation, inefficiency, playing safe, short-termism, reluctance to change;
- loss of competitive edge, risk of takeover, low organizational credibility;
- failure to recognize potential in staff, low morale and commitment, loss of good people;

- high staff turnover, high training costs, poor output;
- errors, failure to improve.

In an exercise to identify how learning can be blocked, the training managers listed over 50 organizational and individual blockages. They then carried out an exercise to compare and contrast a learning culture and a training culture. Having participated in some exercises to make the processes of learning more transparent to the individual, they were asked to identify the appropriate role of trainers in a learning organization. They concluded that their main role was to act as facilitator, coach, counsellor, consultant and option-giver. It was felt that this would help them to enter into partnerships with business units so that HR strategy could be integrated as part of business strategy. The prime objective was seen as working closely with business units to help identify company and individual development needs, and also to develop specialist expertise as facilitators of learning. In addition they saw their role as marketing learning and development opportunities, providing support to help meet individual needs, and guiding individuals and teams through their learning cycles.

For the population of training managers and specialists in the bank this represented a change of focus. In particular, there was increased awareness of the nature of learning organizations; an understanding of the implementation and practicalities involved in becoming a learning organization, and their role in helping bring it about; a new clarity in appreciating the difference between training and learning; and, finally, a commitment to change from being primarily trainers to becoming facilitators of learning within the framework of the company's culture change programme.

As with other organizations it was felt that the learning organization concept would function as an umbrella concept for other initiatives for change, such as increased autonomy, devolution and empowerment.

Seeking to be a trainerless organization: Courage Brewery

The company was facing a very difficult business environment. The national economy was in recession and with a sharp reduction in beer consumption, together with over-supply in the market, was creating a difficult trading environment. Government pressure to prevent monopolies in the brewing industry had created a general shake-up and a strong feeling of uncertainty. The company had recently undergone a merger with another brewery company as part of the restructuring of the industry. As a result, the company had become a specialist in beer production with no retail outlets. Other companies had gone in the opposite direction, specializing in retail outlets with little or no production capacity.

Two other factors contributed to the difficult environment in which the company found itself. Independently of the effects of the recession in the UK economy, there had been a steady decline over many years in the consumption of beer in the domestic market in favour of other kinds of adult beverages. The company was therefore determined to maintain a profitable share of a declining market. The company was subject to the same pressures from developments in information and manufacturing technology that were affecting everyone else in the industry, resulting in major restructuring and head-count deductions. Finally, the company was facing increased competition from large brewery companies in Europe. The company's strategy for change was focused on four key areas:

- improving customer service
- improving quality
- reducing its cost-base
- achieving more through its people.

The last point was particularly significant because the company was seeking higher quality output and improved service to customers from a workforce which had shrunk from 8000 in 1991 to 4900 in 1994. This shrinkage was associated with significant delayering of management and the introduction of new ways of working. It was in pursuit of its business strategy that the company became interested in the concept of learning organizations.

The company believed that achieving more learning on a continuous basis would help facilitate the culture change programme. Secondly, it was felt it would help the company move away from its reliance on a traditional training approach as the basis for achieving significant gains in (specified) learning for specific groups. Thirdly, the company believed that the learning organization concept would help line managers, HR specialists and all employees change their roles.

As part of a wider programme of initiatives, the company had introduced a branded employee development programme entitled 'Encouragement' which brought together within a coherent framework employee benefits, employee development processes and opportunities, and processes for improving the performance of managers.

The development programme included 'Start Your Management Career', a development process open to employees in non-managerial grades who felt they might be interested in progressing into management, and 'Start Your Sales Career', a similar programme for people with no prior sales experience.

The idea behind these two initiatives was to attract and develop the potential of employees who would previously have had no access to sales and managerial jobs. Other initiatives included Learning Centres which provided increased access to open and distance learning materials, foreign language training available to anyone who was interested, a programme of IT training, and personal development for all employees. The processes for improving managerial performance included a new programme of general management development, the introduction of performance management, the development of leadership and people skills and a programme to develop coaching skills in managers and team leaders.

A key objective was to change the role of HR from a potential 'blocker', as seen through the eyes of line managers, to that of facilitator and supporter. But how did the concept of becoming a learning organization relate to the changes that were already under way?

Part of a 10-day management development programme on leading and managing continuous change was devoted to an examination of the significance of learning for the company. The objective was to help managers understand the nature of learning, that is, how easily it is blocked, how it reaches into all aspects of the organization, and the critical role it plays in contributing to the achievement of current goals, and how it can be used to review, and refine, or indeed change, the goals of an organization.

A group of line managers became very excited and decided to focus on the learning organization concept for their presentation to a group of executive directors at the end of the programme. A very powerful and persuasive presentation was made, indicating to the executive directors that the group of managers felt they had developed insights and a new understanding which excited them and made them feel they could really make a difference to the culture change needed and that they could see that a prime role for them as managers was to unleash the talent in the people who worked for them. The four directors listened quietly and did not interrupt the presentation. When the presentation was finished, instead of building on and supporting the new-found energy in the group of highly motivated managers, they replied along the lines: 'That's all very well but what you have got to understand is . . .'. They then went on to tell the group of managers how it really was, and what they needed to do. There was no doubt that some of what the directors had to say widened or at least partially extended the understanding of the group to a bigger picture, but the mistake the directors made was in not seeing how committed and motivated to change the way they worked the group of managers had become. The directors preached to them about empowerment and becoming a learning organization but failed to recognize the energy and drive for change that was in front of them. The effect of their well-intentioned but insensitive response was to dampen the group's enthusiasm.

Notwithstanding this setback, the company continued to progress at a rapid pace. The company was reshaped into local business units across the country, in order to achieve the benefits of, on the one hand, being part of a large multi-national corporation with global and national brands and significant spending and purchasing power and, on the other hand, maintaining a local community and customer focus to the sale and delivery of beers.

The HR function recognized the need to support this new business strategy, and saw in it the further opportunity to move away from the old personnel department approaches of 'doing things' to people—recruiting them, disciplining them, training them, firing them. In its place was a move toward an HR internal consultancy role, which involved sitting down with Business Unit directors in diagnosing and planning an HR strategy that was an integral part of the overall Business Unit Plan.

The number of HR staff was reduced from 200 to 55, and, with the exception of a small core of specialist managers responsible for strategy, the HR managers who were formerly specialists in HR, training, recruitment, etc. were given the opportunity to become 'generalist' HR consultants. This in itself was, of course, the start of a learning process. Consultants were armed with a basic toolkit for survival, including an 'HR Business Workbook' and 'Consultancy Presenter', and spent a number of days together devising and understanding the new vision and ways of working.

Several months into the new roles, the HR consultants were brought together to share their experiences, achievements and disasters, and to work co-operatively in improving their consultancy skills, especially in contracting, facilitating and influencing.

The primary objective in this redefinition of the HR role was to return the responsibility for the company's people back to where it rightly belonged—to individual employees and their line managers. In this respect, the move away from 'doing training' to 'encouraging learning' was implicit rather than explicit, but was underpinned by the new HR role. Large numbers of trainers were no longer available in the company to do training. Instead, the small training resource left at the head office level focused on producing high quality, easy-to-use core skills packages. These were designed for ease of understanding, and to be capable of delivery in flexible ways, and above all to be used by line managers with their teams. Priority was given to those skill areas which supported the move from training to learning, such as coaching skills, or which enabled line managers to take successfully full responsibility for people issues, such as recruitment interviewing, employment law, and performance management.

With hindsight the company realized that the formal presentation on 'the learning organization' to the executive directors was conceptually a bridge too far. The key to progress lay rather in making a start, or perhaps a number of starts, reducing the numbers of trainers and other HR specialists who can usurp the power of individuals and line managers, providing the tools, techniques and materials to enable the line to reclaim their people and their development.

In these ways, and with the continuation of the 'Encouragement' initiatives to foster all employee development, Courage began to establish the psychological infrastructure that would have to be in place to allow a journey toward a learning organization to begin.

Shifting the balance of power

From our own experience, it is a paradox that in relation to the need to change orientation to organizational learning, some of the hardest arguments to win are with traditional trainers. This is understandable given that without careful positioning and a commitment to developing understanding of the concept among trainers, these concepts can appear to be both an erosion of the status of trainers and a negation of the techniques that have been their stock-in-trade. At the same time, the training function is often the key-holder in terms of access to an organization's developmental capabilities, and their commitment to the concept of a learning organization and their reorientation as facilitators of learning can be a key step in achieving change.

Perhaps the power of the control issue is best illustrated by the continuing use on trainer training courses of the Pose, Pause, Pounce technique. Here, trainers are encouraged to maintain audience attention by Posing a question, Pausing for a moment, and then Pouncing on an individual for an answer. In this way trainees will be frightened into paying attention because they do not know when the bolt of lightening will fall on them. This is not a technique which suggests respect for the participant or their autonomy as part of a learning process. It is rooted firmly in an orientation to training as being something that is done to you and not necessarily something that will be particularly enjoyable.

A learning-orientated approach does not demand that trainers' tricks of the trade be abandoned or that classroom techniques have no value. What it does demand is the use of techniques that promote the individual's capacity to learn and contribute to the learning of others and an avoidance of 'dark sarcasm in the classroom' as a means of maintaining control and power.

In practical terms, a key difference implied by a change from training to learning is the increased demands it makes on the trainers', developers', teachers', facilitators' tolerance of ambiguity. While development activity is still planned and while training sessions still have structure, the move from 'chalk and talk' to more facilitatory methods of encouraging learning does imply less certainty as to the minute by minute control of a course or training session.

That these ideas are not just pious hopes but are rooted in the desire to help people learn better is illustrated by recent experience within ICL, the major information technology company which specializes in systems integration. Here, a large scale technical updating programme had been initiated for design and development staff, the courses being run by university specialists and lasting for up to 5 days. The lecturers quickly found that traditional lecture methods—1- to 2-hour lectures—were not working and that their audience were being brought to the point of rebellion by the lack of interaction or active involvement in their own learning. The courses had to be rapidly adapted and some of the lecturing personnel who were uncomfortable with the needs of the participants exchanged.

These changes came about because in this case the learners had the confidence to say that this 'learning' method was not working for them. In training contexts more generally, it is unusual for learners to spontaneously display this level of confidence and as a result time is not effectively used in learning. In our view inspired learners have the confidence to influence others to ensure that they are really learning and in a way that is meaningful to them. (One is forced to ask the question that if long lectures have been shown time and time again not to bring about effective learning, why does anyone still think that they are a good idea for university students?) As we have noted, there is a danger that training can become a matter of the convenience and 'comfort' of the trainer. We would argue that effective learning has the goal of creating inspired learners.

None of this should be taken to imply that there is not a role for high quality didactic approaches to training in the appropriate circumstances, for example, the training of complex procedures. However, as more and more of work involves understanding of issues and solving of problems rather than rote learning of facts or techniques, the role of the trainer must itself develop to encompass individual and organizational learning in its broadest sense.

In the next chapter we

• describe the experiences of two UK organizations attempting to learn from successes, mistakes and failures.

10   Interventions

In this chapter we

- describe in more detail the experience of two organizations in order to learn not only from the successes but also from the mistakes and failures.

Learning organizations strive to make the maximum use of human talent. Liberating this talent and providing an organizational culture or context in which it can thrive offers the benefit of developing and empowering people so that they are better able to respond appropriately and flexibly to changes in the commercial and work environment. At the same time, a learning organization, through the processes of continuous improvement and self-renewal, is better able to anticipate and cope with change.

Empowering people to contribute to organizational effectiveness is not, however, enough in itself. As well as being empowered, people need to be equipped if their abilities are to show through in organizational performance. They also need an operating environment in which that equipment can function. It is little use for managers to tell a group of machine operators to communicate with each other to solve problems if, for example:

- the machine operators have not had the chance to consider the options open to them;
- their supervisors do not allow them time for increased communication and/or are not able to support it;
- the managers have not thought through how to elicit, recognize, reward or react to the problem-solving ideas which emerge.

Paying lip-service to the concept of empowerment is all too

easy. Unless people are equipped to behave in new ways, and an operating environment is created to support and encourage the new forms of behaviour, there is little chance they will take root and flourish.

With this in mind, it is appropriate to look at two organizations which share the aim of bringing about increased organizational effectiveness by equipping as well as empowering people to learn.

In neither example has the organization consciously made a decision to become a learning organization. The underlying reasons for change vary, but the examples have in common a recognition that people were not realizing their full potential (for whatever reason) and that this was limiting organizational effectiveness. As we will see, each case has its own unique life history and its own unique outcomes.

Empowering learners in the nuclear power industry: British Nuclear Fuels

The nuclear power industry in the UK has undergone radical change over the last 10 years. It has moved from being a state-owned, centrally funded organization to being a private sector company competing in a fierce world market. In common with other formerly state-owned industries, a new operating climate brought about the need to review and revise processes at all levels.

At one particular site of British Nuclear Fuels plc, one consequence of these changes was the recognition that improved working practices among skilled craft and trade employees would be vital to success. Structural change in the market for nuclear fuel rods also created pressure for greater efficiency with the run-down of old products and the introduction of new ones. The history of industrial relations at the site, in common with much of British industry in the 1970s, had been of fiercely defended trade and craft demarcations and an inevitable loss of flexibility and efficiency. Thus, the person who was to repair an electric motor (electrician) was not allowed to unbolt it from its current location (normally done by a fitter) and was not allowed to make good any cosmetic damage caused when it was replaced (this was the work of a painter). There was broad agreement at the site that this was not an effective way of working and that additional skilling—enabling people to operate outside their traditional craft area—was essential to future success. In 1989, a programme was introduced to provide people who already had highly developed craft skills (for example, electricians, fitters, machinists) with additional skills outside their own specialism. In this way one person would be able to complete more of any given job.

Up to this point the problem and the proposed response is common to many organizations. It is in the implementation of additional skilling that this British Nuclear Fuels site took steps which can be identified as belonging to a learning organization. At the earliest stage of the Additionally Skilled Craftsmen (ASC) programme it was recognized that attention to the learning process itself would pay dividends in terms of the speed and effectiveness with which new skills were developed. As a first step, all 'recruits' to the ASC programme would take part in an extensive induction course which included off-the-job development to cover health and safety issues, the British Nuclear Fuels business and, significantly, learning about learning. After this induction, designed to equip people to reap maximum benefit from the ASC programme, specific training in new skill areas would be delivered by local colleges as well as by the in-house training function. Part of the impetus for including learning as an explicit part of development was a recognition that many of the potential inductees had been out of formal education for many years. Products of an age where it was naively felt that one set of skills, learned before the age of 20, would equip one for life, there was understandable fear among some inductees at a return to the classroom.

The induction course was designed by facilitating a group of key players—consultants, managers, supervisors and skilled staff—to first experience interventions aimed at pro-moting a more active approach to learning and then to put those approaches to work in designing the induction process itself.

The result was a radically different approach to induction training, which focused on equipping people to take charge of their own learning, for example by identifying different types of learning or by differentiating issues which had to be understood from facts which had to be memorized. In this way, people were encouraged to question the learning process itself and have a direct input into the structuring of their own development. An example of the impact of this approach was in the area of safety policy training, where instead of a series of lectures delivered by managers (the old approach) partici-pants were actively involved in exercises designed to help them understand and contribute to safety policy.

A core group of managers, supervisors and skilled people was developed to be facilitators of the 'learning-to-learn' approach and they then took responsibility for delivering this to the groups of people being inducted into the ASC programme. This overall approach has the important characteristic that it gives explicit attention to the learning process, in this case as part of an induction programme. This confers many of the benefits that have already been described in earlier chapters of this book, namely:

- ownership of learning by learners;
- problem-solving by the people closest to, and best informed about, the problem;
- ownership of the overall process by the people involved in making the process work;
- people empowered and equipped to learn more effectively and to meet organizational aims.

A rolling programme of workshops was established, extending across the whole site. External support continued only for as long as it took to develop in-house facilitators to the point where they could run the induction programme.

No process involving this degree of change is entirely problem free and some important lessons were learned. In retrospect, it was apparent that longer and more flexible workshops which allowed for different learning styles/speeds and gave more time for practice would have been beneficial for the facilitators. It became clear that some facilitators were more comfortable with these new ideas and concepts than others and were thus better equipped than others to carry forward the learning agenda. The result was that concepts which were not fully owned or understood by some facilitators were not shared as effectively with participants during the induction programme.

A particular symptom of this syndrome was careful adherence to a workshop 'script' by a facilitator, with insufficient attention to the learning needs of the group and the overall objectives of a particular learning session. However, explicit attention to the learning process meant that this was quickly recognized and where possible remedied.

From trainer to facilitator

An early discovery during the design of the programme was clearer recognition of the need to consider the role of the training function more carefully. Full involvement of trainers and their development as facilitators is vital if the empowerment of the workforce is not to be perceived as the disempowerment of the training department! There was some anecdotal evidence that at early stages in the process trainers felt sidelined (this being a learning intervention and not a training intervention). This was remedied as trainers became increasingly involved in facilitator development and increasingly grew comfortable with the facilitator role, a role where using the expert power of a 'knowledge holder' to achieve compliance was exchanged for the ability to encourage and develop relationships with fellow learners to achieve understanding. Earlier and more explicit attention to ensuring the full contribution of the training function could have avoided some of these tensions.

Perceived relevance helps

Another point to emerge in feedback from early groups of inductees was that some of the exercises used to explore learning were too generic or remote from everyday working experience. The effectiveness of the learning associated with these exercises would be diluted if their relevance was not readily apparent. While Francis Galton, the 19th century scientist, held that 'there is nothing so practical as a good theory', it is often the case that theories and concepts are best communicated and shared by means of relevant practical processes that enable the link to be made between current experience and new ideas. Thus, exercises have been modified and improved at the site to meet people's learning needs more effectively. This process, like all good learning processes, is ongoing.

A local success

The intervention described above was comparatively small in scale and tight in its focus. There were no organization-wide programmes for change, no directors' seminars to create a vision of the learning organization, no conscious re-engineering of the business (though some of these things happened in parallel). Rather, a small group of people addressed a particular challenge relating to the way in which a group of some 200–300 skilled workers could help themselves to be more effective.

Clearly at this British Nuclear Fuels site the impetus for introducing learning on to the agenda was a very specific one: the need for a more flexible workforce in the shortest possible time. A number of different approaches could have been taken, at both structural and individual level, to meet this requirement, and it should be noted that the interventions described did not happen in isolation nor have those interventions been insulated from sometimes unhelpful changes in the general business climate. What is apparent is that placing learning on the agenda and making learning about learning understandable, relevant and enjoyable has delivered benefits in terms of flexibility. The ASC programme, continuously modified and developed, is a success due to the efforts and abilities of the people most closely involved at the site. For people who have not previously been encouraged to think about how they learn, merely about what they must learn, this also holds the promise of increased personal investment in development and the likelihood of latent talent increasingly being brought to bear on the everyday work of the business.

The full range of interventions and exercises shared with participants during this project were as follows:

- What interferes with or blocks learning?
- How to overcome and deal with internal as well as external blockages to learning.
- Learning to differentiate between different kinds of learning.
- Increasing one's personal range of ways to learn.
- Encouraging a questioning attitude.
- Learning to ask effective questions.
- Using group-based techniques to expand understanding of an issue.
- Using the techniques to help make team decisions and resolve problems.
- Learning in and as a team.

Been there, done that: 3M manufacturing plant

A second example of learning interventions in action is taken from the UK manufacturing operation of a US-owned multinational. Here, as we will see, a series of interventions has helped the organization to manage change processes and empower staff at all levels to play a full part in organizational change rather than to think of themselves as mere recipients of externally enforced change.

Operating in the north of England, the main business of this 3M manufacturing site is the production of non-woven fibres and forming them into a range of filtering face masks. These are of varying specialization and technical sophistication, ranging from simple 'nuisance' masks at one end of the scale, to complex rubber and plastic moulded face masks with highly specified and controlled filtering properties at the other. Some 300 operators on four main production lines (in three shifts) are involved in this manufacture. At the same site, smaller sections of the factory were involved in other activities such as production of absorbent materials, the manufacture of electrical connectors for the computer and telecommunications industry and production of scented coatings for the advertising/publishing industry.

It is with the face mask operation that most of our story lies, however.

The site had experienced a number of changes over the years. Originally set up to supply products to the printing industry, it had made a successful transition to the production of face masks and had introduced innovative products and processes in this area. More recently, however, the production technology for their more standard masks had become widely available and competition, particularly from the Pacific rim, was starting to erode their lead in the production of comparatively low specification products. Here, then, was one of the drivers of change: the need for increased efficiency to meet growing competition.

Beneath this, however, was a deeper motive for change. As part of a multinational corporation there was a recognition that in the future the plant might well experience radical changes in its products and processes as a result of European or global strategies to maintain and increase profitability. While it was impossible to say what these changes might be or when they might occur, it was clear that the more flexible the workforce, the better placed the factory to prosper in the future as well as in the present. How to achieve this flexibility was the task at hand.

The site is a self-contained manufacturing unit with considerable autonomy as to how human resources issues are progressed. This said, as one of three manufacturing sites within the UK operation, it operates within a national, European and global policy framework. So, while able to call on central support and resourcing for any proposed initiatives, in practice the initiatives described below were all driven and resourced by the managers at the factory and in this sense it can be considered as a medium-sized stand-alone operation.

The director of the factory and his project manager for the initiatives described below, were the change agents who took the decision that the site needed to take a radical look at the way it worked, with the dual aims of improving efficiency in the immediate future and developing flexibility to secure the long-term future. It would be a mistake to think that these people took an evangelical approach to these issues; they were instrumental in making things happen not through altruism but because they recognized the need to do things better.

The starting-point

'I want this place to change in such a way that it will stay changed, without people (at all levels) reverting to old habits.'

This quote from the plant director represented early recognition that a deep and persisting change was sought. After a range of possible interventions had been discussed, senior managers at the site agreed that an empowering approach, involving staff at all levels, was the correct way forward. At this stage explicit reference to becoming a learning organization was not on the agenda, though, as we shall see, the initiatives that were developed and the approaches used are all characteristic of a company that is moving towards becoming a learning organization. Previous experience of training-based 'fixes', for example team-building, had failed to have long-term impact. Thus, despite some early suspicion, there was a perception that 'if training has failed, let's give learning a try'.

Empowering and equipping

To return to an earlier theme, people need to be given the equipment to change as well as just the remit to do so. In this instance, the process of equipping was ongoing throughout the project, the aim being to give people the specific skills necessary for completion of particular project stages as well as leaving them with skills that would serve them well in the future.

As a first stage, people across the factory were polled to nominate representatives who would act as 'auditors' as part of what was to become 'Training for Success' (a misnomer, Learning for Success would have been a more accurate title). Once this group had been assembled, it was clear that it would need to be developed to the point where the members could gather information from their colleagues in a systematic and professional way in order to determine the best ways forward.

Thus the audit process started with workshops for 25 people, designed to give them the data-gathering and analysis skills they would need. A 3-day workshop supported by open learning material and designed around the kinds of participative learning techniques already described, covered the creation of an appropriate questionnaire, interviewing skills, critical incident techniques and how to run and manage focus groups for data-gathering. With this equipment, and with appropriate (but small-scale) support, the 'audit' group started the process of canvassing opinion, experience and ideas from across the site. Interview schedules were drawn up, focus groups convened and questionnaires distributed. In this way most of the people on the site played a direct part in contributing information on which to build future interventions.

My people can't do that!

There was initial doubt among both managers and the audit group themselves as to their ability to conduct such an exercise (most of the group were machine operators). In practice the empowered and equipped group were able to perform the data-gathering effectively and efficiently, gathering data of a quality and richness that would have been hard for individual managers or outside consultants to achieve. Ownership of a process which they had been involved in designing, and increasing confidence in the use of the tools they had been given, led to a wealth of qualitative and quantitative data. This approach also served the important purpose of communicating the initiative across the whole site as well as communicating that this approach was rather different to manager- or consultant-driven interventions that they had experienced in the past. As a by-product, it also became clear to those managers and supervisors who were interviewed by operators (or who witnessed them at work) that the team were far more capable than they had previously been given credit for. At the same time, members of the audit team benefited from the experience of interviewing managers from '*mahogany row*', previously unexplored territory for most of them. This was the start of a dialogue which would serve the project well in the future.

It should not be thought that this process of information-gathering was without its difficulties. Some auditors did stumble, some interviewees were less co-operative than others and for some employees the process served to bring to the surface suspicions about what changes might be in the air. This said, however, the benefits of an in-house approach were clear in terms of both communication and the quantity/quality of the information that emerged.

The process of selecting the members of the audit group had been carefully thought through to avoid any perception that 'favourites' were being chosen or that auditors were being imposed on the workforce. Thus auditors were selected by their colleagues, within the constraints of ensuring representative cover of particular factory locations and shifts.

Over the duration of the project, however, it became clear that an individual's alignment with Training for Success had consequences beyond the obvious ones for those most closely involved. Inevitably, perceptions of these people changed. Long conversations with a number of auditors (and those who were later involved as facilitators) made it clear that, for some, relationships with their co-workers and managers were permanently changed as a result of their involvement. For most this was a generally positive experience, but for some it meant that working relationships became less comfortable. It is worth bearing this in mind during any process to 'recruit' facilitators or change agents; people should accept such roles fully aware of the personal changes that can result.

How are we doing,
what can we do better?

Data having been gathered, an important workshop involving all the auditors was convened to complete data analysis and recommend future action. Partial content analysis of the output from interviews, questionnaires and group discussions had already been accomplished by the audit team. The task now was to turn this into an action plan. Once again, the approach was for the auditors to arrive at the plan themselves with the support of facilitators who would provide a process framework. Broadly, over a 3-day workshop, this was achieved with key strengths, weaknesses, opportunities and threats to the business being identified by the group.

The richness of the data did mean that some compromises had to be made. While a range of targets for action was identified and a range of options for action discussed, there was not enough time to agree concrete proposals for the next stage of the project. It should be noted that during this stage of the project only one manager was involved, and he as a member of the audit team. It would be all too easy in this kind of intervention for managers to hijack the output and make a decision as to what should happen next with obvious disempowering results. Happily this was avoided and time was made available for the audit team to report back—both to managers and to their colleagues—before another workshop was convened to decide on the appropriate actions for stage two of the project.

Experience supports the view that too hasty a move to action before a full understanding of the issues has been achieved *and shared* is a common source of disillusion in organizational change interventions. In any move to become a learning organization, time is a key ingredient, necessary for lessons to be assimilated and experience consolidated into an improved understanding. There is, however, a balance to be drawn if enthusiasm and momentum are to be maintained, and for some of the audit team even a short pause (2 weeks) seemed too long when there were issues that they were now keen to address.

Communication

Another quote from a manager serves to illustrate the changed expectations that started to emerge at this point in the project:

'I wouldn't have believed that Rosie and her group could have achieved that six weeks ago.'

The list of issues that emerged from the audit process was a long one and ranged from the very broad (communication between managers and supervisors) to the very specific (operators on a particular machine having insufficient training). The process of communicating these findings was left in the hands of the audit team, who once again surprised their managers and their colleagues with the clarity and professionalism with which they conducted a number of presentations and discussions. Sharing the information at this stage was seen to be vital if the auditors were not to be perceived as a cabal, seeking to control the future of the factory rather than facilitating the development of the whole site.

At this point came the most difficult decision for the whole project: how best to progress? At this point, too, the issue of equipping the group for the next stage surfaced again. Choices had to be made between alternatives which were not all equally familiar or understood.

As has been noted, some very specific issues had emerged from the audit process and there was strong feeling among some of the group that the best way forward was to take initiatives aimed at dealing with these issues. For example, writing a new procedure for shift handover, allowing more time for team meetings, providing better training, persuading supervisors and managers to communicate more. Others in the group recognized that many of these issues had been addressed in similar ways in the past, and that over time little had actually changed. The concept of equipping people with broad enabling skills that would serve across a range of specific issues, in other words of moving towards a learning culture, was not one that was easily communicated or accepted. After much discussion it was agreed that a sub-group of the audit team (who later became the core of the Learning Support Group) would experience some aspects of learning about learning and assess its suitability as a vehicle for the change which was seen as necessary.

A learning organization?

It was at this stage that the concept of a learning organization—as embodied in the balloon analogy—played its part in bringing about a clearer understanding of the multidimensional nature of the task they had set themselves. There was a growing realization that, as well as dealing with specific problem areas, inhibitors and enhancers of learning would have to be considered at both individual and structural level if long-term change was to result. At a final planning workshop this group agreed that a multi-faceted approach to the identified issues would serve them best. Issues of individual empowerment would be addressed by a programme designed to enhance the learning and problem-solving skills of all operators and supervisors. Structural issues would be addressed by reassessing key roles such as that of the supervisor. At the same time, issues of communication across the site would be addressed by specific interventions/workshops designed to focus manager thinking in these areas. This then formed the basis for the work which followed throughout the factory. Throughout, the agenda was governed by the output of the audit group and the process was one of enabling the people most affected and most knowledgeable to reach their own decisions.

Support for learning   As we have seen, a number of the audit group had some experience of enhanced learning techniques as part of their earlier decision-making process. If organization-wide enhancement of learning was to be achieved, it was felt to be important that this experience should be shared with the rest of the workforce. Once again a core group of facilitators was identified, many of them drawn from the audit group but with some additions, their task being to share learning techniques with the rest of the site.

Workshops were designed to develop the facilitator skills of this group and enable them to run workshops on learning for the rest of the workforce. In this way the Learning Support Group was established. Having experienced and practised techniques for enhanced learning themselves, they were now in a position to share them with others as part of a broad enabling strategy. Once again it is important to stress that the Learning Support Group was made up primarily of operators who developed and modified specific techniques to suit their audience. The leap of faith and nerve required in accepting a role as facilitator, and in developing and employing a range of new skills, should not be underestimated. For some, perhaps most, standing in front of groups of their colleagues and managing as well as facilitating learning events was a stressful experience. Practice, support and working as a team helped all the facilitators grow in confidence as the roll-out of the programme continued. Over a period of 6 months, operators across the whole site experienced these learning events.

During this period the facilitators experienced some severe tests of their nerve and their confidence. Most notable of these was a decision taken by senior managers to speed up the implementation process by requiring operators to sign up for learning events rather than leaving it to a process of voluntary nomination. This decision was taken for sound operational reasons, to minimize the disruption to work scheduling for example, but it had a number of effects.

For some operators it was seen as demonstrating management commitment to the process of change; for others it was perceived as the imposition of a heavy-handed management tool. As usual in such circumstances, the decision probably had little effect on those who were unequivocally for the process or on those who were unequivocally against. In the middle, however, were a number of people who remained to be convinced that 'learning' was the way forward and the decision may well have reinforced their cynicism. It is a testimony to the facilitators and to their growing commitment to and confidence in the approaches they were espousing that these attitudes were largely overcome. While not everyone was won over, the more common workshop response was one of surprised enthusiasm for the ideas that had been shared. It is highly unlikely that outsiders delivering the same material would have achieved this level of credibility in the same circumstances.

The work of the Learning Support Group did not end here, however. Specific issues from the original 'hit list' identified during the audit remained to be addressed and a number of sub-groups were established (or, more interestingly, established themselves) to deal with some of these issues. Thus, some were involved in rewriting training material in a way that focused on learning needs and learning processes rather than just job content; others addressed the issue of site safety practices; another group looked at the best way of introducing new equipment on to the site. All those involved were considering the learning agenda when presenting information to others. On a smaller scale, communication was addressed by such means as using in-house publications and notice-boards to keep everyone informed of progress and the activities of the Learning Support Group. These and other process interventions are ongoing.

Parallel processes   While the task of establishing individual enhancers of learning was under way, some of the structural issues identified during the audit were also addressed. In an ideal world, the task of identifying new roles and ways of behaving for supervisors and developing them in these roles would have preceded the initiatives already described. In this way the teaching skills of the operators would have been more likely to find fertile soil in which to grow. For a number of reasons, however, supervisor development did not receive priority until the activity of the Learning Support Group was well under way. While some supervisors had been involved in the process from the start, the majority remained to be embraced by the learning initiative. This produced some inevitable frustrations, for example, an empowered operator suggesting a new way of fault-finding in a machine only to be 'squashed' by a supervisor who did not see that as a part of her job: 'Get back on the line and leave it to maintenance.' While these occurrences were not frequent, they did serve as a barrier to growing a culture of learning and continuous improvement. It was then a matter of some urgency that the role of the supervisor should receive explicit attention to prevent any 'bottom-up' empowerment from being stifled.

Supervisor of the Future

At about the time that the role of supervisor was under scrutiny, other structural changes were taking place at the site, and this is an appropriate time to consider their impact. As we have already seen in the earlier example, the world does not stand still while learning interventions are being planned and implemented.

At the factory, restructuring and a decision to contract out the manufacture of electrical connectors previously done on-site provided a backdrop of some uncertainty. For the supervisors this meant reallocation of work as a result of a number of early retirements. On a positive note, this helped to make clear the need for new ways of working and the impracticality of merely trying to do more of the same; at the same time it was a test of the supervisors' tolerance of ambiguity.

Underpinning the work that was done with the supervisors was, once again, a learning organization characteristic, namely, that of empowering and equipping the supervisors to do much of the work themselves.

The climate of change already engendered by the activities of the Learning Support Group had brought about the realization in many of the supervisors that their role would have to change if they were to be able to 'keep up' with the operators. Thus, as the learning-to-learn programme was being rolled-out in the factory, the supervisors were provided with the skills needed to analyse their own jobs and arrive at competencies that would help define their role and their behaviour in the future. Once again, the approach was to provide the enabling skills through highly participative work-shops, to give support as data was being collected, and then to facilitate a workshop where forward-looking competencies were agreed. These competencies then formed the basis for a development process designed to provide the supervisors with a self-managed route to new ways of operating.

In outline, the full process for Supervisor of the Future involved 11 separate steps, as follows:

1. A workshop to give supervisors job analysis skills and to develop an understanding of the nature of competencies.
2. Supervisors interview managers, subordinates, colleagues, in order to develop an understanding of an appropriate role for them in the future and the patterns of behaviour that go with it.
3. Supervisors visit other organizations to carry out interviews to see how it is done elsewhere.
4. Supervisors gather information from training bodies and educational institutions.
5. A facilitated workshop at which the findings are analysed and a draft role definition and associated competencies are defined by the supervisors and linked to relevant behaviours, and finalized after wider consultation.
6. Supervisors agree an assessment process to measure themselves against the competencies, 'to find out where we are and how far we have to go'.
7. In discussion with the supervisors, a development directory is created, linking specific development activities to competencies.
8. A development centre is created at which supervisors experience a number of exercises designed to assess their performance against specific competencies, e.g. group discussion exercises, role plays, planning exercises.
9. Supervisors are trained to administer and assess the output of the development centres so that the events can be run in-house with minimal outside support.
10. Four development centres are run.
11. Supervisors use the output of the development centres and the development directory to discuss with their colleagues and agree their own self-managed development plans.

Throughout this process, those supervisors who had experienced enhanced learning interventions at an earlier stage grew in confidence in applying those techniques to the data-gathering that formed a critical part of Supervisor of the Future's role. Comments from a number of those involved made it clear that they felt much better placed to approach other organizations, plan visits and make effective use of the information they found as a result of their earlier experience with the Learning Support Group. Their confidence as learners in managing their own development was a critical success factor for Supervisor of the Future.

Once again, any doubts as to the supervisors' ability to develop and apply the skills necessary to make this process work were removed as the quality and rigour of their work became apparent. Ownership of the process, self-managed change and ongoing learning were once again the characteristics that made the intervention possible.

Manager of the Future The third prong in the attack on the structural issues identified during the original audit was to ensure that senior managers at the site were in a position to support the activities of the supervisors and build on the learning initiatives taking place throughout the factory.

As has already been noted, in an ideal world it would have been desirable to have complete alignment between the activities of managers, supervisors and operators, and ideally a cascade of support and encouragement from the top down as well as pressure for change coming up through the organization. In practice, while a number of senior managers had been involved at early stages in the work, others remained to be brought on board. Thus in the autumn of 1993 a workshop was convened at which all the senior managers on site would consider the progress of the various initiatives, experience the learning interventions that were in train and consider their role in supporting learning throughout the site.

The managers first went through the same processes of reviewing learning, considering how to encourage learning and thinking about different types of learning that had been experienced by the early members of the Learning Support Group. At the same time they considered their own styles as supporters of learning and how they could adopt more coaching/mentoring styles with their people before considering specific action needed to support other learners in the factory. A number of initiatives grew from this process:

- The progress of learning issues and initiatives to be a fixed agenda item for senior manager meetings.
- Managers to run a rolling programme of meetings with small groups of operators to ensure clear communication.
- Identification of specific applications where new learning-orientated skills could be brought to bear.
- Less formal, but as interesting, was the decision of two

senior managers to review and monitor their own progress towards a more coaching style of management by getting regular feedback from their colleagues and subordinates, using the Manager as Coach instrument described in Chapter 7.

These initiatives progressed (and are progressing) at varying speeds and with varying levels of commitment as might be expected, but by now learning was literally on the agenda for everyone at the site.

The most up-to-date manifestation of a genuinely empowering approach to the management of the site came in early 1994 when final decisions had to be made about the restructuring of shift/function operations to take account of the structural changes that have already been described. Since the supervisor's role would be the one most affected, managers decided that the new structure would be discussed and agreed at a joint workshop. This represented a considerable move in thinking from a more traditional scenario where the managers would have decided the new structure and told the supervisors to implement it. As it was, the supervisors' ideas held sway and, while broadly similar in nature to the original ideas of the managers, their ownership of the problem and the solution make it much more likely that the new routines will be successfully implemented.

At the time of writing, planning for the Engineer of the Future, an initiative along the same lines as that for supervisors, is under way.

Impact

Measuring and assessing the impact of interventions such as those described above is always problematic. While there is anecdotal evidence in plenty of change (usually, though not always, change for the better) it is difficult to make clear assessments in the short term. Inevitably one is left with the problem of trying to assess how the world would look had something *not* happened. In the example described above, the output of an independent staff attitude survey supported the conclusion that communication was improving and that job satisfaction was increasing. At the same time, however, hard measures such as output figures, staff turnover, or even profitability, cannot accurately be attributed to one influence among many. Thus, while the monitoring of such interventions continues and the search for reliable measures and methods of bench-marking goes on, much of the appraisal which follows is based on the experience and comments of those most closely involved in the processes described.

It would be naive to suggest that this particular site was transformed over a period of 18 months. This said, significant changes in attitude and behaviour have occurred among a significant proportion of the workforce. At the same time, specific initiatives such as those described are delivering, and are promising to deliver clear benefits, for example, improved operator training, greater flexibility and better problem-solving at all levels in the organization. There is clear evidence of more collaborative and cross-functional working taking place and, as has been noted, explicit consideration of learning and self-development processes is now firmly on the agenda.

A senior manager at the site has appraised the project in the following proportionate terms. In his view, roughly one-third of the people on the site have fully bought into the aspirations of the project and are using improved learning skills as a means of seeking opportunities for continuous improvement; these people—at all levels—have been genuinely empowered and equipped to be more flexible and to give more and to get more out of their work.

He feels another third have benefited to some extent from the various interventions, either directly through their own increased repertoire of skills or indirectly through the more flexible and enlightened behaviour and attitudes of others. Thus people are more likely to be asked for their views and experience and are more likely to be asked to contribute to problem-solving.

For a final third his opinion was that the project has as yet had little positive impact. While they are not untouched or uninfluenced by the changes going on around them, they have chosen to play little direct part. In this group, cynicism and suspicion have not yet been removed. Whether this is a result of personalities or of processes it is not yet possible to say.

This, then, is an example of a factory that has started the process of becoming a learning organization (arguably this is a process that never finishes). Enlightened managers have created the space and found the resources to address fundamental questions about the way in which the organization operates. As a result, initiatives have been put in place with the aim of removing or minimizing systemic and individual inhibitors of learning as well as providing strong support for individual learning across the site.

As we have seen, the process has not been one of implementing a smooth, integrated project. In some cases activities have taken place at far from ideal times and in other cases hindsight teaches important lessons about the pace of

interventions and the order in which they should be implemented. What the example does serve to demonstrate is that
progress can be made even when the playing field is not
entirely level, when the goal posts are moving and when
individual players seem to be running towards the wrong
goal. This, after all, is the real world and throughout these
interventions it was necessary for managers to manage, for
supervisors to supervise and for operators to continue to
make thousands upon thousands of face masks.

In the next chapter we

• reflect on our own approach and the experiences of working
  with a variety of organizations to identify some guiding
  principles.

11 Reflections on learning organizations

In this chapter we

- argue that the management of diversity is crucial to becoming a learning organization
- speculate that there are lessons to be learned from naturally occurring learning organizations
- extract the lessons we have learned from over 7 years' experience of trying to help organizations make use of learning processes to facilitate and enhance change.

The management of diversity

The management of diversity is a critical building-block of learning organizations. Organizations that want to survive and thrive in the future cannot afford only to learn to improve their current activities by means of adaptive learning; they must also question, test and challenge what they are doing, and why they are doing it by means of generative learning (Argyris, 1977). To do this, everything must be open to discussion, and knowledge and ideas must flow freely through the organization. However, the challenge and examination of ideas can be impoverished within homogeneous groups because of the overrepresentation or domination of a unified and self-supporting set of views, experience and perspectives. Homogeneity can handicap organizations who want to learn; consequently the achievement of diversity goals can be a significant factor in the quest to become a learning organization and its contribution to sustained organizational success.

The strategic importance of diversity implies that, like learning, diversity must be managed as a long-term asset of the organization. Other members of our team in Oxford have recently created a strategic vision for the management of diversity in organizations (Kandola and Fullerton, 1994). They argue that:

> The basic concept of managing diversity accepts that the workforce consists of a diverse population of people. The diversity consists of visible and non-visible differences which may include factors such as sex, age, background, race, disability, personality, style of working, etc. It is founded on the premise that harnessing these differences will create a more productive environment in which organizational goals are met and an atmosphere in which everyone feels valued and that their talents are being fully utilized.

According to Kandola and Fullerton, the diversity-orientated organization will display six characteristics which they have called the MOSAIC model. First, *mission and core values*, which define managing diversity as a necessary long-term business objective for the organization and a responsibility for everyone in it. Second, *objective and fair processes*. All systems, such as recruitment, selection, induction and performance appraisal, are continually audited to ensure that hindrances to diversity have been removed. Third, *a skilled workforce*, which is aware that diversity is valued, and managers who possess the skills to harness each individual's potential. Fourth, *active flexibility* in terms of policies, practices and procedures. Fifth, the overarching principle of diversity-orientated organizations, which is *a focus on individuals*, not groups. Sixth, *a culture that empowers*, emphasizing openness, trust, responsible authority, information flow and the need for creativity.

Managing diversity has the ultimate aim of realizing the potential of all employees in order to ensure organizational success, and this is one of the goals of learning organizations. It is surprising, in our view , that in the published literature on learning organizations there is virtually no reference to the relationship between managing learning and managing diversity. We believe that there is a synergy between the two approaches, and that by making the links between them explicit, organizations will be in a better position to use the synergy to realize the potential of everyone in the organization. That we have not used this thinking in our work to date is explained by the fact that we have only recently evolved our thinking away from a traditional equal opportunities perspective, with its emphasis on legal frameworks and affirmative action geared to the perceived needs of specific groups towards the concept of managing, harnessing, recognizing and valuing the diversity of all people who comprise organizations, communities, markets and cultures.

Learning organizations are not necessarily diversity-orientated organizations, nor are diversity-orientated organizations necessarily learning organizations. There are similarities and differences. First, the similarities between the two. Ultimately, they have the same aim: to ensure organizational success by realizing the potential of all the individuals within the organization. They are both driven by the business case but may also genuinely believe that what is good for the people of the organization is also good for the organization. Other similarities include empowering culture, managers as coaches, devolved decision-making and teamworking.

On the other hand, there are some major differences. Learning organizations strive to shape their future, whereas diversity-orientated organizations tend to focus primarily on improving their current capabilities, although there may be future vision as well. The tools and processes associated with the two approaches also differ. The tools of learning organizations focus on optimizing organizational learning through the learning of individuals and teams; those of diversity-orientated organizations focus on effectively managing individuals who may be in a minority, who have stereotyping to deal with, and who may be discriminated against. The targets for change are also different: learning organizations introduce working methods to facilitate learning, adaptability and flexibility; the diversity-orientated organization focuses primarily on fair procedures and systems.

These similarities and differences between learning organizations and diversity-orientated organizations lead us to propose a symbiotic model which makes the links between them explicit. In this model, organizational success depends, in part, on realizing the potential of everyone in the organization. We see the management of diversity as maximizing the pool of talent and potential available to the organization, while the learning organization harnesses the learning and achievements of the enriched pool (see Figure 11.1).

Learning organizations strive to harness potential of all the individuals within them, that is, they facilitate learning, and use this learning to shape their future. However, if learning organizations are not diversity-orientated, they risk harnessing the potential of a narrow band of individuals in the organization who may be unrepresentative of the diversity of people in the wider community, markets, etc. Alternatively, organizations seek to iron out differences. This is a little like putting a fruit salad through a blender: individual flavours are lost. Similarly, a diversity-orientated organization that does not learn effectively enlarges and enriches the pool of

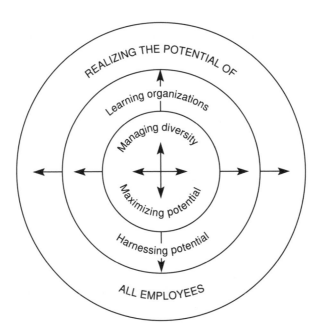

Figure 11.1 The relationship between learning organizations and the management of diversity: a symbiotic approach (extracted from Kandola and Fullerton (1994) and reproduced with permission of IPD Publications, London)

talent, but fails to harness the potential that is available. A diversity-orientation is essential because it maximizes the size and richness of the pool of potential, which learning organizations can then harness. The two approaches are symbiotic, and it is clear that management of diversity is a critical building-block of learning organizations. This symbiotic approach suggests a way in which the potential of *all* employees can be realized for the benefit of the organization.

Natural learning organizations: do they exist?

In an attempt to differentiate levels of management development, Burgoyne (1988) referred to natural management development occurring within newly created entrepreneurial organizations. What lessons can be learned from the characteristics of successful, newly created, entrepreneurial organizations? Success here implies they have survived long enough (months or years) to become viable organizations. Some interesting comparisons can be made between the natural evolution of new entrepreneurial organizations and the way many large organizations wish to be. Because a new entrepreneurial organization has no history, it has no established 'ways we do things round here', no habits, no customs, no acquired inertia. It is nearly always small, and as a result quick to react, flexible and adaptive. Many large organizations want to acquire some of the benefits associated with being small, including the absence of constraining history. New organizations are very sensitive to external changes because they are felt quickly and directly, if not by the owners, then by their employees from whom the owner's physical and/or psychological distance is small compared to that in the multi-level, hierarchical, centralized and functionalized established organizations.

There is often a feeling of excitement and challenge in a new entrepreneurial organization. Overheads are typically small. The culture is clearly led by the founders, whose style and values tend to be prominent. The organization's mission is clear to all. Although it can be chaotic, the newly created entrepreneurial organization has many of the qualities to which learning organizations aspire:

- they are quick to react because chains of command are short and there is a lack of constraining functional structure
- mistakes are felt quickly because the customer is close
- they are adaptive because they are not constrained by an elaborate structure and a stable culture; they are therefore also likely to be innovative
- their energy and sense of challenge are felt directly and are motivating
- they are focused because of the prominence and active involvement of the founder who also creates vision and direction
- they are constantly changing because it is natural for a newly created business to evolve rapidly as it grows.

The fate of many newly created organizations (at least those that survive the first phase of existence) is to become bureaucratic, and thus lose many of the qualities that are critically important in our ever-faster-changing world. In terms of our INVEST model for a learning organization a newly created entrepreneurial organization is likely to be:

- high on
  - vision of learning (everything to aim for)
  - transforming (or lack of a restrictive) structures
  - supportive managers (close to both customers and employees)
  - inspired learners (because feedback loops are so short).

- low on
  - enhanced learning
  - nurturing culture.

The use of enhanced learning techniques and processes may not be necessary in a newly created entrepreneurial organization because feedback loops from customers and employees are very direct. The supportive culture may not necessarily be caring and supportive to the individual's personal needs, but it will be conducive to achieving results and enabling adaptation.

The organization which becomes bureaucratic in nature cannot be a learning organization because it is:

- Low on inspired learners: although there may be concern with individual and professional development, a bureaucratic organization does not encourage challenge, questioning of assumptions or systematic examination of performance. Mistakes are absorbed into a self-perpetuating bureaucracy, and learning is not easily transferred from one part of the organization to another.
- Low on nurturing culture: stability, slowness and risk-averse behaviour tend to characterize bureaucratic organizations.
- Low on vision: the purpose of the organization and a sense of where it is going will have become obscured, or are understood only by a few.
- Low on enhanced learning: bureaucratic organizations tend to be tactical rather than strategic, and have a narrow focus instead of a broad vision. Therefore, they will not use methods and processes which encourage innovative thinking and bring about new learning.

- Low on supportive managers: preoccupation with correct procedures and processes, and not outcomes or results, leads to discouragement of initiative and innovation, which is exacerbated by distance from customers. Belief in the system tends to guide behaviour and decision-making.
- Low on transforming structures: a high degree of segmentation, functionalized roles, and many layers of management will create self-perpetuating activities of varying degrees of true value to the customer.

In many ways, the traditional bureaucracy is the opposite of a learning organization. The bureaucratic organization is dedicated to self-perpetuation in its current form, and under certain circumstances can be effective and may survive for decades. The learning organization is dedicated to transforming itself continuously as the external environment changes. It transforms naturally, just as the bureaucratic organization naturally acquires stability which evolves into inertia and an inability to self-transform. The bureaucratic organization pursues safety by changing little, whereas the learning organization pursues safety by continuously adapting.

Lessons from experience

Over the years of developing tools and working with organizations of all kinds to assist the process of becoming a learning organization, certain lessons have emerged or have been strengthened in the light of experience. They can be summarized as follows:

- Involve the people most affected at the earliest possible stage.
- Champions for a learning organization need to understand how they and other people learn.
- Diagnostic and analytical processes are crucial.
- Managers must learn early on to facilitate learning as a prime activity.
- Evolution is better then prescription.
- One of the biggest obstacles to the achievement of a learning organization is the gulf between managers and the managed.
- The learning organization is a quest not an end state.
- The business case for becoming a learning organization should be supported by a vision and values that inspire.
- Mystique-busting is also essential early on.
- Equipping is the key to empowerment and empowerment is one of the keys to a learning organization.
- An orientation to quick action and reaction rather than reflection can be a major block to becoming a learning organization.
- Interventions should be fitted to the organization, not the organization fitted into a pre-conceived model of a learning organization.

Early involvement of affected people

It is important to involve the people most affected at the earliest possible stage. In our experience learning on behalf of others and then passing on the benefits of that learning is inefficient. Similarly, planning complex processes or events on behalf of other tends to produce solutions and plans that may look good on paper but will not necessarily be the best course of action. If the view is taken that the affected group should not be involved because they do not understand the wider picture, or because the issue is too sensitive, or too complex, then the organization has identified a learning need rather than a reason for taking action on their behalf. If a group is perceived to be not capable of carrying out a certain task, e.g. planning the winding-down of their own department, then they may need equipping with the necessary information, understanding, or skills, in order to be able to perform the tasks. It is a fundamental principle guiding our work that participative methods involving representative samples of the organization should be a major feature of the development of understanding and the creation of processes to move towards becoming a learning organization.

Champions need to understand the nature of learning

Champions for a learning organization need to understand how they and other people learn. Too often we have seen senior managers in organizations espousing commitment to the learning organization concept or to empowerment and yet displaying behaviour consistent with mind-sets that seem to contradict their own words (e.g. that they continue to know best). By understanding the sometimes uncomfortable nature of learning and also the excitement that can be associated with learning, change champions may talk in a way that encourages rather than inhibits support, contributions and challenge from others. One of the most useful things that most senior managers can learn is that they themselves can be blinkered by old habits, blinded by inappropriate mind-sets, artificially comforted by defensive routines, and that they, like others, can lack core skills in thinking systemically or for that matter creatively. It can be a humbling experience for top managers to realize that they are not exempt from the same processes that trap and limit the thinking of everyone else, but a degree of humility may be a necessary attribute in empowering learning at all levels in an organization.

Diagnostic and analytical processes are crucial

Although considerable insight can be gained from group discussions into the nature of learning blocks at organizational and individual level, data derived from systematic audits and surveys using instruments such as the Learning Climate Questionnaire or the Learning Audit across an organization can give a better feel for the extent of the learning blocks. It can also permit comparisons within the same area over a period of time, and comparisons between areas and between organizations for bench-marking purposes.

Prime role of management

Managers must learn early on how to facilitate learning as a prime activity. In an organization that regards the optimization of learning of all its members as a prime objective, it follows naturally that facilitation of continuous learning among work groups and teams should be a prime objective of the management role. Encouraging and sustaining learning in individuals and groups is a key component in the process of equipping staff with the competencies necessary for working effectively in a high-involvement culture. To the extent that managers and team leaders succeed they will be able to tap into the latent and unrecognized 'intelligence' and wisdom available within the workforce.

Evolution is better than prescription

By its very nature a learning organization is dynamic and evolving. It is dangerous to think that it is possible to become one by signing up to five dimensions or 11 characteristics in the belief that all the benefits of becoming a learning organization will thereby be achieved. A great deal can be attained but the organization must be ever alert to new possibilities that have not been thought of by proponents of learning organization theory. It would be difficult to describe Ricardo Semler's Semco (Semler, 1993) as anything other than a learning organization and yet it does not appear to subscribe to any one view or model of a learning organization. In one organization we worked with, the 'global expert' on learning organizations was so imbued with Senge's five learning disciplines that he would brook no opposition or challenge, thus alienating his audience in the way he communicated with them. As is so often the case, the expert even on an issue like learning organization theory displayed little evidence that he understood basic learning processes. As we noted earlier, no-one since the dawn of time has been privileged with knowing all the answers, and the most dangerous time for a teacher is when their views are treated with unquestioning respect.

The gulf between managers and the 'managed'

One of the biggest obstacles to the achievement of a learning organization is the continuing gulf between managers and the 'managed'. In our work we have seen and experienced many instances of this prevailing gulf. It is usually biggest among senior managers who are often physically separated from the people for whom they have direct or indirect responsibility, but it also exists among first line supervisors who have been selected and encouraged in the belief that the majority of workers cannot be trusted to do things for themselves even when they possess most knowledge of their jobs. The gulf between the managers and the 'managed' is a variation of the classic 'them and us'. 'Them' varies in different contexts, but is frequently applied to:

- those managers who believe that it is their job to know best on behalf of those that they are there to manage;
- experts who believe that they are expected to have all the answers otherwise their credibility and perceived usefulness will be undermined;
- professional and functional specialists who protect their territory, status and power by upholding the belief that years of training and formal qualifications are necessary before an opinion relevant to their work can be expressed, let alone influence the way they work.

One of the goals and benefits of becoming a learning organization is to break down this artificial barrier to problem-solving, decision-making, and creativity.

A quest not an end state

The learning organization is a quest not an end state. We argued strongly at the beginning of this book that the single-state learning organization did not exist and that it was unhelpful to think of organizations as either learning organizations or not learning organizations. Just as there are many different ways in which organizations can be successful, there are many different ways in which an organization can strive to add the adjective 'learning' to the many that could be applied. The desire to mobilize the intelligence of every member of an organization, and in ways that result in the transformation of the organization so that it thrives now and in the future, is a quest which reaps benefits along the way rather than a state to be achieved.

Inspiring vision and values

The business case for becoming a learning organization should be supported by a vision and values that inspire. There is a danger that the learning organization concept is becoming more talked about than practised. One consequence is that it is seen as a passing fad whose time will come (all too quickly) and that therefore nothing needs to be done because top management's interest will soon blow over. It is clearly part of the role of organizational leaders to ensure that an internalized understanding and commitment is achieved and that this understanding is cascaded in a consultative and involving way throughout the organization, not as something nice to know, but as something crucial to the organization's survival and success. Another risk is that people pay lip-service to the idea, even attending workshops and finding the whole subject interesting, but not in a way that deeply changes their own behaviour or understanding of their role as managers.

By creating a vision of the future that members of an organization would want to be part of, expressing a set of values that give dignity and meaning to everyone involved, there is a reasonable chance that organization members will be inspired to contribute to the achievement of the organization's goals. The business case fits into the bigger picture with a coherence that would not otherwise be available, creating a synergy between the needs of the organization and the needs of its members.

Mystique-busting

Mystique-busting is also essential early on. Many people have heard of the concept of learning organizations and of arcane-sounding processes such as systems thinking and paradigm-shifts and are not sure whether to admit that they do not really understand what they are. There is also a sense in which some managers, and indeed some consultants, talk about learning organizations as though they have been initiated into dark and portentous secrets not available to the uninitiated. Part of the appeal of the learning organization concept, apart from the potential to help organizations secure their capacity to thrive in an unpredictable future, is the essential simplicity of the core ideas which can easily be worked out by a group of employees within a suitable participative process. If the mystique is not busted early on, there is a risk that understanding of the nature of learning organizations will reside with a chosen few who will be seen to preach from the mountain top but who will be ignored by the majority.

Commitment to equipping and empowerment

Equipping is the key to empowerment and empowerment is one of the keys to a learning organization. This book is not about empowerment. Whereas isolated pockets of empowerment can be achieved without becoming a learning organization, it is not possible to become a learning organization without a high commitment to empowerment. Empowerment, in terms of devolved responsibility and decision-making, is unlikely to work well if so-called empowered groups are not equipped with the necessary skills and knowledge. Supporting and encouraging learning in the workplace is essential to a learning organization which may have things in common with an empowered organization, but an empowered organization is not the same as a learning organization. The difference lies in a learning organization's commitment to learn to transform itself in the face of evolving and difficult to predict changes in its external environment.

Review and reflect

An orientation to quick action and reaction rather than reflection and review can be a major block to becoming a learning organization. In our experience of working with many organizations we have seen a readiness to react and act rather than to review and reflect as the hallmark of an organization's culture. Many organizations admire and reward managers who get things done quickly, who overcome obstacles, and who succeed in the face of opposition. There is an impatience with processes that take longer than the expected time-span between action and outcome. In these organizations there is a tendency to opt for actions that get early results rather than reflecting on alternatives, perhaps arrived at by the application of systems thinking, which might achieve better results. Systems thinking is possibly the most powerful antidote to the quick-fix mentality characteristic of so many organizations. Even in organizations who have entertained the learning organization concept, the predilection for quick action and quick results can prevent them fully committing to the longer-term benefits. As a result, the concept my be wrongly discarded as only marginally helpful to the organization.

Fitting interventions to the organization

Interventions should be fitted to the organization, not the organization fitted into a preconceived model of a learning organization. This should be self-evident. Unfortunately many large and sophisticated organizations are only too ready to sign up to expensively implemented systems which appear to work for a while but which eventually do not bed into the organization, and very quickly begin to atrophy. In our view the commitment to becoming a learning organization should come from within, if only as a result of awareness-raising workshops. The diagnosis of what needs to be done and the planning and implementation of action programmes should evolve from the initially developed understanding of the significance of learning for the organization. Failure to do this risks achieving only superficial and short-lived gains, and as a result the interest in being a learning organization will be seen as a passing phase rather than a deep-rooted fundamental change in organizational thinking and behaviour.

These lessons from experience capture much of our thinking about organizational learning and the challenges involved in helping organizations to unleash the potential 'locked up' inside themselves. Since our experience is not complete, however, we would expect these lessons to be extended and modified in the light of our and other peoples' experience. As we have been at pains to emphasize, learning processes are ongoing and we would not seek or expect to find a definitive or prescriptive list of lessons, interventions or tools, for then *we* would have stopped learning.

As our examples and illustrations have suggested, we do not believe that there is 'one right way' to becoming a learning organization. At the same time, we have been fortunate enough to have the opportunity to work with organizations across the whole spectrum of corporate and industrial endeavour: large and small, public and private, commercial and industrial, traditional and innovative. The 12 lessons described above are based on communalities of experience drawn from all these and are, we believe, a robust base from which to start building a learning organization.

Final thoughts   In talking with people about organizational learning, two common reactions occur; innocent enthusiasm for the latest management idea that will transform the organization, or world weary cynicism that here is yet another management 'flavour of the month' that will have limited impact and will last only as long as it takes for consultants to produce the next great break-through. Both reactions implicitly categorize the idea of a learning organization among that class of one-off organizational fixes that have surfaced over the last 40 years and which, like a patent medicine, promise cures without any serious change in behaviour. In our view, becoming a learning organization is more like changing one's habits to arrive at a healthier and more adaptive lifestyle than it is like taking a tablet to treat a symptom: it is an orientation and change of life-style rather than a vaccination. It is at least as much about promoting organizational health as it is about curing organizational malaise.

In this book we have tried to outline some of the reasons for our belief that the idea and gradual realization of a learning organization offers much more than a one-off cure or a quick fix but instead offers a framework for organizations to achieve conscious evolution and self-transformation on a continuing basis. At the same time we have described our experience of tools and interventions designed to help move towards a learning organization. If this is where we have come to, what of the way ahead?

As the pace of change increases, driven by a whole host of

factors which are technological, environmental, social and political, at national and at global levels, then arguably the quest to be a learning organization will become a necessity rather than an option. The choice will be between conscious organizational and individual adaptation or allowing 'natural selection' to determine organizations' evolutionary outcomes, which for many will mean decline and ultimate cessation. History tells us that reliance on size and strength are not enough (as the dinosaurs discovered), and that perfect adaptation to one evolutionary (or market) niche does not serve well when that adaptation can actually limit ability to deal with ever-changing niches, and evidence suggests that such change is a certainty.

If the competitive environment does bring about a situation where only learning organizations survive, what then? What happens when all organizations are learning organizations? The short answer is that no one can know but some of the implications for individuals and organizations can be guessed. Tolerance of ambiguity, flexibility, adaptability and, above all, the ability to learn, will be the most highly prized commodities for individuals, teams and organizations as a whole. Process and systems thinking will be as important as expert technical knowledge. Managers will be appraised on the basis of their change agency and learning skills as well as on their ability to facilitate these approaches in others. Organizational structures will transform to enable continuous parallel processing of information rather than intermittent serial processing. Organizations may increasingly model themselves on that most flexible of information processing devices, the human brain, where functional specialization is much less important than the neural network that creates the adaptable linkages between centres of activity. All this with the aim of being better at adapting and improving than competitor organizations. What pleases the brain is challenge, stimulation, curiosity, intrigue and inventiveness. What pleases the whole person is doing something worthwhile, being valued, having a sense of purpose and belonging, and pride.

If organizations of all kinds can achieve their mission by pleasing both the brain and the whole person of *all* the people who comprise the organization, then more people will manage to find fulfilment, or at least partial fulfilment, through work rather than having aspirations which lie completely outside the realm of their working lives. If the aspirations of the individuals who comprise an organization are aligned with, or are compatible with, the needs of the organization then greater commitment and contribution should result from everyone involved. The quest to be a learning organization holds out this prospect.

If this vision of the organizational future were to be anything like accurate, then most organizations have a long way to go. As we suggested earlier, natural selection is ruthless and a fundamental choice exists between conscious learning that enables adaptation and management of the environment or acceptance that organizations are almost helpless in the face of external factors. Unlike the species that evolution chose or discarded, organizations have choices about the kind of evolutionary system to which they wish to subscribe. Whatever other decisions organizations make to ensure that they thrive, the need to learn—at all levels—is not negotiable.

Finally, we would like to assert our fundamental belief, which we hope is apparent throughout this book, that learning is too important to leave to chance, to managers, to experience, to HR specialists, gurus and to past paradigms. It should be the responsibility, joy and enrichment of everyone. Learning organizations ensure that it is.

References

ARGYRIS, C. (1977) 'Double-loop learning in organizations', *Harvard Business Review*, September–October, 115–125.

BURGOYNE, J. (1988) 'Managerial development for the individual and for the organization', *Personnel Management*, June, 40–44.

KANDOLA, R. A. and FULLERTON, J. (1994) *Managing the Mosaic*, London: Institute for Personnel and Development.

Annotated bibliography

ARGYRIS, C. (1977) 'Double-loop learning in organizations', *Harvard Business Review*, Sep–Oct, 115–125

Organizational learning is the process of detecting and correcting errors that inhibit learning. Single-loop learning occurs when the organization learns to do better what it is currently doing. Double-loop learning is the learning that results from questioning organizational goals and policies; and this is the learning that organizations must have for future success. Double-loop learning is inhibited because people in organizations have a 'theory-in-use' which leads to information being withheld, or being vague and ambiguous. To change these behaviours, individuals must change their private assumptions, or theories-in-use. This change involves: (1) becoming aware of the private assumptions; (2) understanding how these assumptions inhibit double-loop learning; (3) developing new assumptions to facilitate learning; and (4) developing the skills necessary to implement the behaviours which follow from the new set of private assumptions. The aims of the new private assumptions are to help people produce valid information, make informed choices, and develop internal commitment to those choices. So, in the new model, the power of double-loop learning comes from: (1) reliable information; (2) competent people; and (3) continually monitoring the effectiveness of decisions.

See also ARGYRIS, C. and SCHON, D., *Organizational Learning*. Addison-Wesley, 1978. This book fully develops the single-double-loop distinction.

ARGYRIS, C. (1990) *Overcoming Organizational Defences: Facilitating Organizational Learning*, Boston: Allyn and Bacon.

Expanded treatment of the notion of defensive behaviour. Highlights the seven 'worldwide errors' that managers believe violate the principles of sound management, though they still make them. (1) Actions intended to increase understanding and trust often produce misunderstanding and mistrust; (2) blaming others or the system for poor decisions; (3) organizational inertia; (4) upwards communications for difficult issues are often lacking; (5) budget games are necessary evils; (6) people do not behave reasonably, even when it is in their best interests; and (7) the management team is often a myth. These errors are the source of defensive reasoning. Six steps towards overcoming organizational defences are highlighted: (1) make a diagnosis of the problem; (2) connect the diagnosis to the actual behaviour of the participants; (3) show them how their behaviour creates organizational defences; (4) help them to change their behaviour; (5) change the defensive routine that reinforced the old behaviour; and (6) develop new organizational norms and culture to reinforce the new behaviour. The answer is not to make laws against organizational defensive routines; rather, individuals must become self-managing and create organizations that reward self-responsible actions.

ARGYRIS, C. (1991) 'Teaching smart people how to learn', *Harvard Business Review*, May–June, 99–109.

Being smart, smart people have infinite capacity to blame others, to rationalize away failure. And they are defensive, very defensive. There is a marked difference between the way people think they are acting and the way they really act: what Argyris terms espoused theory, and theory-in-use. Managers at the top need to evaluate and change their theories-in-use, to overcome their tendency to reason defensively and to recognize the negative consequences of that defensive reasoning. Only then will they begin to be able to learn.

ARGYRIS, C. (1994) 'Good communication that blocks learning', *Harvard Business Review*, Jul–Aug, 77–85.

Argues that double-loop learning does not take place often enough in organizations for two reasons: (1) social—people do not like to put other people on the spot, and prefer to avoid the negative; (2) psychological—people reason defensively to avoid vulnerability, risk, embarrassment and the appearance of incompetence. Corporate communications can act as a block to learning. The allocation of 'employees' as 'information-providers' and 'managers' as 'decision-makers' can create a bias against personal learning and commitment. The focus on extrinsic, as opposed to intrinsic, rewards also opens a door to defensive reasoning. Managers must demonstrate a new level of self-awareness, candour and responsibility if they are to develop employees who think constantly and creatively about the needs of the organization with as much intrinsic motivation and as deep a sense of organizational stewardship as any company executive.

ATTWOOD, M. and BEER, N. (1988) Development of a learning organization—reflection on a personal and organization workshop in a district health authority, *Management Education and Development*, 19, 201–214.

The authors' organizational development work with Mid-Essex Health Authority is described. A learning organization addresses six issues: (1) the role of management; (2) the role of organization development and personnel staff; (3) the shared responsibility of staff for the learning process; (4) the robustness of the learning process; (5) the continuity of feedback; and (6) the rate of learning. Three issues are identified which must be continually monitored if progress is to be made: (1) liberating structure; (2) organizational sub-climates; and (3) the notion of responsible freedom. Seven future actions which the Health Authority must carry out to move it towards becoming a learning organization are highlighted: (1) effective operation and maintenance of the individual performance review scheme; (2) involvement of non-managerial staff in learning organization thinking and practice; (3) the use of individual development methods which are consistent with the characteristics of the learning organization; (4) selection and induction procedures which convey the Mid-Essex culture as a learning organization; (5) a management style which is consistent with the district's guidelines for management practice; and (7) new and appropriate interventions.

BALL, C. (1992) *Profitable Learning*, London: Royal Society of Arts.

Follows from the earlier report *Learning Pays* (1991) with a 10-point action plan to help create a learning society in the UK, a *learning society* in which the vicious circles of the 20th century—low productivity and profits, low investment, low standards, low skills—will be replaced by the virtuous circles of the 21st century—high aspirations, high standards, high skills, high salaries, high satisfaction. Notes that at its best learning is continuous and often informal; existing models of education and training overemphasize the initial and formal aspects of learning. The report's three major findings are that learning pays, that in a learning society the principle of lifelong learning should be the informing idea of education and that it is the supply side of education and training that must change first if a true learning society is to be created. The role of learning is put in a broader business context in a subsequent RSA report, *Tomorrow's Company: The Role of Business in a Changing World* (1994). The report advocates the inclusive approach as the route to sustainable competitiveness; an approach based on learning. This inclusive approach is characterized by: (1) distinctive values and purpose; (2) consistent message; (3) recognition of interdependence; (4) reciprocal relationships; and (5) informed decision-making in areas of conflicting interests.

BALLÉ, M. (1994) *Managing with Systems Thinking: Making Dynamics Work for you in Business Decision-making*, Maidenhead: McGraw-Hill.

A book which provides a method and specific, simple techniques to use systems thinking in practice. Systems thinking though is not about solving corporate problems; it is about thinking. The limits of rationality are described and static mental models are clearly not sufficient to capture the dynamic complexity of contemporary organizations. Systems thinking provides an alterative rationality; one which is analytical, holistic and pragmatic. It focuses on relationships not parts, patterns not events, and sees causality in terms of circles rather than straight lines. The systems thinking framework is built on five concepts: (1) feedback loops; (2) delays; (3) influence; (4) structure as the driver of systems behaviour; and (5) leverage. As a guide, seven steps to systems thinking analysis are suggested: (1) what is the symptom?; (2) who are the players?; (3) what is the growth engine?; (4) what are the main limiting factors?; (5) expand the frame; (6) operational action points; (7) communicate.

BEARD, D. (1993) 'Learning to change organizations', *Personnel Management Journal*, Jan, 32–35.

Describes the model through which BT's UK sales force has become a 'learning organization'. Involves three levels of learning, applying and developing. The first level is individual; participants attend a development centre, review their performance and abilities and apply the learning to their work and career development. This is completed on a regular basis and includes reviews with line managers. The second level deals with teams; team managers facilitate team reviews and learning through team meetings and coaching. The third level is organizational learning and is still developing. It involves learning, reviewing and developing by the top management team, with inputs from the other two levels.

BECKHARD, R. and PRITCHARD, W. (1992) *Changing the Essence: The Art of Creating and Leading Fundamental Change in Organizations*, London: Jossey-Bass.

Fundamental change involves changes to the essence of organizations, and this book identifies the key issues for top managers who set out to implement fundamental changes. Three characteristics of a fundamental change strategy are highlighted: (1) a clear vision of the desired end state; (2) a conscious decision to move to a learning mode, where both learning and doing are equally valued; and (3) a clear commitment from the top to making a personal investment in achieving the vision. This book is written for leaders, because they have a crucial role to play: their behaviours must be congruent with the articulated vision, they must make a personal commitment to that vision, and they must enrol the commitment of other key players. To lead a vision-driven change, top managers must: (1) create and set the vision; (2) communicate the vision; (3) build commitment to the vision; and (4) organize people and what they do so that they are aligned with the vision. This alignment requires the integration of roles, systems and rewards. A fundamental role of the leaders of thriving organizations is to create the conditions that produce commitment and creative actions by the people in the organization.

BUCHANAN, D. and McCALMAN, J. (1989) *High Performance Work Systems: The Digital Experience*, London: Routledge.

The development of work design theory and practice is described.

The resurgence of interest in new work organization strategies is attributed to the strategic imperatives of the 1980s. DEC's implementation and evaluation of high-performance work groups is described in detail. Nine guidelines for managers are set out, falling into three categories. First, get the *purpose* right: (1) the change demands a strategic trigger; (2) the work organization must be supported by the overall employment and rewards package; (3) technology must be selected for its flexibility, not because it is the 'latest thing'. Second, get the *people* right: (4) encourage flexibility, quality, creativity and skills development; (5) develop a management style consistent with the approach; (6) design support systems that are consistent with the strategic goals. Third, get the *process* right: (7) establish clear responsibility for project management of implementation; (8) plan the nature and timing of wider employee involvement; (9) develop systematic training and development to equip everyone for the high-performance organization. The realities of practice show that 'effortless excellence', implied by prescriptive approaches is simply a myth; the process is painful.

CARRÉ, P. (1991) 'The self-learning gamble: an examination of the issues involved', in Nyhan, B., *Developing People's Ability to Learn*, Brussels: Eurotecnet Technical Assistance Office, Inter-university Press.

An examination of the concept of self-learning and the key differences from traditional training. There is the need for a transformation from 'learning as consuming' to 'learning as production and action'. *Seven Pillars of Self-learning* are identi-fied: (1) a project-orientated pedagogy; (2) a threefold training contract; (3) a mechanism for induction and pre-training; (4) a resource centre with free access; (5) guides for self-learning; (6) new roles for trainers; and (7) a continuous three-level support mechanism. The implications of the seven pillars for society, professional training, and continuous improvement within companies, are spelled out.

CARRÉ, P. (1992) *L'Autoformation en Formation Professionelle*, Paris: La Documentation Française.

Aims to give trainers, researchers and human resource profes-sionals a global view of the state of the art in international research on self-learning. Contains an overview of what Carré sees as the seven prevailing streams of research (mainly in France, the UK and Canada), a chapter on the American concept of self-direction in learning, one on practical applica-tions of the concept in a training context and conclusions for future research and action.

CARRÉ, P. and PEARN, M. (1992) *L'Autoformation dans l'Entreprise*, Paris: Editions Entente.

A review of how the training systems in organizations can use the new technologies of training and multi-media to encourage self-directed learning. The book also describes the implementation model which forms part of *Tools for a Learning Organization* (Pearn and Mulrooney, 1995).

CASEY, D. (1993) *Managing Learning in Organizations*, Milton Keynes: Open University Press.

A practical book focusing primarily on bringing about learning in teams, i.e. small groups, management teams and self-directed teams. The author draws heavily on his personal experiences and presents a case study of the learning consultancy of which he is part at Ashridge. The final chapter on organizational learning examines how insights can be gained by drawing on other disciplines ranging from transactional analysis and family therapy to anthropology and even marine biology.

COLLINS, J. C. and PORRAS, J. I. (1991) 'Organizational vision and visionary organization', *California Management Review*, Fall, 30–52.

These authors note that most mission statements are ineffective. The one universal requirement of effective leadership is to catalyse a clear and shared vision of the organization. Without a vision, organizations have no chance of creating their future, they can only react to it. They provide a framework which provides clear concepts and useful tools for developing a vision. An effective vision has two elements: A *guiding philosophy*, made up of the organization's values and beliefs and its purpose; and a *tangible image*, which comprises the mission and a vivid description. The guiding philosophy is a system of fundamental motivating assumptions, principles, values and tenets. The tangible image is a concrete picture of the future. Numerous examples of each of the components are given. They conclude that building an organization with vision is more important that having a single charismatic individual with vision as the CEO.

CUNNINGHAM, I. (1994) *The Wisdom of Strategic Learning: The Self-managed Learning Solution*, Maidenhead: McGraw-Hill.

Strategic learning is contrasted with bureaucratic training. For organizations, strategic learning means that: (1) the organization values learning; (2) the culture supports learning; (3) the strategic direction of the organization is clear; and (4) the organization selects good learners and helps each individual to learn to their maximum potential. Self-managed learning (SML) is put forward as a strategic approach which captures what good learning is all about. The principles of SML are outlined, as are the tactics for implementing the four strategic processes: (1) *preparing*—start-up events, maps, diagnostic activities, handbooks and learning contracts; (2) *resourcing*—learning resources and learning budgets; (3) *collaborating*—learning sets, learning communities, networking and assisting learning; (4) *judging*—assessment and evaluation. The importance of providing support for SML is emphasized. The self-managing learner: (1) adopts an active role; (2) uses formal learning situations for maximum benefit; (3) translates learning across contexts;

(4) takes responsibility for his/her own actions; (5) prepares for the future through learning; and (6) maintains a strategic view, and is able to link detail with the bigger picture.

DICHTER, S. F. (1991) 'The Organization of the '90s', *The McKinsey Quarterly*, no. 1.

Organizations based on the 'command-and-control' principles of the 1910s are too costly, too slow to adapt, too unresponsive to customers and too limited in creativity and initiative to respond effectively to the competitive challenges of the 1990s. Offers these actions: take stock of your efforts to date; visit other organizations attempting transformation; renew your vision; build a leadership team; lead more; manage less; eliminate layers; break down the organization; experiment; create new management forums.

DIXON, N. (1994) *The Organizational Learning Cycle: How We Can Learn Collectively*, Maidenhead: McGraw-Hill.

Organizational learning is the intentional use of learning processes at the individual, group and system level to continuously transform the organization in a direction that is increasingly satisfying to its stakeholders. Organizational learning is strengthened when the meaning structures of individuals are accessible to others, and when the collective meaning structure is made explicit so it can be tested and changed as necessary. This requires three things: (1) systematic processes; (2) a culture that supports learning; and (3) the skills and knowledge that facilitate collective learning. Dixon develops Kolb's notion of the individual learning cycle and applies it to organizational learning. There are four elements to this cycle: (1) widespread generation of information; (2) integrate new or localized information into the organizational context; (3) collectively interpret information; and (4) provide authority to take responsible action based on the interpreted meaning. The later chapters examine how the organizational learning cycle can be accelerated; how managers can be developed for organizational learning; and how to define a culture that supports learning. The final chapter suggests that organizational learning is essential for organizations who want to make the transition towards Handy's (1992) notion of organizational federalism.

DODGSON, M. (1993) 'Organizational learning: A review of some literatures', *Organization Studies*, 14, 375–394.

Dodgson discusses the two reasons usually put forward for positioning the role of organizational learning: competitiveness, and responsiveness to a turbulent environment of technological change. He argues that the dynamic and integrative nature of learning also makes it an analytically valuable concept. 'Individuals are the primary learning entity in firms', and this paper uses the psychological and organizational conceptualizations of individual learning as an analogy to inform the discussion of organizational learning. Three main areas are addressed: (1) the goals of organizational learning; (2) the processes of learning;

and (3) factors facilitating and impeding learning. A learning organization is characterized as one which moves beyond 'natural learning' and systematically uses its learning to progress beyond mere adaptation.

DONEGAN, J. (1990) 'The learning organization: Lessons from British Petroleum', *European Management Journal*, 8, 302–312.

For BP, the learning organization means improving the organization through people. All the essentials are in published values and mission statements but the author (a BP manager) worries that inability to believe in the creative potential of people is too deep-rooted among managers for whom status, power and control are the only things which matter. This essentially Western position is contrasted with Japanese management approaches.

DOWNS, S. and PERRY, P. (1984) *Developing Skilled Learners. Learning to Learn in YTS*, Research and Development Report 22, Sheffield: Manpower Services Commission.

Describes a research project which examines the role of learning to learn as part of the government's Youth Training Scheme. Two themes of the research are: (1) how must learning interactions change so that trainees are encouraged to take responsibility for their learning; and (2) to examine ways of learning, learning decisions and learning skills, to see how these could be deliberately and overtly developed. Following a preliminary study, a 2-day course for YTS course supervisors was developed. The course focuses on the importance of using appropriate approaches to learning how to memorize, understand and do something. The study illustrates that the 2-day course is an effective introduction to the developing skilled learners approach.

DOWNS, S. and PERRY, P. (1987) *Developing Skilled Learners. Helping Adults to Become Better Learners*, Research and Development Report 40, Sheffield: Manpower Services Commission.

The premises of the Developing Skilled Learners approach are outlined: (1) learning involves a relationship between learning processes and the material to be learned; (2) three types of learning process: memorizing, understanding and doing; (3) learning skills can be identified, learned and practised; (4) learning skills are most effective when they are overt; (5) people must take responsibility for their own learning in order to improve their learning skills; (6) the learning environment must be supportive; (7) error is important in developing understanding, but to be avoided in memorizing or doing; (8) there are blockages which hinder learning; (9) everyone can be helped to develop their ways of learning. Four tools are described in detail: (1) a 5-day course to improve learning skills; (2) the ways of learning questionnaire: a tool to help individuals identify how they learn; (3) the job learning analysis: a tool which analyses jobs in terms of their learning requirements; and (4) the learning blockages questionnaire: a tool to identify the

factors inhibiting learning. Organizations must (1) realize the
Developing Skilled Learners approach is a reversal of most
accepted practices, and (2) demonstrate commitment to the
approach and to the trainers introducing it.

EASTERBY-SMITH, M. (1990) 'Creating a learning organization',
Personnel Review, 19, 24–28.

Although the inability to learn may not be the only reason
organizations get into difficulty, it certainly compounds their
problems. Organizational learning is the process of improving
actions through better knowledge and understanding. Three
different forms of improving action are highlighted. This
involves changing (1) structure; (2) systems; and (3) culture of
the company. There are three things companies can do to
facilitate organizational learning: (1) learn about organizational
learning; (2) promote experimentation; and (3) regulate awareness through good communication. The obsession with activity
may be the major block for an organization trying to foster a
learning environment, and the role of reflection in effective
learning is highlighted. There are no simple procedures for
introducing learning and innovation into organizations,
because if there were, they would by definition lead only to
single-loop learning.

GARRATT, R. (1987) *The Learning Organization and the Need for
Directors who Think*, London: Fontana/Collins.

The problem of non-performing directors is addressed. Organizations do not specify the performance they expect from their
directors, and do not design and implement an induction,
inclusion and development process for their top managers.
Directors become blocks to the development of the organization. Garratt asks 'What can be done?' and 'How can we get
there?' Ten necessary characteristics of an effective director are
described: (1) focus not on specialist functions, but on links
with other functions; (2) adopt an integrated view of the
performance of the total business; (3) delegate and coach; (4)
provide staff with support when they need it; (5) be less
political inside the organization, but more politically aware
externally; (6) learn to be competent in the true director's role;
(7) balance achieving and nurturing; (8) consider the community as a stakeholder in the organization; (9) learn to design the
future rather than react to it; (10) be seen to have time to think.
These ten characteristics form a director's manifesto for learning
organizations.

GARRATT, R. (1990) *Creating a Learning Organization: A Guide to
Leadership, Learning and Development*, Cambridge: Director
Books.

From his work with directors, Garratt describes five preconditions
for unblocking organizations: (1) a clear strategic role for the
top team; (2) time and space for the top team to reflect on their
role; (3) the creation of a true team at the top; (4) delegation of
problem-solving activity to operational levels; and (5) a will-

ingness to accept that learning occurs continuously. The director's role is to create a climate where people can learn to learn through work and to move their learning to where it is needed in the organization. Five conditions for such a climate are outlined: (1) a perception that learning is a cyclical process; (2) an acceptance of the different roles of policy, strategy and operations; (3) a free flow of authentic information; (4) people are valued as the key asset for organizational learning; and (5) the ability to reframe information at the strategic level.

GARVIN, D. A. (1993) 'Building a learning organization', *Harvard Business Review*, Jul–Aug, 78–91.

The author suggests there is a need to look beyond the grand themes and examine the nitty-gritty of practice. He defines a learning organization as one which 'is skilled at creating, acquiring and transferring knowledge and at modifying its behaviour to reflect new knowledge and insights'. He suggests five guidelines for practice, which he describes as the building-blocks of the learning organization: (1) systematic problem-solving; (2) experimentation with new approaches; (3) learning from past experience; (4) learning from others; and (5) transferring knowledge. He also emphasizes the importance of measurement and suggests a complete learning audit must include three elements: (1) cognitive and attitudinal; (2) behavioural; and (3) performance improvement. He provides a range of case studies which give practical examples of these details of practice.

DE GEUS, A. P. (1988) 'Planning as learning', *Harvard Business Review*, Mar–Apr, 70–74.

The author describes his experience at Shell, where 'planning means changing minds'. Based on the fact that one-third of the Fortune 500 listed in 1970 had vanished by 1983, he surmises that companies are slow to adapt. The primary task is to understand how best to accelerate institutional learning; a process which begins with the calibration of existing mental models among key decision-makers. He describes Shell's use of scenarios as a tool for 'learning by playing'. Working with scenarios help managers to surface their implicit mental models and enables each individual's mental model to become a building-block of the institutional model. This process encourages managers to continually revise their views of the world and accelerates learning. This in turn provides the company with a sustainable competitive advantage.

HAMMER, M. and CHAMPY, J. (1993) *Re-engineering the Corporation: A Manifesto for Business Revolution*, New York: Harper Business.

Re-engineering is 'the fundamental re-thinking and radical re-design of business processes to achieve dramatic improvements in critical, contemporary measures of performance, such as cost, quality, service and speed'. This approach is at the other end of the spectrum from Kaizen, the persistent, almost relentless, pursuit of incremental improvement. As the authors put it, the

key words in the definition are *fundamental, radical, dramatic* and
processes (the latter defined any input–output activity or
activities which give value to the customer). The book describes
practical tools and draws heavily on the experience of Ford,
IBM Credit, Wal-Mart, Kodak and other companies.

HANDY, C. (1992) *Managing the Dream: The Learning Organization,*
London: Gemini Consulting.

Describes the basis of learning organizations: the assumption of
competence, where each individual performs close to the limit
of his/her capabilities with minimal supervision. To support
this, a climate of curiosity, forgiveness, trust and togetherness is
necessary. Focuses on the wheel of learning, a recurring cycle
made up of four elements: (1) questions; (2) ideas; (3) tests; and
(4) reflections. Five principles for keeping the wheel moving are
outlined: (1) subsidiarity; (2) clubs and congresses; (3) hori-
zontal fast-tracks; (4) self-enlightenment; and (5) incidental
learning. The leader's role is to drive the wheel and this can be
achieved by providing: (1) vision; (2) encouragement; and (3)
example. Handy concludes that organizations have no alternative but to learn if they are to survive a future which is
unpredictable.

HASTINGS, C. (1993) *The New Organization: Growing the Culture of
Organizational Networking,* IBM/McGraw-Hill Series, Maidenhead: McGraw-Hill.

Challenges the traditional way of organizing and refers to the
organization of the future as the 'new organization'. The
hallmark of this organization is outlined early in the book,
with the remaining chapters devoted to describing in detail
eight case studies or 'pathfinders'. The case studies include a
wide range of organizations and serve to illustrate the
practical skills available to managers in order to achieve the
'new organization'. The notion of networking is a strong
theme and involves both hard (electronic) and soft (process)
networks, project working, sharing know-how and teamworking.

HONEY, P. (1991) 'The learning organization simplified', *Training
and Development,* July, 30–33.

Creating a learning organization requires two things of people:
(1) to take continuous improvement seriously; and (2) to
actively encourage others within their sphere of influence to do
the same. Success is more likely if five assumptions underpin
the drive for continuous improvement: (1) learning is a good
thing; (2) good quality learning is deliberate and not left to
chance; (3) learning is continuous; (4) learning is more easily
sustained if it is shared, not done in isolation; and (5) learning is
typically not on the conscious agenda of most organizations
and a simple behaviourist recipe for addressing this is given.
First, choose the learning behaviours to encourage. Then
identify the antecedent events which act as triggers and the
consequent events which reinforce those learning behaviours.

Finally, make sure those triggers and reinforcers occur and the desired learning behaviours will follow.

HONEY, P. and MUMFORD, A. (1989) *The Manual of Learning Opportunities*, Maidenhead: Honey.

Contains ten instruments: (1) the learning diagnostic question-naire; (2) the four approaches to learning; (3) principles of effective learning; (4) learning opportunities review; (5) trans-formational learning opportunities; (6) factors influencing learning; (7) personal experiences of learning; (8) identifying learning skills; (9) identifying and using support for learning; (10) drawing up a personal development plan. These instru-ments build on the learning cycle as a model of learning processes. The materials can be used in three ways: (1) to help with individual counselling; (2) to help on courses, particularly in sessions dealing with development processes; and (3) to help audit the learning organization, particularly the learning diag-nostic questionnaire and the learning opportunities review.

JONES, A. M. and HENDRY, C. (1992) *The Learning Organization: A Review of Literature and Practice*, London: HRD Partnership.

A literature review which addresses five questions: (1) what is a learning organization? (2) what does a learning organization look like in theory and in practice? (3) how are learning organizations created? (4) what are the benefits of adopting the concept? (5) what are the implications of adopting the learning organization model? The learning organization concept is a challenging one that dares organizations to *think* differently, and not just to do things differently. The first step is to create 'what could be' by removing blockages to learning within the organization. From this beginning, they describe five learning phases learning organizations go through: (1) foundation; (2) formation; (3) continuation; (4) transformation; (5) transfigura-tion. They conclude that there are five key factors in creating a learning organization: (1) team learning; (2) changing power structures; (3) leading change; (4) giving vision; (5) expressing concern for social and ethical issues.

KATZENBACH, J. R. and SMITH, J. R. (1993) *The Wisdom of Teams: Creating the High-performing Organization*, Boston: Harvard Business School Press.

According to this book, teams are not to be confused with teamwork, empowerment or participative management. Also, drawing on the experience of Kodak, Motorola, 3M and others, the book describes how teams can be used to bring about improvements in organization performance, ranging from total quality and customer service to innovation. Based on extensive discussion with over 50 teams in 30 different companies, the authors describe practical ways in which a team has unique potential to deliver results and argue that teams will be the principal building-blocks of company performance in the future.

KIECHEL III, W. (1990) 'The organization that learns, *Fortune*, 12 Mar, 75–77.

The old control-and-command model of organizations will not be fast, keen, smart or sensitive enough to succeed in the future. The learning organization is a potential route to success: it offers the next stage in empowerment; a clear role for middle managers; and a bold goal for communications, i.e. people in organizations must tell it as it is. The learning organization does a number of things that make it different: (1) takes the idea of continuous improvement seriously; (2) understands the difference between learning and training; (3) acknowledges and exploits the benefits of different learning styles; (4) reconciles the needs of the individual with those of the organization as a whole; (5) looks beyond functional boundaries; (6) sets up cross-functional project teams; (7) gives middle management a coaching function; and (8) helps people to feel free to speak their minds about what they have learned. Although no 'learning organization' exists, Honda may come close. A Honda manager is quoted: 'The Honda philosophy is a way of life. It is characterized by closeness, communication and frankness at all levels.'

LAWLER III, E. E. (1986) *High Involvement Management: Participative Strategies for Improving Organizational Performance*, London: Jossey-Bass.

High involvement management is the competitive advantage available to countries with educated, achievement-orientated workforces who want to perform effectively, whose core values support participative decision-making, and who can engage in substantial amounts of self-regulation. Discusses the 'new design' plant which was meant to supply the physical and social arrangements for implementing participative strategies. The Digital investigators (Buchanan and McCalman) comment tartly that Digital did not have the luxury of implementing their high-performance work organization strategy in a new plant.

LEONARD-BARTON, D. (1992) 'The factory as a learning laboratory', *Sloan Management Review*, Fall, 23–37.

A learning laboratory is defined as 'an organization dedicated to knowledge creation, collection and control', and Chapparell Steel is used as a detailed case study of a factory as a learning laboratory. A learning laboratory can not be constructed piecemeal; there is interdependence between the incentive systems, education systems and corporate strategy. The case study examines the activities, values and management systems that support the four subsystems of a learning laboratory: (1) owning the problem and solving it; (2) garnering and integrating knowledge; (3) challenging the *status quo*; and (4) creating a virtual research organization through networking.

LESSEM, R. (1991) *Total Quality Learning: Building a Learning Organization*, Oxford: Basil Blackwell.

Argues that the two dominant factors in organizations in the 21st century will be *quality* and *learning*. Western quality management adopts the techniques but not the spirit of quality.

Learning is the heart of productive activity. So learning and quality are linked, as both are dependent on the interweaving of thought, feeling and action: learning is the process, quality the end. The two factors are fused to form a more fundamental concept for learning organizations: total quality learning. The book is structured around the idea that there are three fundamental arenas of learning: (1) thinking; (2) feeling; and (3) acting. The combinations of these give rise to seven different learning styles which make up the spectrum of learning. The author uses this concept to examine how managers can develop both themselves (identifying your learning style; develop yourself as a manager; charting the seven life paths; from apprenticeship to mastery; knowing yourself as a whole) and the business (transforming the business functions; rediscovering the core of business) towards total quality learning; two activities which are the foundation of holographic, or learning, organizations.

MARSICK, V. J. (ed.) (1987) *Learning in the Workplace*, London: Croom Helm.

Contains two particularly useful pointers. First, Mezirow's 10 principles of learning in the workplace, in which employees: (1) participate freely and fully in collaborative problem-solving; (2) share progressively in decision-making; (3) take different perspectives regarding their work; (4) ask questions, receive accurate and considerate feedback and reflect on themselves; (5) think critically and reflectively and question basic assumptions; (6) experiment without suffering serious consequences; (7) make inferences from daily activities that help them learn how to learn; (8) respect one another's self-worth; (9) feel free to pursue self-directed learning; (10) are helped to learn through mentoring, coaching and small group work. Second, Marsick's nine characteristics of a learning environment: (1) reflection on practice; (2) conscious evaluation of goals, norms and values; (3) concern for setting the problem as well as solving it; (4) experimentation and inquiry leading to new approaches to action; (5) use of team and group learning; (6) enhancement of self-esteem, self-discovery and self-directedness; (7) value given to the whole person, including feelings and emotion, in learning; (8) emphasis on internal motivation through empowerment; (9) fostering of continuous, informal, on-the-job learning.

MOSS-JONES, J. (1992) *The Learning Organization, Corby: Institute of Management.*

Argues that learning organization theory is part of the family of ideas which attempt to help organizations cope with the turbulence of rapid, difficult-to-predict and complex change. Responds to the question 'what is the learning organization?' with the advice 'not to get hooked on a name', emphasizing instead the importance of the ideas underpinning the concept of the learning organization. The author traces the genealogy of the thinking which led to the concept: Burns and Stalker's notion of the organic system, Revans' view of the organization as a learning system, Bateson's work on the importance of the double-loop and learning how to learn, Schon and Argyris' reminder of the importance of learning from experience, Beer's Viable Systems Model, and Deming's work in total quality management. He also identifies five key themes which recur in the literature: (1) the role of mind-sets; (2) the leadership group; (3) systems thinking; (4) people and learning; (5) organizational adaptiveness.

MOSS KANTER, R. (1994) 'Collaborative advantage—the art of alliances', *Harvard Business Review*, Jul–Aug, 96–108.

Describes the findings of an extensive research project examining business partnerships and what makes them succeed. The author argues that managing the partnership in human terms is just as important as the financial aspects of the partnership. There are three elements to a successful business partnership: (1) the benefits go beyond the immediate reasons for entering the relationship; (2) the relationship involves creating new value together; and (3) the relationship depends on a dense web of interpersonal connections that enhance learning. Three varieties of relationship are discussed: (1) mutual service consortia; (2) joint ventures; (3) value chain alliances. A five-phase model of successful alliances is proposed, built around the metaphor of a marriage: (1) selection and courtship: the emphasis is on attraction and compatibility; (2) engagement: specific plans are made and committed to; (3) housekeeping: the stage at which different ideas about the relationship begin to emerge; (4) bridging: mechanisms for overcoming these differences are put in place; (5) internalization: where the partners in the alliance change themselves as a result of learning from the alliance. Moss Kanter concludes intercompany relationships are a key business asset and knowing how to nurture them is an essential managerial skill.

NONAKA, I. (1988) 'Towards middle-up-down management: Accelerating information creation', *Sloan Management Review*, Spring, 9–18.

The concepts of top-down, or deductive, management and bottom-up, or inductive, management are about an organization's capability to process information. But organizations must also create information. Organizations with a high level of information creation and a high level of pressure for a quick response should use the middle-up-down approach to the management of knowledge creation. At different organizational levels, different characteristics become important for promoting information creation. For the individual, the critical factor is autonomy; for the group, interaction; and for the organization, structure. Middle management is central to knowledge creation because it is equipped with the ability to combine strategic

macro-level information with hands-on micro-level information. Middle managers should: (1) establish creative chaos;
(2) form a self-organizing team to create meaning out of that
chaos; (3) synchronize concept creation with top managers and
frontline employees; (4) transfer learning and unlearning to
other parts of the organization. Top managers create an overall
theory, while middle managers create a middle-range theory to
test empirically within the framework of the entire organization.

NONAKA, I. (1991) 'The knowledge-creating company', *Harvard
Business Review*, Nov–Dec, 96–104.

Many organizations are information-processing machines, rather
than knowledge-creating organisms. Such organizations must
learn from the Japanese approach to knowledge creation, which
depends on the tacit and often highly subjective insights,
intuitions and hunches of individual employees and make
those insights available for testing and use by the company as a
whole. Knowledge-creating companies constantly encourage
the process whereby personal knowledge is made available to
others (articulation) for them to use to extend their own tacit
knowledge base (internalization). Articulating tacit knowledge
is a three-stage process which uses: (1) metaphor; (2) analogy;
(3) model-building. The fundamental principle of designing
knowledge-creating companies is to design redundancy into
the organization. Gives the example of Canon, who uses the
principle of internal competition. Project teams are divided into
groups to develop different approaches to the same problem.
Two implementation issues are also discussed. First, new
knowledge should be evaluated qualitatively as well as quanti-
tatively. For example, does the idea embody the organization's
future vision? Second, middle managers have the key role in
knowledge creation, because they integrate the tacit knowledge
of frontline employees and senior executives.

NYHAN, B. (1991) *Developing People's Ability to Learn*, Brussels:
Eurotecnet Technical Assistance Office, Interuniversity Press.

Part one describes how rapid technological change has led to the
need for a new learning paradigm. The self-learning knowledge
worker will be self-motivated and possess a high degree of self-
awareness and self-control. Such people cannot exist in a
vacuum. The organizations in which they work must support
learning, with learning as a key element of the strategic plan to
achieve organizational and business goals. Part two examines
the issues surrounding the new learning paradigm; firstly the
methodological issues involved in developing self-learning
competency and secondly, the organizational and management
issues. The key message is the interconnectedness between
learning and the ability to compete commercially, open new
markets, anticipate change and build the society of tomorrow.
While the task of creating a total learning environment belongs
to everyone, three groups are especially important: (1) policy-

makers at government level; (2) managers of companies; (3) training professionals.

PASCALE, R. T. (1990) *Managing on the Edge*, London: Viking.

Of the 48 'excellent' companies described in the bestselling *In Search of Excellence*, fully half no longer qualify as 'excellent'. How did they lose their edge? How could they get it back? Based on extensive interviews with Japan's and America's most innovative business leaders, the book describes how companies can survive by mixing 'hard' and 'soft' qualities. It concludes that the transformation of organizations is tied to the growth of those people who manage them. This growth is encouraged when people stay in touch with what is really going on, because such reality checks may often highlight the need for a new way of thinking. This new way of thinking, or paradigm, is a vital ingredient of successful transformation. However, the quest is not simply for a new management paradigm that works in the present, but for a way of thinking that is continually open to the next paradigm and the next and the next . . . .

PEARN, M. A. and DOWNS, S. (1991), 'Developing skilled learners: The experience of UK companies', in Nyhan, B., *Developing People's Ability to Learn*, Brussels: Eurotecnet Technical Assistance Office, Interuniversity Press.

Developing skilled learners is vital for changing organizations: 'If people can be helped to increase their capacity to understand, they have a mechanism within themselves by which they can learn to cope with change'. Two assumptions underpin the focus on learning rather than training: (1) people do not have to be trained in order to learn; (2) people often learn in spite of the training they receive. Ten characteristics of skilled learners are outlined. Skilled learners: (1) take responsibility for their learning; (2) distinguish between different types of learning; (3) use more ways of learning and apply them appropriately; (4) do not try to memorize when they need to understand; (5) consciously choose how to learn; (6) ensure they learn despite poor teaching; (7) ask questions to ensure they learn effectively; (8) seek feedback; (9) realize that difficulties in learning are frequently due to poor delivery; (10) are confident to take on new learning opportunities. The application and consequences of this approach are described in case studies of ICI's agricultural division and a Shell blending plant.

PEDLER, M., BURGOYNE, J., BOYDELL, T. and WELSHMAN, G. (eds) (1990) *Self-Development in Organizations*, Maidenhead: McGraw-Hill.

Self-development means learners taking the freedom and responsibility for choosing what, how and when to develop. In Part one, the historical perspective of self-development is presented. In Part two, 10 examples of current practice of self-development are given. These 10 examples break down into two broad approaches: the first focuses on the personal development of the individual, the second on ensuring a tight fit between the development of the individual and the development of the organization. Part Three addresses the challenges and questions for the future of the self-development approach. Two key issues emerge: the role of differences in self-development and the role of learning organizations in self-development.

PEDLER, M., BURGOYNE, J. and BOYDELL, T. (1992) *The Learning Company*, Maidenhead: McGraw-Hill.

The authors set out to apply their knowledge and experience of individual learning to understand and master the art of corporate learning. The learning company, the term preferred to 'organization', is an idea which fits in with the context of UK companies in the 1990s. An 11-point blueprint for the learning company is set out. Learning companies will display these characteristics: (1) learning approach to strategy; (2) participative policy-making; (3) infomating; (4) formative accounting and control; (5) internal exchange; (6) reward flexibility; (7) enabling structures; (8) boundary workers as environmental scanners; (9) inter-company learning; (10) learning climate; (11) self-development for all. These elements are distilled into five core areas of activity for the learning company: strategy, looking in, structures, looking out and learning opportunities. The main body of the book focuses on 101 'glimpses' of the learning company, in which practical approaches to each aspect of the 11-point blueprint are outlined.

PETERS, T. (1991) 'Get innovative or get dead, part II', *California Management Review*, Winter, 9–23.

Here it is what the author has to say about teams which registers most. For instance, to become project-focused means more than just appointing teams. Teams and task forces have often ended up adding to, rather than subtracting from, bureaucracy. Part I of the article is in the Fall (1990) issue of the *California Management Review*.

SAFIZADEH, M. H. (1991) 'The case of work groups in manufacturing operations', *California Management Review*, Summer.

Points out that we have not as yet devised a satisfactory method of engaging workers' minds with their jobs. Work groups are only one way of involving workers in the design-making process. A significant obstacle to adoption of work groups appears to be managers' and supervisors' reluctance to let workers have the necessary autonomy and responsibility for the effective functioning of groups.

SCHEIN, E. H. (1993) 'How can organizations learn faster? The challenge of entering the green room', *Sloan Management Review*, Winter, 85–92.

Three distinct types of learning are identified and barriers to each are discussed: (1) knowledge acquisition and insight; (2) habit and skill learning; (3) emotional conditioning. Suggests that the anxieties of change can be managed. The first step involves providing evidence which disconfirms the validity of current ways of doing things. The second step is to create an anxiety associated with continuing to do something which will fail eventually; which overcomes the inertia of anxiety caused by an unwillingness to learn something new because it appears difficult or disruptive. Third, a psychologically safe environment must be created: this can be promoted by providing opportunities for practice; by providing support and encouragement; by rewarding efforts in the right direction; and by establishing norms that legitimize errors and experimentation. Suggests eight practical steps to help organizations learn faster: (1) leaders must learn something new; (2) a change management group must be created; (3) the steering committee must go through its own learning process; (4) the steering committee must design the organizational learning process; (5) the steering committee must establish task forces to create specific change programmes; (6) the task forces must learn how to learn; (7) the steering committee must maintain communication throughout the process; (8) mechanisms to support continual learning must be put in place.

SEMLER, R. (1993) *Maverick! The Success Story Behind the World's Most Unusual Workplace*, London: Century.

An inspiring account of the author's transformation of his father's Brazilian-based organization 'Semco' from a traditional pyramidal structure of 12 management layers to that of a structure based on three concentric circles. Among the changes introduced in the past 11 years is the abolition of rule books, policies and receptionists/PAs/secretaries and the treatment of all employees as responsible, trustworthy adults. Workers set their own production quotas; managers set their own salaries; everyone gets a vote regarding big decisions and profit sharing and managers are evaluated 6-monthly by those who work below them. As Semler put it, 'Bosses don't have to be parents and workers don't act like children'.

SENGE, P. M. (1990) 'The leader's new work: Building learning organizations', *Sloan Management Review*, Fall, 7–22.

Senge quotes the CEO of a large insurance company: 'If the learning organization is so widely preferred, why don't people create such organizations?' The answer, he says, is leadership. People have no real comprehension of the type of commitment it requires to build such an organization. Senge goes on to discuss the qualities leaders need. Leaders, he says, are designers/teachers/stewards. They need new skills, the ability to build shared vision, to bring to the surface and challenge prevailing mental models. In short, leaders in learning organizations are responsible for building organizations where people are continually expanding their capabilities to shape their future. He suggests there are five learning disciplines: (1) systems thinking; (2) personal mastery; (3) mental models; (4) building shared vision; (5) team learning. Considerable emphasis is placed on the value and benefits of systems thinking, which he describes as 'the cornerstone of learning'.

See also SENGE, P. M. (1990) *The Fifth Discipline: The Art and Practice of the Learning Organization*, New York: Doubleday.

SENGE, P. M., ROBERTS, C., ROSS, R. B., SMITH, B. J. and KLEINER, A. (1994) *The Fifth Discipline Fieldbook*, London: Nicholas Brealey Publishing.

This is an amazing book. Written by Senge and four co-authors, an additional 52 people have contributed to the book. It is structured around the five disciplines and offers a variety of models and tools for building learning organizations. The book is designed to answer the question posed by many people after they had read *The Fifth Discipline*: 'This is fascinating, but what should I do, where should I start?' It is essentially a practitioners' book, with many of the exercises to be performed by individuals or by a group described in a step-by-step fashion like a cookbook. The book also contains further theoretical development of the 'deep learning cycle in the domain of enduring change' and above it the 'implicate order' which is known by inference and transcends the deep learning cycle and may represent a higher level of learning that guides and inspires human enterprise. The Fieldbook is rich in ideas, techniques, sources, case studies, and will be a valuable aid to anyone seeking to become a learning organization. It is not, however, complete; for example, it lacks any discussion of analysing the current state of learning in the organization.

SENGE, P. M. and STERMAN, J. D. (1992) 'Systems thinking and organizational learning', *European Journal of Operational Research*, 59.

Helping the organization to learn is widely acknowledged to be vital. The next challenge is to move beyond generalizations about accelerating learning, to tools and processes that help managers. One of the biggest blocks to accelerating managers' learning is that their cognitive skills and capabilities are often limited in comparison to the increasingly complex systems they are called upon to manage. One possible tool for helping managers become more systemic and dynamic in their thinking about the complex systems they deal with is the learning laboratory. A learning laboratory is a 'flight simulator for managers'. A detailed case study of a learning laboratory developed with Hanover Insurance is described. Four key lessons for implementation emerge: (1) focus on conceptualization; (2) promote reflection; (3) evaluate the role of the computer; (4) continually make links between the 'virtual world' and the real world. The authors argue that learning laboratories provide a practise field for management teams akin to those used by sports teams and this opportunity to practice and learn can increase managers' capabilities to meet the challenge of thinking globally, while acting locally.

SHIPPER, F. and MANZ, C. C. (1992) 'Employee self-management without formally designated teams: An alternative road to empowerment', *Organizational Dynamics*, Winter, 48–61.

Discusses the experience at W. L. Gore (of Gortex) where there are no managers or bosses, but lots of leaders. At Gortex they talk about 'unstructure'. A lattice system allows all associates to interact directly with whoever they need to. So-called sponsors (mentors?) are used to help associates, not managers. Innovation, teamwork and independent effort are valued. Gore relies heavily on fluid, temporary self-developing teams, but concedes that relying on self-developing teams without managers will not suit all businesses. Perhaps the lattice works best in start-up companies led by dynamic entrepreneurs.

STAHL, T., NYHAN, B. and D'ALOJA, P. (1992) *The Learning Organization: A Vision for Human Resource Development*, Eurotecnet Technical Assistance Office, Brussels: Commission of the European Communities.

The learning organization is a vision of a new type of organization, with new relationships between work activities and learning. It is a vision which is derived from the competitive challenge of flexibility and quality. In learning organizations, the most important qualifications will relate to self-managed learning, as it is through these qualifications that new learning will occur. Learning organizations 'turn the strategy, structure and culture of the enterprise itself into a learning system'. Learning organizations are organized in a distinctive way. Typically there is: (1) integration of learning and work; (2) new orientation of HRD departments; (3) self-learning at the workplace is the learning pattern; (4) planned innovation; and (5) facilitation of learning. The final chapter notes that nearly 72 per cent of all the people working in Europe work for small or medium-sized enterprises, and the relevance of learning organization theory to such companies is discussed.

STATA, R. (1989) Organizational learning: The key to management innovation', *Sloan Management Review*, Spring, 63–74.

The author describes his work with people like Forrester, Senge and de Geus on the issue of organizational learning, which he concludes 'may become the only sustainable source of competitive advantage'. Organizational learning (1) occurs through shared mental models; and (2) builds on past experience. This means that organizations can learn only as fast as the slowest link within them and that they must develop institutional mechanisms to retain knowledge. The author illustrates how organizational learning has served as a unifying principle in Analogue Device's approach to: (1) systems thinking; (2) planning; (3) quality improvement; (4) organizational behaviour; (5) information systems, and gives practical examples of how this has affected the organization. He concludes that the changes introduced have put the company back on the right track, but notes that 'these results do not come free; they require a major investment of time and resources'.

STEWART, T. A. (1991) 'GE keeps those ideas coming, *Fortune*, 12 Aug, 19–25.

Jack Welch, pioneer of taking out the boss element, has come up with three new management techniques called Work-Out, Best Practices and Process Mapping. Work-Out opens the doors that keep employees out of the decision-making process; Best Practices seeks to smash the 'not invented here' syndrome and to spread good ideas quickly from one part of GE to another; Process Mapping is the tool the others most depend on. All foster employee involvement. Combined, they are designed to sustain the rapid growth in productivity that, Welch says, is the key to *any* corporation's survival in the competitive environment of the nineties.

SWEDISH WORK ENVIRONMENT FUND (1988) *Towards a Learning Organization*, Stockholm: Swedish Work Environment Fund.

By learning organization is meant making good use across a broad front of the skills and ability of personnel to develop. Training and education are seen as part of everyday life. Includes concrete examples of training activities, the design of work organizations for learning (including Saab) and the creation of new contact lines within companies. Learning is seen very much in the perspective of working life.

SWIERINGA, J. and WIERSMA, A. (1992) *Becoming a Learning Organization: Beyond the Learning Curve*, Wokingham: Addison-Wesley.

A learning organization is built around co-operative processes which learn through co-operation and co-operate while learning. The approach focuses on collective learning. It is noted that this can only be achieved through individual learning, which is a necessary but not sufficient condition for organizational learning. A model of collective learning and organizational change, which builds on the work of Argyris and Schon, is put forward. Single-loop learning equates to organizational improvement, double-loop to renewal, and triple-loop to development. An organization must learn how to learn before it can successfully transform itself. Based on this model, they suggest three activities to provide leadership for collective learning: (1) management of the operational process; (2) management of the organization's internal interfaces; and (3) management of the relationship between the whole organization and its environment. This is done successfully in learning organizations, which are capable of learning, and of learning to learn. However, a learning organization is not paradise; learning together and agreeing on principles is burdensome, difficult and sometimes very painful. The final section examines the role of those who provide assistance with organizational learning and the phases which must be gone through to implement a course intended as the first step on the road towards creating a learning organization.

THURBIN, P. J. (1994) *Implementing the Learning Organization: The 17-Day Programme*, London: FT/Pitman.

Learning organizations are about learning at three levels. (1) *The enterprise* needs to learn how to: (a) interface with its environment and provide stakeholder satisfaction; (b) be efficient and effective in its internal affairs; (c) create an internal environment in which people can be effective. (2) *Groups* need to learn how to: (a) manage interfaces with other groups; (b) satisfy customers and stakeholders; (c) make tacit knowledge explicit; (d) work together more effectively and efficiently. (3) *Individuals* need to learn how to; (a) master the local environment; (b) contribute to the team; (c) pursue personal development and growth. This book provides a structured approach and tools to help the reader to address a number of key issues: (1) the learning organization—myth or reality?; (2) clarifying the purpose; (3) reviewing the organization; (4) creating the vision of the learning organization; (5) identifying the culture and opportunities for change; (6) assessing the benefits; (7) implementation. The final chapter consists of 16 case studies based on the author's experience and the existing literature.

TOBIN, D. R. (1993) *Re-educating the Corporation: Foundations for the Learning Organization*, Vermont: Oliver Wight Publications.

The learning organization focuses on harnessing not only the company's potential, but also that of each individual employee in order to create its own future. For any organizational transformation to succeed, the organization must be a learning organization. Five principles underpin learning organizations: (1) everyone is a learner; (2) people learn from each other; (3) learning enables change; (4) learning is continuous; (5) learning is an investment, not an expense. At the core of the book is a close examination of the five foundations of the learning organization: (1) visible leadership; (2) thinking literacy; (3) overcoming functional myopia; (4) building and sustaining effective teams; (5) managers as enablers. A self-assessment checklist of the five foundations is included as an appendix. Nine action steps for breathing life into the learning organization are given: (1) learn about learning organizations; (2) assess the organization's current status; (3) plan how to develop the five foundations; (4) allow everyone to buy into the idea; (5) make an act of commitment to kick-start the process; (6) develop and deliver appropriate training; (7) implement learning practices; (8) reinforce new learning and practices; (9) remain open to new ideas. Three processes are required to nurture learning in the long term: (1) continuous inquiry; (2) information capture; (3) information dissemination.

WATERMAN, R. (1994) *The Frontiers of Excellence—Learning from Companies That Put People First*, London: Nicholas Brearley Publishing.

This book explores in depth the strategic and organizational reasons why a handful of American firms do so well. The best firms are the best because of their organizational arrangements. This means they are better organized to meet the needs of their people and their customers. Organizing around people provides five things for the people within the organization: (1) control; (2) something to believe in; (3) challenge; (4) lifelong learning; (5) recognition. Organizations achieve sustained advantage from the way they organize, not from a great idea or strategy. There are however three fundamentals to any successful strategy: (1) continuous innovation; (2) customer satisfaction; (3) cost. The book includes 11 'case study' chapters, from which four key lessons are drawn in the epilogue. Companies that remain successful: (1) break themselves into small, fairly autonomous units; (2) organize to please their customers and motivate their people; (3) smoothly switch to the adhocracy mode of organizing; (4) show staying power and very long-term commitment.

Index